A heart-breaking tale of family and loss, set against the backdrop of a WWII and a war torn Germany. The author's knowledge of the war shines through in this novel, from the horrifying details of the frontline as experienced by Franz, to the heart-aching wait for families left behind hoping to see their loved ones again.

'The Letter' by Barry Cole follows Franz Mayer, a sergeant in the German army struggling to survive on the Eastern Front and on the way home to his family before braving the threat of war once more. Throughout the novel there's great characterisation, even for the characters we meet for a brief time, the author makes sure they are rounded out. It's subtle enough to not detract from the plot, but clear enough to hammer home that despite the broad descriptions of war - the country vs country commentary - the reality involves countless unique and complex individuals. This style of writing made 'The Letter' feel even more poignant and emotive to me. Combined with the detailed descriptions of the horrors witnessed and the poverty endured, 'The Letter' is a powerful story that emphasises the loss and pain experienced on all sides. There are moments of hope scattered throughout, and I found Wolfgang in particular helped to bring some levity to the story during the times we spend with Hannah.

This was a fascinating historical war drama. There's twists and changes that keep you turning the pages, hoping for a positive outcome, but never certain. I think that the author has succeeded in delivering an emotional and immersive story. 'The Letter' is a compelling and brilliant look at loss, at family and at the personal costs of war.

... LoveReading Review

THE LETTER

HE HAD ESCAPED THE WAR,
BUT NOT HIS CONSCIENCE

BARRY COLE

Michael Terence
Publishing

First published in paperback by
Michael Terence Publishing in 2022
www.mtp.agency

Copyright © 2022 Barry Cole

Barry Cole has asserted the right to be identified as
the author of this work in accordance with the
Copyright, Designs and Patents Act 1988

ISBN 9781800941899

No part of this publication may be reproduced, stored
in a retrieval system, or transmitted, in any form or
by any means, electronic, mechanical, photocopying,
recording or otherwise, without the prior
permission of the publisher

Front cover image
Copyright © Bundesarchiv (Bild-183-B22531)

Rear cover image
Courtesy of Barry Cole

Cover design
Copyright © 2022 Michael Terence Publishing

He had often wondered where soldiers
like himself went when they died.
After all the killing they had done he hoped it
wasn't hell because he had been there already.

It was called Stalingrad.

One
Potsdam Railway Station
Late December 1945

BUNDLED UP AGAINST the biting cold of a Berlin winter, a group of elderly men armed with makeshift wooden shovels finished clearing away the overnight fall of snow from the wide platform. With the curved glass and wrought iron canopy which covered the station reduced to a cat-cradle of tangled metal, it was becoming a daily task. Moments later, hissing like a snake a DRB class 50 locomotive, its rusting boiler covered in layers of soot pulled into the station. The steam venting from its cylinders engulfing everything in a billowing white cloud. No sooner had it screeched to a halt when flinging open the carriage doors the train's passengers, mostly elderly men and, women spilled out onto the platform their worldly possessions crammed into cardboard boxes and battered suitcases. Positioned at intervals along the platform armed Russian soldiers cocooned in their warm greatcoats, watched disinterestedly as bunched together like a herd of sheep the train's occupants shuffled along in silence towards the glass-fronted booking hall at the far end of the platform.

Perched in his cab, wiping the sweat and grime from his face with a grubby rag the engineer watched as the orderly line of passengers filed past below him. It seemed as if the whole country was on the move. The remnants of a defeated nation. Each person like a piece in a giant jigsaw, all hurrying back to their allotted place in the puzzle in the hope that it would make Germany whole again. Fat chance of that he thought to himself, tying the piece of cloth around his neck. But then again with *The Little Corporal* (Hitler) dead and the war finally over perhaps the future should be viewed with a sense of optimism. A belief that his beloved Germany would rise again like a Phoenix from the ashes. The thought bringing a smile to his weathered face.

Carrying a heavy suitcase, its bulging sides secured by a leather strap a young boy wearing a three quarter length overcoat with a red woollen scarf wound around his neck jumped down onto the platform. Putting the suitcase down, he turned to the open door, and with arms outstretched he helped his four-year-old sister down from the carriage. The boy's name was Wolfgang and he was eleven years old. His sister, dressed in a full-length double-breasted overcoat with its wide velvet collar turned up to protect her ears from the cold was called Trudel.

Following behind them, framed in the carriage doorway the woman hesitated for a moment, staring down at the platform such a long way below her. Although only in her late twenties she looked much older. Her once rounded cheeks had lost much of their firmness, her skin pale and lustreless. In an attempt to brighten her complexion she had applied a dark red lipstick to her mouth. A flower-patterned silk headscarf covered her shoulder-length auburn hair and she was wearing a long woollen winter coat, the fabric a little worn around the cuffs. The knee-length boots she wore, although badly scuffed and in need of polish were made of good quality leather. Clutched tightly to her chest, wrapped in a hand-knitted shawl with tiny primroses embroidered along its edges, a gift from her kindly neighbour Frau Junker was a month-old baby. In her other hand was a heavy suitcase. The woman's name was Hannah and she was the children's mother.

Seeing her hesitating, grinning from ear to ear a young Mongol soldier strode forward, and taking the suitcase from her he helped her down onto the platform. Touched by his action, Hannah rewarded his kindness with a smile. Acknowledging the gesture with a simple nod of the head, the soldier returned to his post. Watching through slanting eyelids as Hannah and her two children joined the crowd of people walking towards the exit.

Like the rest of the station, the impressive booking hall had also suffered from the constant Allied bombing raids. The end wall had fared worse, split from top to bottom by a vertical crack large enough to push a fist into. To save it from collapsing altogether, a massive plank of wood had been placed horizontally across its width braced by two heavy wooden beams. With a third beam wedged between the floor and a roof joist to support the sagging ceiling. Thanks to their heavy wooden shutters, the panes of glass in most of the building's windows had survived intact. The cracked ones being held together by strips of brown tape.

Inside it was a different story however. The walnut veneered panelling and wide dado rail which had lined the room were gone, stripped away from the walls to expose the horizontal rows of brickwork it had once hidden. Also missing were the ticket booths with their ornate arched windows and two-way counters which had stretched from one side of the room to the other. All torn down and carted away. Every scrap of timber turned into firewood by people desperate for fuel during a bitter winter, where coal was worth more than gold.

Set against one wall was a large cast-iron stove that had been salvaged from what remained of the station master's office. Tasked with feeding its voracious appetite with lumps of chopped wood was an old woman with a scarf wound around her head like a Bedouin tribesman. The only furniture was a ten-foot-long trestle table and a pair of high-backed chairs. Seated on the more comfortable of the two was a Russian officer. A stocky, muscular man in his early forties, clean-shaven his dark pomaded hair slicked back in the style of Rudolph Valentino. The olive-green uniform he was wearing was freshly pressed, its single row of gold buttons gleaming brightly in the glow from a naked light bulb suspended from the ceiling. Placed on the table in front of him was his peaked cap. Its enamelled badge, a single Red Star embossed with the emblem of the hammer and sickle clearly visible to people as they approached the table. A reminder if one were needed of who was in charge now. Occupying the chair next to him was an elderly, thin-faced man dressed in the uniform of a Reichsbahn official. Tell-tale patches of faded material and remnants of thread revealing where sleeves and epaulettes had been stripped of their Nazi insignia. The badge and gold braid had also been removed from the cap he was wearing.

Eventually, after what seemed an intolerable length of time Hannah and her children suddenly found themselves being ushered into the booking hall. Once through the door, a Russian soldier sweltering in his thick greatcoat, prodded Hannah forward with the barrel of his rifle. Obediently, Hannah approached the desk. Setting down her suitcase, she dipped her hand into a coat pocket and withdrew a folded piece of paper. Nervously, head lowered she placed it in front of the Russian officer facing her on the other side of the table. Sitting with his arms folded across his chest the officer looked down at the piece of paper. Confused as to why he hadn't picked it up Hannah forced herself to look up and meet his gaze. But the man simply stared back at her stony-faced and although she knew her document was in order, icy fingers suddenly began running up and down her spine.

Then, like a cat bored of playing with the mouse it had caught with a slight movement of his head the officer directed his gaze onto the paper and nodded. Instantly, she understood. Reaching out a hand, Hannah picked up the paper and quickly unfolding it she placed it back on the table. A smile tugged playfully at the corner of the officer's mouth. The point had been made. Picking up the travel permit he began scrutinising it, poring over its single page as though determined to find an irregularity. Occasionally, just for a second or two, he would look up at Hannah his gaze lingering on her face for a moment. Anxiously, heart-pounding, Hannah waited for the questioning to begin. But he never spoke.

Major Anatoly Borovkov had been sitting at this table for four hours now. His backside was numb and the absurdity of this bureaucratic nonsense bored and enraged him in equal measure. What angered him most however was having fought street by street to the very heart of this accursed city, even standing on the steps of the ruined Reichstag while men from his unit clambered onto its roof and raised the flag of the victorious Motherland, that this should be his reward.

During those four long hours hundreds of people, men and women had passed in front of him. Each face as miserable-looking and forgettable as the last. But this one was different. Even with the dark shadows under her eyes, she was very attractive. The lipstick was a mistake of course but despite that, she was quite beautiful and pleasing to look at. So why shouldn't he take his time, he deserved a moment of indulgence, didn't he? A little compensation for being assigned to such a thankless task.

In a pretence of checking their identities, his gaze fell on the two children. The boy first, standing there with his tight angry mouth. Despite being a bit skinny he appeared well-nourished. He had his mother's eyes but little else of her. Still, boys tended to be more like their fathers, Anatoly reminded himself. What was it they used to say? 'Like father like son?' It could mean something else entirely of course. He couldn't be sure. It wasn't a saying Russians tended to used very much. The girl however was different. She shared the boy's pale blue eyes but her oval-shaped face, with its petite freckled nose and butterfly lips were all characteristics of her mother. She would be a real beauty one day that he was sure of. A heartbreaker for sure. Drawing pleasure from the thought, with a final glance at the woman, Major Borovkov handed the sheet of paper to the man seated next to him and with a wave of his hand, gestured for Hannah to move along.

Taking hold of the permit with his nicotine-stained fingers, the Reichsbahn official applied the freshly-inked stamp to the allotted space on the paper. Satisfied with the result, without looking up he reached out his arm and handed it to Hannah. Overwhelmed with relief Hannah took the permit from him, slipping it into her coat pocket for safekeeping. Then, shooing the two children ahead of her she picked up her heavy suitcase, and together the small family walked towards the exit doors.

At the rear of the building an area had been cordoned off by a makeshift barricade manned by a squad of armed Russian soldiers, the collars of their long overcoats turned up, their fur caps pulled down over their ears. Corralled behind this temporary barrier, passengers anxiously scanned the faces of the people waiting on the other side. Suddenly, voices began ringing out. A name shouted out loud, an arm raised as a friend or family member was recognised by someone in the waiting crowd. Clutching their meagre possessions, the fortunate ones pushed their way to the front of the barrier. Looking on, sheltered by the wall of the building the NCO in charge dragged another mouthful of nicotine-infused smoke into his lungs. Exhaling it through his nostrils like some fire-breathing dragon he barked out an order. Immediately two soldiers hurried across to the barrier and pulled a section of it aside.

Emerging from the building into the fading daylight, Hannah instinctively pulled the shawl tightly around her infant before moved forward into the throng of people. The numbers of passengers were thinning already as more were allowed through the barricade. Throwing themselves into the arms of their waiting loved ones, the air filled with cries of delight and muffled sobs of relief.

Hemmed in by the waiting press of people a tall, broad-shouldered man probably in his early sixties, dressed in a black padded jacket with patches sewn into the elbows and wearing a grease-stained engineer's cap, scanned the passengers as they emerge from the booking hall. Spotting Hannah and the children he began pushing his way through the milling crowd. His strong arms held out in front like the prow of a boat. Reaching the barrier, he shouldered his way to a point opposite to where Hannah was standing. Then lifting an arm in the air he began waving it back and forth. Calling out at the same time in a loud voice. 'Hello!'

Attracted by the man's gesturing and the sound of his voice rising above the hubbub Hannah looked towards him. Was it her he was waving at or some other family? Satisfied that it was her he was signalling to, Hannah picked up her suitcase and with mounting apprehension, she made her way toward him. Relieved that she had spotted him, the man looked across to one of the soldiers. Catching the man's eye, he gestured for him to come over and remove the barrier. But the soldier simply looked back at him disinterestedly. The man gestured again, more urgently this time. Scowling, the soldier stared back at him and for one horrible moment, the man worried that unwittingly he had somehow antagonised him. You could never tell what mood these bloody Ivan's were in. To his relief, the soldier's features softened and shouldering his rifle he strolled over to where he was standing. Separated by the barrier, a yard apart, the two men stared into each other's faces. Weighing each other up like two belligerent bull elephants. Then quite unexpectedly, letting out a great roar of laughter curling back his lips to reveal an impressive row of gold teeth the soldier gripped the barrier with both hands and dragged it aside.

Pushing the children ahead of her, Hannah walked through the gap in the barricade and quickly found herself standing in front of someone who was a stranger to her. Sensing her uncertainty, smiling warmly the man extended a large glove-less hand.

'Frau Mayer?' he said in a distinctive Berlin accent.

While his accent was a little strange to her, his youthful tone of voice was not at all what she expected from such a big gruff looking man, nor was the warmth of his smile. Reassured by both, she shook his hand.

'Yes, I am Frau Mayer.'

'I am Herr Neusch. Otto Neusch. Welcome to Potsdam.'

'It is very kind of you to meet us,' Hannah said, setting down her heavy suitcase.

'Nonsense! We are so glad that you have come. Did you have a good journey?'

'Yes. The journey was good, thank you.'

'Excellent! Said Herr Neusch. Turning to face the boy

standing beside her, 'And this must be young Wolfgang?'

'Yes sir,' Wolfgang replied, clearly impressed by the fact that the man was wearing a train driver's cap.

'I am very pleased to meet you, Wolfgang Mayer,' said Herr Neusch holding out his hand.

Delighted by such an adult gesture, Wolfgang reached out his hand, palm open, watching with some concern as it was swallowed up in the man's huge fist. After exchanging a proper handshake, conjuring up a broad smile Herr Neusch then fixed his eyes on Trudel. 'And who have we here, then?'

Unsure of the man, clutching a handful of her mother's coat, Trudel quickly disappeared out of sight behind Hannah's legs.

'Her name is Trudel,' said Wolfgang, speaking up for his younger sister. 'She is quite shy.'

Hanging his head in a show of disappointment, Herr Neusch focused his attention on the Shawl. Reaching out a finger he carefully pulled back a corner, peering down at the sleeping infant.

'I have called him Franz,' Hannah said, knowing the man would understand.

'It is a fine name, Frau Mayer. A good German name.'

Hannah smiled weakly. Pleased by the man's words.

'But come,' said Herr Neusch in a cheery voice. 'We must get you home. Frau Neusch will have heard the train and she will be worrying that you were not on it.' With that, picking up Hannah's suitcase as though all it contained were feathers he turned and leading the way he guided his charges through the dispersing crowd and into the adjoining street.

Turning the corner into Zum Wasserturm they were greeted by the sight of *Trummerfrauen* (Rubble women) clambering down the slopes of crumbling masonry which was piled up on both sides of the road their faces and clothes covered in a layer of dust. They were a mixture of old and young. Age was not a discriminating factor. If you could work you worked. They were paid of course. Not much, but these days something was everything. Enough anyway to put food in their children's bellies until their men came home. Those who were coming home. Like most German towns and cities, Berlin was populated by widows. All of them wore a scarf or a cap of some description, their thin figures bundled up in layers of assorted clothing or button-less overcoats tied around the middle with a belt or strap. Some had on a man's jacket padded with old newspapers or pieces of cardboard for insulation. Anything to keep out the bitter wind whipping down the street. All of them were wearing a pair of shapeless gloves.

Towering above them were the windowless facades of apartment buildings, their plasterwork pitted and scarred by bullets and shell holes. Protruding from the mounds of rubble, twisted into bizarre sculptures were the rusting metal girders which had once reinforced them. A narrow avenue had been cleared down the centre of the street, just wide enough for a single vehicle to drive down. At intervals along its length, cleaned of their old mortar, were piles of reclaimed bricks. All neatly stacked in waist-high rectangular blocks, each brick patiently waiting to play its part in rebuilding a city ravaged by war. At the intersection, with Am Stellwerk a line of young blonde-haired children had formed a queue at the water point. Each holding some kind of receptacle to collect the precious liquid in; buckets mainly, most without a handle, or pots and pans of varying shapes and sizes. One of them, a lanky boy wearing trousers which were too short for his long skinny legs carried a watering can. Its swan-necked spout hammered flat so that when it was filled none of the water would escape.

Walking in single file along the narrow strip of road with Herr Neusch leading and Wolfgang and Trudel close on his heels, Hannah found herself glancing across at the line of women filing past in the opposite direction their expressionless faces lined by exhaustion, eyes devoid of life. Most ignored her. Others meeting her gaze and scowling back at her angrily. Occasionally one would offer a benign smile. After all, they were all in the same boat. Some pulled a small cart or pushed a battered, hoodless pram, their wheels threatening to fall off every time they encountered an obstacle. Each one loaded with items they had scavenged from the piles of rubble, anything which could be traded on the black market. Even a single pair of worn shoes had their value. One cart contained an old gramophone its Bakelite Horn, miraculously still in one piece. Another was filled with a pile of folded linen sheets looted from a cupboard that nobody was ever likely to use again. Occasionally, a few lucky ones stumbled upon a piece of treasure in the rubble, a small silver photo frame perhaps, or a finely engraved cigarette case. All quickly hidden away in a pocket. The less fortunate ones carried armfuls of wood they had gleaned from the heaps of brick and plaster: Chair legs, pieces of floorboards, anything which would feed their stove for an hour or two. Sometimes a body would be pulled from the rubble. It was rare, but it happened. Just two days earlier they had discovered the corpse of a young girl in the ruins, entombed in an understairs cupboard where she had taken refuge to escape the bombs. Her favourite doll still clutched in her arms.

Up ahead, Herr Neusch turned into a narrow passage between two buildings. Shouting over his shoulder 'Almost there.'

The passage, which was not even wide enough for a horse and cart quickly led them into Bodelschwingh Weg a narrow back street sandwiched between the towering walls of apartment buildings on one side and the marshalling yards on the other. Facing the street which was still clogged with slabs of concrete and fallen masonry were the front doors of eight terraced houses. Three stories high with a tiled Mansard roof, they had been constructed to house railway employees and their families. Each had a small rear garden enclosed by a low brick wall that backed onto the ribbons of metal rails that snaked into the nearby station. Miraculously, even though all had a few tiles missing the row of pretty brick houses had somehow survived the daily bombing raids on the city without serious structural damage. And while it was true that two of them had lost their chimneys and several front walls were now just a jumbled pile of broken bricks. All things considered unlike the buildings in the surrounding streets Bodelschwingh Weg had come through the war relatively unscathed.

Standing at the far end of the row, while one of its second-floor windows was now boarded over, giving the facade the appearance of a face wearing an eyepatch the Neusch's house had suffered the least damage of all. Even three of the four window boxes Herr Neusch had made from a couple of old pallets still occupied their respective windowsills. Although missing a few bricks, even the front wall was still in one piece. Beyond it, leading up to the front door was a narrow gravelled path. It was a good solid wooden door, freshly painted with engine blacking from a tin Herr Neusch had discovered among the ruins of the locomotive sheds.

'Here we are,' said Herr Neusch, pointing towards the house with his free hand. 'Home sweet home.' Then with a gentlemanly bow, he pushed open the gate and ushered them inside. Smiling with satisfaction as the gate swung open effortlessly on its new brass hinges. Hinges he had recently appropriated from an impressive mahogany door belonging to the ruined apartment building opposite. Approaching the front door, Hannah was distracted by a sudden movement at one of the downstairs windows. Glancing towards it she glimpsed the face of an elderly woman peering out through one of the panes. A moment later and whoever it was disappeared. The curtain falling back into place.

First to reach the front door, before Wolfgang's bony fist could make contact with it, the door was suddenly pulled open, and there standing in the doorway was the imposing figure of Frau Neusch. Almost as wide as she was tall, with a bosom like a pouting pigeon she peered down at Wolfgang with small watery blue eyes. Terrified, Wolfgang stared back at her. With her iron-grey hair pulled into a bun and secured by a tortoiseshell comb and wearing a plain ankle-length black dress with a lace collar and cuffs she looked exactly like the wicked witch from Hansel and Gretel. In fact, if Frau Neusch's face hadn't broken into a beatific smile, it was extremely likely that Wolfgang would have dropped his suitcase and fled. But smile she did and so all was well.

'Come in! Come in!' she said. 'I was worried that you might not be on the train.' At which point Herr Neusch gave Hannah an, I told you so look. Happy to oblige, Wolfgang quickly followed by Trudel, stepped into the long windowless hallway. Faded honeysuckle patterned wallpaper lined the walls and running down the centre of the tiled floor was a threadbare runner. There were two doors, both closed. One on the left and one at the far end. Midway between them was a narrow staircase leading up to the floors its treads covered in worn linoleum. The door on the left opened into a sparsely furnished sitting room containing a two-seater sofa with an antimacassar draped over each arm and a small freshly polished circular rosewood table, partially covered by a lace tablecloth. Occupying one of the two alcoves was an ornately carved double-fronted cabinet, complete with brass key, its glass doors protecting an array of porcelain figurines. A faded Afghan rug covered most of the parquet flooring and hanging above the empty fireplace, set in a heavy frame was a picture of a Bavarian landscape complete with a fairy tale castle.

'Put your suitcase on the stairs, Wolfgang,' Herr Neusch called out. 'We will take you up to your new room after we have eaten.'

Obediently, Wolfgang placed his suitcase on the bottom tread, and taking hold of Trudel by the hand he followed Frau Neusch through the door at the far end.

As soon as they entered the Neusch's kitchen, the children were immediately enveloped in a cloud of warm air infused with the aroma of cooking. The delicious smell emanated from a large, lidless enamel pan sitting on top of a coal-fired range set against the back wall. Its ironwork blackened to within an inch of its life. Also contributing to the room's warmth was a small open fire, the lumps of coal nestling in its cast-iron grate glowing like a steelwork furnace. Standing in the middle of the room was an oblong wooden table, its surface bleached and scrubbed until it was white. Surrounding it were an assortment of chairs. The two with padded armrests belonging in front of the fire. The two lighter ones having been brought down from one of the bedrooms by Herr Neusch earlier that day. The remaining chair was actually a tall stool. Acquired by Herr Neusch at the black market in the Tiergarten in exchange for an old

Leica camera he no longer used. Its four chromium-plated legs and padded seat in surprisingly good condition considering it had been salvaged from a bombed-out building. Placed in front of each of them was a blue china soup bowl and a silver spoon. All that remained of the set of cutlery Herr Neusch had bought his wife for their silver wedding anniversary. The knives and forks having been traded for food. In times of war, need is far greater than sentiment. Adding to the unmistakable aroma of boiled vegetables was the intoxicating smell of six thick slices of corned beef each coated in a creamy batter made from acorn-flour sizzling gently in a large copper-bottomed frying pan on the adjoining hot plate. Purchased at the same time as the stool in exchange for a sack containing a few precious lumps of coal.

The back wall of the kitchen was dominated by a solid wooden door furnished with an impressive iron bolt and a metal coat hook, which Frau Neusch always complained was too high for her to reach. A rectangular window with a full-length curtain on either side held back by a sash, looked out onto a small back garden covered in a carpet of freshly fallen snow. Standing in pride of place on the wide sill was a terracotta plant pot containing a small tree branch which Frau Neusch had lovingly transformed into a Christmas tree with tinsel and small coloured candles.

Last, to enter the kitchen, Herr Neusch removed his padded jacket and positioning himself with his back to the fire he watched with quiet satisfaction as Hannah handed the infant to his wife while she removed her coat and scarf. Smiling at the look of joy on his wife's face as she gently rocked the sleeping baby back and forth in her arms. Wolfgang had already taken off his overcoat and by standing on tiptoe, stretching out his arms, he had managed to hang it up on the hook beside Herr Neusch's jacket.

'Nice and warm, aye?' said Herr Neusch to nobody in particular. 'No need of a coat in here.' Adding by way of an explanation. 'A train driver never goes short of coal.'

Tutting at her husband's boastful words Frau Neusch handed the baby back to Hannah.

'Come now, sit yourselves down, you must all be starving after such a long journey.'

'We had some bread and cheese to eat so it was not so bad,' said Wolfgang taking a seat on one of the bedroom chairs.

'And Kuchen too,' said Trudel. Reminding her brother of the cake they had eaten.

'Yes, but I am still hungry,' Wolfgang added quickly, just in case the old woman might think that he had lost his appetite.

Frau Neusch smiled, clearly delighted to have children in her kitchen. Especially the boy. With Trudel sitting happily up on her high stool she crossed to the stove and picking up a wooden spoon she gave the contents of the pot a final stir. Satisfied, with hands impervious to the heat she lifted the heavy pot by its handle's and carried it to the table. Setting it down beside a wicker basket filled with roughly cut slices of bread.

'It's not much, I'm afraid,' she said apologetically. 'Mostly potatoes and swede with a little grated sausage.'

'But you are forgetting the corned beef, mother.' Herr Neusch piped up somewhat aggrieved at having his prize purchase overlooked.

'Yes, and a little meat Herr Neusch managed to acquire from goodness knows where,' said Frau Neusch a little begrudgingly, while giving her husband a hard look.

Doing his best to keep a straight face, Herr Neusch glanced

across at Wolfgang, and tapping the side of his nose with a finger he winked knowingly. Huffing at her husband's annoying gesture, Frau Neusch began ladling the steaming soup-like mixture into the bowls. With them all filled to the brim she returned to the stove and removing the frying pan from the hot plate, taking a wooden spatula one by one she carefully turned over each of the fritters. Happy that they had all crisped up nicely, frying pan in hand she returned to the table and carefully placed a fritter into each bowl. Watching with disappointment when instead of floating on top as she had hoped, her golden delights slowly sank beneath the murky surface of the broth.

Wolfgang was the first one to finish his meal and after giving his spoon a final lick he placed it on the table. The lick however did not go unnoticed and after exchanging a look with her husband, pushing back her chair Frau Neusch got up from the table and walked across to the range. Returning with the frying pan in her hand, with a flick of the spatula she deposited the last of the fritters into Wolfgang's empty bowl. Smiling with delight, grabbing his spoon Wolfgang attacked the fritter as though he hadn't eaten for a week. Thankfully, before the succulent morsel entered his mouth he spotted the disapproving look on his mother's face.

'Thank you.' He muttered rather apologetically.

Smiling with pleasure Frau Neusch ruffled his mop of hair with her free hand.

It was at that moment that the baby began crying. A sound which was so alien to the old couple that it took them quite by surprise.

'Is there somewhere I can go to?' Hannah asked. 'Only I need …'

Before she could finish her sentence, Frau Neusch turned

on her husband.

'Well don't just sit there like a fool husband!' And when Herr Neusch showed no sign of moving. 'Shoo! Shoo! Out you go. And take the children with you.'

Fearing that the frying pan his wife was holding might be used for something other than frying fritters, Herr Neusch scrambled to his feet.

'Come now children. Time for some fresh air I think.'

With that he plucked his jacket and the children's coats off the coat hook and pushing a hand into a sleeve he opened the door. Ushering the children outside even before they had time to put their coats on.

Smiling at their pantomime exit, unbuttoning the front of her dress Hannah pulled down the cup of her brassiere. Seating herself in a chair, Frau Neusch gazed lovingly at the baby as it suckled contentedly at Hannah's breast.

'Now all the family are fed.'

Hannah nodded. Smiling at the old woman's words.

'You have both been so kind to us.'

'Nonsense,' said Frau Neusch fluttered her fingers as though she was brushing away an annoying fly. 'It's no more than you would have done for us had circumstances been different. Besides which you are family now and that's how you will be treated.'

Overcome with emotion, tears welled up in Hannah's eyes. But these tears were different. They were tears of happiness. For while the past must never be forgotten, she and her children had embarked on a new life now and in her heart, she believed that it would be a good one. With nothing more to be said, the two women turned their heads and stared out through the window.

The Letter

Outside in the garden, Herr Neusch had eventually managed to get an excited Trudel into her coat; though not all the buttons were in the correct buttonhole. In the meantime, Wolfgang was busy at work, his small ball of snow quickly growing in size as he rolled it back and forth across the garden. Keen to begin making a snowball of her own, with a little help from Herr Neusch, Trudel was soon copying her brother. Within a few minutes, satisfied that the size of his snowball was sufficient for the snowman's body, oblivious to the cold Wolfgang began sculpting it into shape. After convincing a reluctant Trudel that her snowball was now large enough to make his head, rounding it into a ball Herr Neusch carefully placed it on top of the snowman's body. Confident that it wasn't going to fall off, dipping a hand into his coat pocket, the old train driver removed three small lumps of coal and handed them to Wolfgang. Smiling as Trudel began jumping up and down with excitement as she watched her brother pushing them into the snowman's head. Two for the eyes and the larger one for his nose. Clapping her hands together in delight when as a finishing touch Herr Neusch placed his cap on top of the snowman's head.

'Well Wolfgang Mayer,' said Herr Neusch resting a hand on the young boy's shoulder as they stood admiring their handiwork, 'now that we have made ourselves such a fine-looking snowman do you think you and I could build a radio set?'

Two

The Cauldron – Stalingrad
Late December 1942

PUSHING BACK HIS peaked cap, *Hauptmann* (Captain) Schlesser raised his field glasses a second time and surveyed the ground in front of him. A no man's land littered with the gutted shells of burnt-out buildings, their blackened, windowless walls reduced to piles of rubble by the months of constant shelling. A sight which still sickened and angered him. A once vibrant city reduced to an apocalyptic wasteland by man's ability to destroy. An attack was coming. He could sense it just as a wild animal senses danger. Knowing when that was the trick. Normally he would have sent out a small patrol to investigate, to probe the enemy position. But with his company reduced from one hundred and eighty to just twenty-eight men he could no longer afford such a luxury. To the north, the eerie howl of Katyusha rockets, nicknamed Stalin's Organs by the German soldiers could be heard. Here it was the eerie silence that concerned Hauptmann Schlesser.

'It's too quiet,' he said voicing his concern to the soldier standing beside him. 'Just too quiet for my liking.'

A half-smile touched the soldier's gaunt, unshaven face. A few inches shorter than his captain but broader in the shoulder, he wore a long overcoat belted around the waist its collar turned up. Although the epaulets were gone, the left sleeve still bore the insignia of *Hauptfeldwebel* (Sergeant

The Letter

first class). The soldier's name was Franz Mayer.

Both men had joined the 71st Infantry Division just before the invasion of France in June 1940 and had served together in the 211th Infantry Regiment ever since. For Schlesser soldiering was in the blood. Both his Great Grandfather and his Grandfather had fought in the Franco-Prussian War and his father had lost an arm at Verdun. So it was something of a family tradition. For Mayer, it had been an act of patriotism. Ignited by the Fuhrer's desire to see the Sudatenland returned to the Fatherland. But sadly for him, Hitler had wanted more. Much more. Two men from vastly different backgrounds now comrades in arms.

Together with elements of the 305th Infantry Division supported by tanks from the 4th Panzer Division they had entered Stalingrad in early September and for four gruelling months had fought to drive out the Russian defenders. Fighting doggedly for every house, every factory every street. Sometimes battling for days at a time for a single building. Hundreds of German soldiers being sacrificed for a few yards of ground. And yet even when the enemy had been driven back to the banks of the Volga River still they resisted, fighting with the tenacity of men devoid of all hope. Their only reward a glorious death.

Then winter arrived with its howling blizzards and sub-zero temperatures. And with the changing of the seasons came another change. Un-foreseen. Unexpected, and for some unwelcome. In mid-November five Russian armies, over half a million soldiers spearheaded by the 21st Guards Army in the north and the 64th Army in the south smashed through the weakened German flanks and sweeping across the snow-covered steppe in a giant pincer movement by the 23rd November they had encircled the city. Trapping the 6th Army in a ring of iron. A career officer, Schlesser had always doubted the wisdom of committing such an elite mobile force as the 6th Army to this type of urban warfare. In his opinion, it was a criminal waste of men and machines. Especially as day after day, he watched his company strength being whittled away. His men dying senselessly fighting for every building, every cellar. Even engaging in deadly hand-to-hand combat in the city sewers. *Rattenkrieg* (rat war) the soldiers called it. To him, this battle for a city that had little tactical importance was becoming nothing more than an obsession for Hitler simply because of its name. And now they were encircled. An army of 330,000 men trapped in a *Kessel* (cauldron) of death. But all was not lost. They still retained the ability, the firepower to smash their way through the Red Army encirclement with ease every soldier knew that. But just as their hopes were being raised Von Paulus and his generals received the fateful Fuhrer Order. "There was to be no breakout. Stalingrad must be held at all costs. If necessary they must fight to the last bullet."

They slaughtered the cavalry horses first. Then the heavy horses which had been used to pull the howitzers and heavy flak guns. And when they had eaten the flesh they made a thin watery soup by boiling the animal's bones. On the 19th November 1942 the ledger of the Deputy Quartermaster of the 6th Army showed a total strength of 330,000 men. By the 6th January 1943, this number had been reduced to 190,000. In fifty-one days 140,000 men had been lost. Killed in battle or died from hunger or their wounds. For the living, it meant a little more soup in your mess-tin. A few extra grams of bread. A little longer to live before you too were struck off the ledger.

No sooner had the words left Schlesser's lips when from beyond his field of vision came the sound of a whistle being blown. A heartbeat later and a great roar went up. Urra! Urra! Urra! The bone-chilling battle cry of hundreds of Russian soldiers. Followed moments later by the sound of an engine coughing into life.

'Are the men in position?' Asked Schlesser, knowing already what the answer would be.

'Yes Hauptmann.' Mayer replied calmly.

This was the second attack the Bolsheviks had made in the last three days and each of the twenty-eight men, the remnants of the one hundred and eighty strong company which had entered the city knew what was expected of him. The constant fighting had become almost routine. The ever-present fear of death hovering over them like an invisible cloud. For some, those who had seen first-hand the appalling conditions of the field -hospitals; cellars choked with an endless stream of torn and bleeding bodies. Planks of wood for operating tables. Exhausted surgeons, sustained by black coffee and Pervitin operating with a scalpel and saw. Slicing through flesh to extract a piece of shrapnel. Sawing off arms and legs like branches from a tree. And everywhere the stench of festering wounds; the thought of being wounded was more terrifying than being killed. For those fearing both prospects, the problem was solved by putting a gun to your head and pulling the trigger. And so they waited. Some with a farewell letter carefully folded and tucked inside their pay-book. A letter they prayed would never be posted. While others, old soldiers like Giebeler thought this sort of thing was tempting fate. Tell them about it when you get home was his philosophy. They were no longer fighting for the Fuhrer and Fatherland anymore. They were fighting for each other. Fighting so that somehow against all the odds they might survive this nightmare. That they would be rescued from this hell hole and return home safely to their loved ones.

The range marker, an innocuous piece of timber stuck upright in a pile of brick rubble, was set at fifty meters, and not a shot was to be fired until the first of the enemy reached it. Even without his field glasses, Schlesser could see them now. Not yet as individuals, just a solid wall of men. A tide of olive green rushing towards them with just one thought. To kill. In amongst them, its chains rattling, plumes of inky black smoke belching from its exhaust was a tank.

'It's a T-70!' Somebody shouted out from a forward position.

'Thank you Giebeler,' said Schlesser, recognising the man's voice.

'Thank fuck it's not one of their T-34's eh Hauptmann?' Another soldier called out.

Schlesser smiled. 'Then we would most definitely be in trouble,' he replied, before turning to Mayer. 'One for Bauer and Kaufmann I think?'

Mayer nodded and scrambling over the rubble-strewn ground he crossed to where two soldiers were positioned behind a triangle of brickwork that had once been the corner of a house. Armed with a Panzerfaust and a small satchel, the pair shuffled away disappearing moments later into the gutted shell of an adjoining building.

The Spandau MG-42 opened up first. A hundred and fifty rounds fired in short bursts of twenty to thirty seconds, to begin with. Moving from left to right along the leading ranks of Russian soldiers, the 7.92 mm rounds ending lives as easily as snuffing out a candle. But still, they came. Urged on by pistol-waving commissars screaming out their patriotic slogans. Those with any sense taking shelter in the wake of the T-70 as it rumbled forward over the crumbled ruins. Now the remainder of Schlesser's men, all armed with a Karabiner rifle took up the battle. Each selecting a target and taking aim. No fancy headshots. With ammunition so scarce, each bullet was priceless. So just a single round in an enemy's body was all that was required.

With Kaufmann close behind him, the Panzerfaust slung over his shoulder Bauer made his way down a short flight of wooden steps into a cellar. Quickly adjusting to the gloomy interior, clambering over lumps of fallen masonry the pair made their way towards the far wall. Scrambling up a sloping pile of brick rubble, they emerged into a cave-like opening just high enough for a man to crawl through. The unsupported section of the building's outer wall hovering over it like the blade of a guillotine. Moments later, above the crackle of gunfire and the rhythmic bursts from the Spandau they heard the unmistakable roar of the oncoming tank. Dropping onto one knee behind a concrete beam that had once supported a ground floor window, Bauer pulled the Panzerfaust from his shoulder. Gripping the tube-like weapon in the palm of both hands, a finger hovering over the firing lever he aimed it through the opening in front of him. Kneeling beside him, Kaufmann opened the flap of the satchel and began fiddling with the bomb's primitive timer. Gauging the setting of its fuse on the time it would take the tank to reach where he and Bauer lay in wait. Information gleaned from the increase in the tank's engine noise and the clanking of its caterpillar tracks as they rumbled over the stunted remains of walls and buildings. Not an exact science but experience was a good teacher and Kaufmann had proved to be a worthy student. Watching as the legs and lower bodies of advancing Russian soldiers, oblivious of their presence passed in front of them, Bauer and Kaufmann counted off the seconds. And then, suddenly the T-70 lumbered into view directly opposite them. Its great metal bulk less than fifteen meters away. No need for the sights this time thought Bauer as his finger pressed down on the firing lever.

Concealed by a partially collapsed building, Mayer watched with satisfaction as the Panzerfaust's warhead exploded against the side of the Russian tank sending lumps of mangled metal skywards and bringing the vehicle to a grinding halt. A moment later he spotted Kaufmann emerging from the ruined house. Watching as he raced across the rubble-strewn ground and tossed the satchel-bomb under the belly of the tank. Seconds later an explosion ripped up through the T-70, the shock wave lifting Kaufmann off his feet and propelling him back towards the opening in the wall far quicker than his legs could have carried him. Smiling with relief as he watched Kaufmann scrambling to safety, resting his rifle on the brick wall in front of him Mayer focused his aim on the tank's turret. He didn't have long to wait before its hatch cover was pushed open and a member of its crew emerged. With the round from Mayer's Karabiner buried in his chest, like a puppet whose strings had been cut the man toppled sideways and began sliding down the side of the tank. Dying before he reached the ground. Pulling back the bolt, Mayer loaded another round into the breach and waited. When the second of the two-man crew appeared in the open hatch he was already a human torch. So without a flicker of emotion, Mayer turned away. Quickly seeking another victim for his next bullet among the on-rushing ranks of Russian soldiers.

And then, as quickly as it had begun it was over. Unable to withstand the slaughter any longer, deaf to the vitriolic cries of the commissars first in ones and two's then in dozens crazed with fear the surviving Russian soldiers turned and fled. Trampling over the bodies of their dead and wounded comrades in a desperate bid to escape the carnage. With the last bullet fired, a profound silence settled over the scene. Punctuated by the cries and groans of the mortally wounded littering the rubble-strewn ground. The pitiful

The Letter

voice of a son calling out to his mother. Words she would never wish to hear. Not even in her darkest moments.

Cursing his twisted ankle, Kaufmann climbed to the top of the cellar steps and supported by Bauer the pair made their way back to their position where they were greeted by a hearty pat on the back from Mayer. Followed by a caustic remark.

'Not so nimble anymore eh Kaufmann? I suppose you'll expect our beloved quartermaster to find you a crutch?'

The soldier glared back at him gloomily and then they both began laughing. The pair had fought together side by side for a long time and Kaufmann knew this was Mayer's way of saying "well done". A brief moment of levity helping to lift the sombre mood hanging over them all. It was always the same, a kind of fatigue mixed with relief. Relief that it was not you lying out there, your life-blood seeping into the ground like those poor Bolshevik bastards. You had lived to fight another day as the saying goes. And that was something to be thankful for in a place where life expectancy was no longer measured in days, only in hours and minutes.

The companies bunker was located in a cellar. The building above having been reduced to a pile of brick-rubble by the shelling. Its low ceiling, constructed of a thick layer of concrete was badly cracked in places but was in no immediate danger of collapse. Or so private Giebeler, someone who could always be counted on for an opinion confidently assured his less optimistic comrades. Thankfully for them, Hauptmann Schlesser didn't share Giebeler's optimism ordering two stout lengths of timber to be used as pit props to provide some additional support. The cellar's dirt floor was covered in strips of threadbare, colourless carpet with a short flight of steps leading up to the entrance concealed behind a canvas sheet. A small cast iron stove, set up on bricks occupied one corner. Its makeshift chimney disappearing above ground through a hole in the cellar wall. At the far end were four wooden cots, each occupied by two soldiers, all dead to the world. Three less fortunate souls their shaven heads covered in scabs, their eyes glittering with hunger huddled together around the stove. The rooms remaining furniture comprised of a makeshift table and an ornately carved wooden chair. Hanging from a nail driven into each of the wooden props a pair of paraffin lamps did their best to give the subterranean room a modicum of light.

Seated at the desk, Hauptmann Schlesser cranked the handle of the field telephone for the third time and held the handset to his ear. Silence.

'Damn in hell!' The expletive wasn't spoken loudly but the officer's frustration was obvious. 'Corporal Deifel go and relieve Sergeant Mayer. Tell him I need him.'

Reluctantly, Corporal Deifel relinquished his place by the stove, and without a word, turning up the collar of his greatcoat he climbed the steps and disappeared through the bunker entrance. Moments later, the canvas sheet was drawn back and Sergeant Mayer descended the steps. Removing his gloves, he crossed to the table watching and waiting as the officer finished what he was writing.

Setting down his pen, tearing the page from his notebook, Hauptmann Schlesser reached out and offered it to Mayer.

'The telephone line is down again. Go and see what you can scrounge from the quartermaster. For what it's worth I've listed what we need but see what you can get anyway.' Then looking up into Mayer's face. 'We must have ammunition.' He said, emphasising the word 'must'.

Taking the sheet of paper from him. Mayer pushed it into a pocket.

The Letter

'Yes Sir.

Then pulling on his gloves he turned away and began walking towards the steps.

'Take Neubauer with you,' said Schlesser as an afterthought. 'Who knows when he sees the state of the poor lads face it might soften the old bastard's heart eh?'

His foot on the bottom step, trying hard not to smile Mayer turned towards the officer.

'Can't hurt I suppose Hauptmann.'

And with that, he climbed the remaining steps and left the bunker. Behind him, pencil in hand Schlesser returned to his notebook. There was a report to write and Kaufmann's bravery must also be noted.

Situated on Heroes Square the Univermag Department Store was one of Stalingrad's newest and most prestigious buildings. Positioned at the junction between two wide avenues its imposing frontage thrusting out into the large T-shaped square like the prow of some great ocean-going liner it commanded attention. Standing four stories high it was constructed in the Monumental style of architecture with stuccoed walls inset with rows of plain oblong windows, the first and fourth floors stylized by an ornate balustrade. Sitting atop the building was an impressive square turret embellished with five large Greek-style urns. At ground level, its sweeping curved entrance, approached by a flight of wide steps was supported by eight large pillars; four rounded ones, and behind them four square ones. The gaps between them allowing access to the five sets of glass panelled double doors that opened into the store's spacious, brightly lit interior.

Requisitioned by the 71st Infantry Division for its headquarters, this once-proud edifice was now little more than a roofless, fire-ravaged cavern. Its smoke-blackened façade pockmarked by bullet holes and rocket shells. Miraculously, all of the eight pillars which supported the curved portico had survived the deluge of shells that had claimed many of the neighbouring buildings, reducing them to piles of rubble. Stretching out in front of it the vast snow-covered expanse of Hero's Square was littered with the burned-out shells of vehicles and artillery pieces; Tanks resting on shattered tracks their turrets pierced by shell holes. Howitzers abandoned because there were no shells for them to fire. A pair of ack-ack guns, their twisted muzzles pointing skywards in a forlorn gesture of defiance. At the far end, lying spread-eagled on the ground like a dead bird was a Junkers 52 its fuselage peppered with bullet holes. Radiating out from its centre in long symmetrical lines, their scorched and burned branches giving them the appearance of used pipe cleaners, were long rows of young lime trees.

After finding a gap in the ring of barbed wire which encircled the square, as Mayer and Neubauer clambered over the wall of sandbags at the front of the building one of the remaining front doors swung open and two soldiers, bundled up in scarves and greatcoats emerged. Relieved, the two sentries who had been huddled around a makeshift brazier for warmth, handed their weapons to the new guard detail before quickly making their way into the building. Unchallenged, Mayer and Neubauer followed them through the open door the shards of glass from the shattered windows crunching under their feet as they crossed the marble floor of the foyer. Nothing was left of the mahogany display cabinets which had once greeted shoppers as they entered the store. Their wood burned, their glass tops shattered. All that remained in their place were mounds of rubble and an eerie silence broken momentarily by the sound of the sentry's boots as they descended the stone stairs into the basement below. Leading, Mayer crossed to the staircase the doors which once barred the entrance already removed, and with Neubauer a step behind, the pair made their way below ground.

By the time Mayer and Neubauer reached the foot of the stairs, the two sentries had disappeared. Confronting them was a wide corridor leading off right and left, illuminated by a string of naked light bulbs hung at intervals from a single cable. From somewhere within the bowels of the building the steady throb of a generator reverberated along the corridor.

'This way,' said Mayer, turning towards the direction the sound was coming from. 'We'll try down here.'

Making their way along the subterranean passage, up ahead of them a door suddenly opened and a soldier clutching a sheet of paper appeared. After giving the pair a cursory glance, the soldier hurried away disappearing down a narrow side passage like a rabbit down a hole. As they carried on past the half-open door they heard the crackle of radio static and the rhythmic chatter of a Morse key coming from inside. A few yards further along the corridor the sound of muffled voices emanated from a door-less room. A tangled web of wires snaking out from it and into the hall before vanishing through a hole in the ceiling. Hearing Mayer and Neubauer approaching, one of the switchboard operators turned towards them.

'We need the stores,' said Meyer. 'Which way?'

Holding his headphones away from his ears, the operator stared at Mayer.

'The stores. Which way?' Mayer repeated.

Raising his arm the soldier gestured in the direction they

were taking. As Mayer nodded his thanks, another operator swivelled around in his chair.

'Do you have an appointment?'

'Why do we need one?' Asked Mayer.

'No.' The man replied before turning away. 'But if you get in without one be sure to let me know and I'll see you're recommended for a Knight's Cross.'

A set of double doors marked the end of the corridor. Pinned to one was a sign with a single word written on it in bold letters "Quartermaster". Gripping the handle Mayer quickly realized that the door was locked. Annoyed, he clenched his fist and began banged it hard against the door. Getting no response, he hammered on the door a second time. Nothing! Contemplating using the butt of his rifle, before he had time to put the thought into action, from beyond the door Mayer heard the sound of a bolt being drawn back. A moment later the door was pulled open and a young soldier, his head swathed in a blood-stained bandage peered out.

'The stores are closed. No one is…'

Before he could complete the sentence, Mayer reached out a hand, and pushing hard on the door he forced the young soldier aside, and closely followed by Neubauer, he strode into the room.

Once used as a storage room for crockery; everything from porcelain dinner sets to everyday items of chinaware, the rows of tall wooden shelving now held items of a more military nature each marked by a stencilled label. Piles of neatly folded grey blankets, tinned food, and boxes of ammunition and grenades. The upper shelf was reserved for loaves of bread. Each row neatly stacked one on top of the other like bricks. A precaution against foraging vermin.

Which as it turned out was quite unnecessary as whatever rats there were, had been killed and eaten weeks ago. In the far corner were a few hessian sacks filled with potatoes. Light was provided by two large naked light bulbs suspended from the white-washed ceiling. An oil heater, pushed up against a side wall did its best to keep the room a few degrees above freezing. Hanging above it in a frame that had previously contained a photograph of the Fuhrer was a picture of Raphael's Madonna and child. A page torn from a magazine which an employee had forgotten to take home with them when they had finished work for the day perhaps?

Strategically placed between door and shelving was a large neo-classical style mahogany pedestal desk. Acting as both barricade and counter its usefulness had ensured its escape from the jaws of the building's many stoves. Behind it, seated on a comfortable-looking chair was Wilhelm Haussegger the regiment's Quartermaster affectionately known to all as Big Willi. A nick-name attributed no doubt to his size; after all the man was at least six feet tall, squarely built with a broad chest and a ponderous belly which his uniform trousers had trouble accommodating. Of course, there were a few nameless individuals who maintained that the attribute referred to the size of his penis. Although no one it seemed had been brave enough to verify whether this was true or not. With his clean-shaven head and a pair of metal-rimmed spectacles perched on the bridge of his hawkish nose, he gave the appearance of being a nightclub bouncer masquerading as a Jewish moneylender. Placed in front of him on a fine porcelain plate, the last one to have survived were the remains of a half-eaten meal.

'You heard what he said. The stores are closed. Now bugger off.'

Even Quartermaster Hausseggers voice was big. A deep

bass tone, effortlessly delivered.

The old bastard hasn't changed much thought Mayer as he stepped closer to the desk.

'What's this then? Are the Wehrmacht keeping shopkeepers hours now?'

'The stores are open when I say so. Now bugger off before I send for the Felgendarmarie.' (Military police) Said the Quartermaster without even bothering to look up.

'You can send for the Fuhrer himself for all I care,' said Mayer grim-faced. 'Maybe he would have something to say about your opening hours eh?'

Angered, Haussegger lifted his head and stared hard into Mayer's face.

Thinking perhaps he gone a step too far, Mayer softened his voice.

'Look I can see we have come at a bad time. Go ahead and finish your meal. We can wait.'

Placated by the man's words, Haussegger settled back in his chair and pondered for a moment. Finally, not relishing a cold supper without replying he picked up his spoon and returned to his half-eaten meal.

Absent-mindedly picking at one of the pustules on his face with a dirty fingernail while mentally licking his lips, Neubauer stared down at the Quartermaster's plate. Whatever he was eating smelled delicious and it was taking all of his willpower to stop him from reaching down and grab the man's plate. Spooning the last of the meal into his mouth, after mopping up the thick brown gravy with a crust of bread Haussegger leaned back in his chair and belched. Suitable relieved, looking up from his empty plate he studied Mayer's face. Somehow the man seemed vaguely familiar but for the life of him, he couldn't remember why. But it would come to him. There may be parts of him that didn't work too well but thankfully his memory wasn't one of them. With his square jaw and cold blue eyes, he looked a hard bastard. Not someone he was likely to forget.

'What's your regiment?'

'211th,' Mayer replied. Relieved that the man was even taking an interest in his request for supplies. Perhaps there was hope yet.

'Your battalion?'

'Second battalion' said Mayer, adding 'Third Infantry Company,' just in case it might make a difference.

Wiping the hand he had used to soak up the gravy on the front of his jacket, Haussegger pulled open a desk drawer and removed a heavy-looking book with a worn leather cover.

Opening it to the relevant page, peering through his glasses the Quartermaster began running his index finger down the page. Stopping halfway down.

'According to my records, your next supplies aren't due for another two days.'

Leaning forward, Mayer planted both his hand's palms down onto the desktop.

'In two days- time, we won't need any of your stinking rations. Because we'll all be fucking dead.' Mayer replied angrily.

Haussegger stared up into Mayer's face. Somehow the anger in the man's voice had triggered a memory. Ah yes, now he remembered. France nineteen forty. In a small village just outside the town of Amiens. Smiling to himself as he recalled the incident. The man standing in front of him now had been bawling out a soldier he'd caught trying to put his hand up a young French girl's skirt before grabbing the poor sod by the scruff of the neck and throwing him into a ditch. Yes, that was him alright. Not somebody you forgot in a hurry. An old sweat like himself. And now here they were together again. Only this time things were different. This time they were both well and truly in the shit.

'Look at least give us some bloody ammo, so we can die like soldiers,' said Mayer the anger in his voice evaporating.

Haussegger leaned back in his chair. My God, so this was to be their only salvation. An honourable death.

'I'll need a requisition form signed by your officer.'

Taken by surprise at the quartermaster's words, Mayer quickly pulled off his gloves and removing the page from Schlesser's notepad from his pocket he handed it to Haussegger.

'Will this do?'

Taking the page from him, the Quartermaster began running his eyes over the list of items.

'Quite a shopping list eh? What does this officer of yours think? That Christmas has come early perhaps?'

Mayer shrugged his shoulders apologetically. 'He has always been an optimist.'

'Has he know,' said Haussegger closing the ledger. 'Not something I'd recommend in our line of business eh?' And reaching into the drawer once more he pulled out a pad of official requisition forms. Removing a pencil from a top pocket he placed it on top of the pad.

'I'm promoting you' Haussegger said, pushing pad and pencil across the desk. 'Sign your name at the bottom.'

Picking up the pencil, Mayer quickly scrawled his signature.

The first explosion had little effect. The one that followed though was much closer, causing the light bulbs to flicker ominously and fragments of the ceiling to fall onto the floor. Pushing back the chair Haussegger climbed ponderously to his feet.

'Ivan's lullaby,' he said in a resigned voice. Then taking two blankets from one of the racks he moved towards the door. 'Follow me. No sense in you venturing out until morning. They'll probably keep it up all night.' Adding with a note of envy 'They never seem to be short of shells.'

And with that he disappeared through the doorway, quickly followed by Mayer and young Neubauer. After walking a few yards Haussegger turned off the main corridor and into a narrow unlit passage, its grey concrete walls running with water from a ruptured pipe in the ceiling. Fortunately, thanks to a step the floor of the small room the Quartermaster led them into was relatively dry. Reaching up, Haussegger flicked his lighter into life, touching the flame to the wicks of two candles stuck to a wooden ledge by dribbles of wax.

'It's not the Adlon,' said Haussegger, referring to Berlin's prestigious hotel on Unter den Linden. 'But it will do you for the night. Then handing each of them a blanket he turned towards the doorway.

'We're grateful but what about our supplies?' Asked Mayer anxiously.

'Come and see me in the morning and I'll see what I can do.'

And then the man was gone. The sound of his feet splashing through the puddles receding with every step until all that remained was the drip-drip of water trickling down from the ceiling. The light from the candles revealed two metal beds, each covered by a thin stained mattress. After prodding each in turn with a fist, removing his helmet Mayer sprawling out on what he believed to be the more comfortable of the two and covering himself with the blanket he closed his eyes. With Neubaur quickly following suit, in less than a minute both had fallen into a deep sleep.

Mayer heard it first. The splashing of feet wading through water, and even before the young orderly entered the small room he was sitting bolt upright his rifle aimed at the doorway. Although startled by the sight of the Mauser point directly at him, thankfully the young soldier held his nerve and the two tin plates he was carrying didn't end up on the floor.

'Apologies,' Mayer muttered, putting down the rifle. 'It's become a habit.'

Recovering his composure, the young orderly stepped forward and handed a plate containing boiled potatoes and diced portions of meat all swimming in a dark rich gravy, to each of the two soldiers.

'Complements of the Quartermaster,' he said cheerfully. Then remembering the two spoons in his top pocket, he handed one to each of them. Grinning from ear to ear at the look of bewilderment on the faces of Mayer and Neubaur as they surveyed the plates of food.

'Tell him we appreciate his kindness,' said Mayer before spooning up a lump of meat.

'Oh he looks a mean old bastard,' said the young soldier 'but he's not a bad sort really.'

And then by way of explaining his continued presence. 'I am to remain here until you have eaten. Every plate and spoon must be accounted for.'

The Letter

Shrugging his shoulders Mayer popped the lump of meat into his mouth and began chewing. Amazed at how tender it was he looked enquiringly at the young storeman.

'Oh it's not human if that's what you're thinking,' he said, sniggering at the sound of Naubauer almost choking on his mouthful of food.

Ignoring the remark Mayer continued eating, savouring every mouthful. Seated on the bed opposite, having recovered from the thought of becoming a cannibal Neubauer wolfed his food down. Stuffing lumps of meat and potato into his mouth as though he were entered into an eating competition. Finally, after licking the last trace of gravy from the plate Neubauer pronounced confidently.

'That was the best meal I've ever eaten.'

'I am pleased that you enjoyed it,' said the young storeman taking the plate and spoon from Neubauer.

'Come on then,' said Mayer, handing his plate and spoon to the orderly 'So what have we just eaten then?'

The young storeman smiled. 'You have just eaten the last of Major Neist's Doberman's.'

Mayer smiled, a rare thing and not something Neubauer had ever seen before.

'Well God Bless Major Neist and his Doberman I say.' And with that Mayer sprawled back onto the bed and closed his eyes.

A corner of the portico laid in ruins. Destroyed by the previous night's shelling. Trapped beneath it was the broken bodies of the two sentries. One door remained intact, gently swinging back and forth, a plaything of the icy wind blowing up from the Volga River. Emerging from the building, an ammunition belt for the MG-42 machine gun slung around their necks, Mayer and Neubauer scrambled over what remained of the wall of sandbags. It had snowed again during the night, the crystallised flakes nestling in the cracks and crevices of the burned-out buildings, covering everything in a mantel of white. Squeezing through a gap in the coils of barbed wire, each holding one end of an ammunition box walking side by side they made their way along the rubble-choked road. Their feet leaving a trail of footprints behind them like a present-day Robinson Crusoe and Man Friday. After about half a mile the road opened out into a small square, enclosed on all sides by the remains of what had once been elegant buildings their skeletal spires pointing upwards towards the heavens like accusing fingers. At its heart was an ornate marble fountain with the figure of a Dolphin as its centrepiece. Protruding from its mouth was a small water pipe with an icicle shaped like a unicorn's horn hanging from its lip. A shell had breached the outer wall allowing the water to drain away, forming a halo of ice around its circular base. Both men were struggling under the weight of the ammo box, especially Neubauer. With a stomach unused to consuming such a protein-rich meal he had spent much of the previous night vomiting its contents onto the floor. Now, ashen faced and plagued by stomach cramps, he was beginning to wish he had never heard of Major Neist and his bloody Doberman.

Old soldiers will tell you that you never see or hear the gun that kills you. For Neubauer, this proved to be true. The crack as the firing pin of the Mosin-Nagant made contact with the bullet's primer reaching his ears when he was already dead. The 7.62 calibre armour-piercing round striking Neubauer's helmet at the point where it curved down from his forehead and burning through his brain. Exiting out through the other side engulfed in a crimson mist.

Even as the globules of Neubauer's blood and brains splattered against his cheek, knowing the likelihood of a second bullet following the first Mayer was already throwing himself to the ground. A split second later he was proved right when the corner brick of the low wall he had thrown himself behind suddenly exploded in a shower of fragments. The sound of the shot echoing around the enclosed square. Spotting what looked to be the entrance to a cellar, freeing himself of the ammunition belt, on hands and knees Mayer began crawling towards it. Finding himself greeted by a set of narrow stairs with his arms extended out in front he slithered down them on his belly into the stairwell below. Pushing himself upright, gulping in mouthfuls of air Mayer rested his back against the wall. In his weakened condition, any physical exertion quickly exhausted him. Allowing his eyes to become accustomed to the gloomy interior, he discovered that he was at the entrance to what appeared to be a narrow passage. With no option other than to see where it was leading to, Mayer entered the inky blackness and with a hand pressed against both walls, he inched forward his boots scraping on the uneven surface of the dirt floor. After what seemed like an eternity, just when he was beginning to wonder if the passage would never end it suddenly dog-legged to the right and up ahead, exposed by a shaft of daylight was a flight of stone steps. With his rifle slung across his shoulder, climbing the rubble-strewn steps one at a time Mayer emerged into what appeared to be the atrium of a large imposing residence.

The heart of the house was a void. The chequered tiled floor littered with the shattered remains of the glass skylight and fragments of the ceiling. Above, the shells of windowless rooms were exposed to the heavens, their furniture reduced to matchwood. Strips of wallpaper fluttering like pennons in the biting wind. In the spacious hall, clinging precariously to an inner wall a wide staircase with an ornate balustrade spiralled upwards. Testing each tread Mayer slowly climbed to the first floor. Reaching the wide landing, getting down on hands and knees he crawled across to the blackened remains of a window. Removing his helmet, he peered over the charred sill and looked out into the square. Hidden somewhere in the buildings opposite there was a Russian sniper. The trajectory of the bullets had given Mayer a clue. Head high, not from above. So he focused his search on the ground floor windows. But then a sheet of corrugated iron laying on the top of a pile of rubble outside one of the ruined houses attracted his attention. His suspicions heightened when where he would have expected the snow to have settled there wasn't any. Reasoning that somebody may have disturbed it, unslinging his rifle with his eyes focused on the rusting sheet of metal Mayer settled down to wait. He had all day. He also had a very good reason for wanting to kill whoever might be hiding under that sheet of iron.

At first, he thought he had imagined the slight movement. But he was quickly proved wrong when a foot appeared, then another. Followed by a pair of legs. Resting his rifle on the window ledge Mayer took aim, his finger hovering over the trigger. Waiting until the sniper had slithered into full view, he fired. Watching with satisfaction as the body jerked and then lay still. Working the bolt, Mayer fed another bullet into the breach and fired another round into the body. If fighting in Stalingrad had taught him anything it was that where Russians were concerned, it always paid to be sure.

Approaching from behind, rifle held at waist height his finger on the trigger, Mayer walked slowly towards the prostrate figure. Stretched out full length and wearing a tight-fitting olive green padded jacket and a pair of mud-brown trousers the dead sniper looked quite frail. Even the

The Letter

fur cap with its customary ear-flaps seemed too big for the head it was covering. Sticking out a foot with relative ease, Meyer turned the body over onto its back. Even for a battle-hardened soldier like Mayer, the sight of the young woman's lifeless eyes staring up at him was a bit of a shock. My God, what has it come to? Now even our children are killing each other. Retrieving the sniper's rifle, smashing the stock against a pile of bricks he tossed it away into the rubble.

Looking up as Mayer stepped in through the entrance to the bunker, Schlesser was relieved to see that the sergeant was carrying a laden sack. Resourceful as always though the officer half-smiling.

'Any ammunition?' Schlesser asked before Mayer was halfway down the steps.

'Yes Hauptmann,' said Mayer crossing to the table. 'Corporal Deifel is distributing it now.

Five belts for the MG and twenty rounds for each of the men.'

'Is that all our dear quartermaster could spare?'

Mayer shrugged. 'He said we are due more in two days. But for now, that's all there is.'

But Schlesser wasn't listening. His gaze moving towards the steps. Before he could ask the question Mayer knew was coming, stepping forward the sergeant reached into his pocket and pulling out the broken half of the identity disc and the pay-book he had removed from Neubauer's jacket pocket he placed them on the table.

'A sniper got him. Shot in the head so he didn't suffer.' The words spoken matter-of-factly.

Overwhelmed by sadness, Schlesser slumped back in his

chair. His eyes fixed on the small strip of metal and the small book with its crumpled brown cover.

'Dear God not Neubauer, he was just a boy.' Then reaching out he picked up the tag, squeezing it tightly in the palm of his hand. '*Gott im Himmel*, (God in heaven) has this stinking war no conscience?' he cried out angrily. Striking the table with his clenched fist. Mayer remained silent for a moment. Waiting for the officer's anger to subside.

'For what it's worth she won't be doing any more killing.'

'She! You mean a woman killed Neubauer?' Schlesser asked in disbelief. Clearly shocked by the revelation.

'Yes, a slip of a girl. Probably younger than he was,' said Mayer before lifting the sack he was carrying and emptying its contents onto the table; A few loaves, some potato's not half-rotten like the ones they were used to getting and a dozen tins of meat. 'This should cheer the men up,' said Mayer changing the subject.

Surveying the meagre pile of food Schlesser smiled. The sergeant understood his moods. And so he should, they had been in this bloody war together for a long time. He was a good NCO. A good man. Perhaps, someone, he could have as a friend after all this is over. Who was to say?

'Yes, quite a feast. Wake Giebeler and let's see what he can cook up for us.'

Grinning, Mayer walked across to the stove and nudged one of the sleeping soldiers with the toe of his boot.

'Wakey-wakey! Giebeler. Saint Nicholas has not forgotten us after all.' Getting no response Mayer kicked him a little harder. 'Come on up now. Your culinary skills are required.'

With no other option other than to relinquish his place by the stove reluctantly, Giebeler climbed to his feet.

Stretching some life into his arms, keen to see what delights the sergeant had managed to acquire he walked across to the table. After picking through the collection of tins, he tested the quality of the bread by banging one of the loaves against the leg of the table. Praying that the bread would come off worse. It was rumoured that the division's bakery was out of action because there was not enough firewood for the ovens. And if this was true then only the Good Lord and Hanns Wedderhauser the head baker, really knew how fresh the bread was. Still, he reminded himself, bread was bread no matter how old it was. The allowance for soldiers, even those in the front line was just 200 grams. A single slice. Not a thick slice either only about the width of a finger. Just enough to dip into your cup of horse-meat soup to make it more palatable. It was then that Giebeler noticed the small packet in amongst the Potatoes. Picking it up he began reading what was printed on the side.

'And what the hell am I expected to do with a packet of condoms?' he asked, staring at Mayer accusingly.

'They are a gift from the Quartermaster Giebeler. It seems that the Fuhrer has such high regard for the wellbeing of his beloved 6th army that he has sent us enough condoms to keep the whores of Hamburg supplied for a year.'

Not at all amused by the sergeant's prank, Giebeler opened the packet, and removing one of the condoms he began tearing open its foil wrapping.

'Perhaps,' said Giebeler, sarcastically, taking hold of the thin rubber tube and stretching it out between his fingers, 'as it looks like an octopus's leg I could make you a nice plate of calamari Sergeant?'

Before Mayer had a chance time to remind the ignorant bugger that an octopus doesn't have legs, Schlesser beat him to the punch.

'An excellent idea Giebeler. Then we can all imagine ourselves sitting outside a café on the Amalfi Coast on a warm summer evening enjoying a chilled glass of Albarino and a delicious bowl of squid and caponata. Yes? Schlesser joked.

Far from happy, Giebeler stuffed the offending object back into its box and wishing that the Fuhrer had also sent along a few whores with the consignment of "rubbers" he scooped up an armful of potatoes and walked back towards the stove. At least they would have kept their cocks warm.

With his coat collar turned up Mayer wedged himself into the corner between the two brick walls. Anywhere to escape the icy wind whistling through the gaps in the ruined buildings. An impatient wind the soldiers called it because rather than going around it went straight through you instead. Pressing the bottle to his lips he swallowed another mouthful of brandy, the liquid burning his throat on its journey to the pit of his stomach. An unexpected gift from Big Willy. Across the Volga River to the east, the rumble of Russian heavy artillery rolled in like distant thunder. To the north, ribbons of tracer rounds began lighting up the night sky. The noose is tightening thought Mayer. Yet even though we have been abandoned still we fight on. Then suddenly the sound of a voice interrupted his reflective mood. A challenge from one of the sentries. Recognising the man's voice, screwing the top back on the bottle, Mayer stuffed it into a pocket and made his way to the soldier's sentry post.

'What's the trouble, Kleiber?'

'We have visitors Sergeant,' the young soldier replied, gesturing towards a group of men.

But before Mayer could do or say anything one of the group stepped forward. An officer, the silver shoulder epaulette's of his bottle-green, double-breasted greatcoat embellished with a single star.

'Good evening Sergeant. I wish to see your commanding officer.' The man spoke quite matter-of-factly. Not with the usual condescending tone adopted by many of the younger officers, thought Mayer so he had got off to a good start.

'Yes, Oberleutnant. He's in the bunker over there,' said Mayer pointing. Kleiber here will take you.

With a curt nod, the young officer walked away. Curious as to why they were here, Mayer turned towards the group of soldiers huddled together in a tight group. Running his eyes over them he spotted somebody he recognised. It was the young storeman. His blood-stained bandage, partially hidden by a helmet that was far too large for his head.

'What's all this about then? What are you doing here?' Said Mayer, confronting the young soldier.

'Haven't you heard the news Sergeant?' said the young storeman, 'Von Manstein is coming. We are saved! We are saved! He replied excitedly. The flame of hope flickering brightly in his eyes.

Mayer stared back at him.

'Good news indeed,' Mayer replied somewhat unconvincingly. Then patting the young soldier on the helmet he turned and walked towards the bunker. Could it be true Mayer wondered? Amazed at how, even when all seemed lost, the very mention of the man's name could conjure up such feelings of hope. A belief that the impossible was somehow possible.

Schlesser was still sitting at the table when the young officer walked down the steps.

Turning towards him, he watched as the Oberleutnant came

to attention and raised his left arm in a Fuhrer salute. 'Hauptmann Schlessser?' the young officer inquired.

Pushing back the chair, Schlesser climbed slowly to his feet. Once upright, he raised his left arm in what was meant to be a salute but was little more than a token gesture.

'Yes, I am Schlesser. And you are?'

'Oberleutnant Freisler Sir. From Division HQ,' the young officer replied.

'Welcome to our humble abode Oberleutnant Freisler.'

Removing the pair of hand-made leather gloves he was wearing Freisler turned towards the stove, his head turned up slightly.

'Something smells good.'

'Ah Oberleutnant we have an excellent chef and this is one of his specialities. Eh Giebler?' He said, turning towards the company's unelected cook hovering over a large battered saucepan, occasionally stirring its glutinous contents with what looked like a chair leg.

'Yes Hauptmann,' Giebler replied cheerfully, 'a speciality of the house.'

Leaning towards the young Oberleutnant, in the pretence of sharing a secret, Schlesser whispered. 'Though it's better if you don't enquire what the ingredients might be.'

Realising that he was being subjected to some kind of a joke, Freisler stiffened slightly.

'I have orders from division.' He said pointedly and unbuttoning his greatcoat he removed a slim brown envelope from an inside pocket and handed it to Schlesser.

Opening the envelope Schlesser removed the single sheet of paper and began reading.

The Letter

'As you can see Operation Winter Storm has begun,' said the young Oberleutnant confidently. 'And with its success, we can at last break out of our encirclement. Ignoring the interruption, Schlesser continued reading. Glancing up momentarily when Mayer entered the bunker before returning to the letter.

'So!' Said Schlesser, laying the sheet of paper down on the table, 'Papa Hoth and his Panzer's are coming to our rescue eh? But why from the south? Surely from the west would be better?'

'Who can say Herr Hauptmann but we must trust in our Generals. Yes? Besides the news is good. In their latest report, the 6th Panzer Division have confirmed that they have crossed the Mishlova River at Vassilevska.'

Frowning, Schlesser crossed the bunker to where a detailed map of Stalingrad had been pinned to the wooden slats that lined the wall. Beside it, draped over a length of string were a handful of Christmas cards that had arrived several days ago, their tinsel adornments twinkling like stardust in the lamplight.

'Given that Vassilevska is at least fifty kilometres to the south,' said Schlesser pointing to a spot on the map with his finger. 'And that between them and us are two Russian armies I would say your optimism is a little premature Oberleutnant. Wouldn't you agree?'

'Not at all Hauptmann,' Freisler replied, undaunted by Schlesser's observation. 'Headquarters have been informed that by tomorrow the 17th Panzer Division will also have crossed the Mishkova River and joined forces with the tanks of 6th Panzer. Faced with such an iron fist, the Bolsheviks will run like frightened rabbits.'

With a resigned shrug, Schlesser turned away from the map.

'Well, then we must live in hope. I know our brave Panzers will do their best.' With that said, crossing to the table he turned to Mayer, 'See that the men are given a hot meal first Sergeant, and then tell them we are moving out.'

'Can I tell them where we are going, Hauptmann?'

'Yes,' said Schlesser retrieving the letter and holding it aloft. 'You can tell them that we are to join the 297th Infantry at Businovka. Tell them also that Hoth's Panzer's are coming to our rescue. That should cheer them up.'

'What about supplies?' Mayer enquired, more in hope than expectation.

Schlesser looked enquiringly at Freisler.

'Regrettably, I have only enough rations and ammunition for my own men Herr Hauptmann,' Freisler replied firmly.

Schlesser gave a half-smile. It was what he had expected the man to say.

'Although perhaps I can spare some grenades. But that is all.'

'Thank you Oberleutnant,' said Schlesser, acknowledging the officer's generosity. I take it you will not be accompanying us on our little outing then?'

'Regrettably not Herr Hauptmann. My orders are to take over your position and to hold it at all costs.'

Picking up his cap from the table, buttoning up his greatcoat Schlesser walked over to the young officer.

'Then I wish you well Oberleutnant Freisler,' said Schlesser, holding out his right hand.

'Thank you, Herr Hauptmann,' Freisler replied gripping the older officer's hand with his own. 'I wish you well also.'

It was snowing when the small company of soldiers made

The Letter

their way through what remained of the freight depot. Not heavily, the flakes no bigger than a nail-head but enough to blur a man's vision. The once busy goods yard with its web of sidings had been shelled so many times that had it not been for the wrecked, burned-out freight wagons and buckled lengths of track it would have been unrecognisable. Just another ruined enclave in a devastated city. Desperate to escape the bitter wind, several of the larger craters had been covered over with makeshift rooves, and like burrowing animal's small groups of soldiers had converted them into shelters. Miraculously, looking for all the world like an exhibit in a museum an old Class E freight locomotive was still standing on an intact section of rail. Its blackened boiler with its pepper-pot chimneys riddled with bullet holes. Its cab and cowling mangled by shrapnel. A dozen yards away laying on their sides in a neat line was a string of goods wagons. Still connected by their couplings, it was as though a giant hand had pushed them over one by one just for the sheer hell of it. It was then that Mayer noticed that one of the freight wagons had remained on its wheels, the makeshift chimney poking out of its roof giving it the appearance of a Romany caravan. Curious as to who its residents might be Mayer walked over to where the planking in the end wall had been prised away to form a doorway and pulling back the strip of carpet covering the entrance he peered into the wagon. Cowering in the semi-darkness huddled together for warmth were a large group of soldiers. Most were wrapped in a blanket with scarves covering their heads like a monk's cowl, their mitten-less hands pushed into the pockets of worn-out greatcoats. Each emaciated face turned towards the small iron stove in the centre of the floor. Each pair of lifeless eyes fixed on the flickering orange glow in its belly.

'What's your regiment?' Mayer called out, his voice reverberating in the enclosed space. But nobody replied.

Not a single head turned to look at him. The sound of his voice greeted by a deathly hush. Starving, and devoid of hope these men were no longer soldiers, simply people who had lost the will to live patiently waiting for death to end their living nightmare. Allowing the strip of carpet to slip from his hand, filled with a mixture of disgust and anger Mayer turned and walked away.

Moving in two separate columns, one on each side of the railway line, the small group of soldiers followed the single, narrow-gauge track as it snaked its way south through the desolate wilderness of skeletal buildings. Each soldier's eyes nervously scanning the windowless, fire-blackened brick walls. Then a machine-gun opened fire, its staccato bursts shattering the silence.

Kleiber tried to scream but his lungs were already filling with blood. The same blood which was seeping into the front of his greatcoat from the terrible wounds in his chest. Behind him, another soldier had also been caught in the hail of bullets, his body convulsing as though a powerful electric current were passing through it before falling lifeless onto the ground.

'Down!' Screamed Mayer instinctively.

But he was wasting his breath. To a man, the remainder of the company were already scrambling to find whatever cover they could as the machine-gun opened up again. Sprawled on their stomachs, sheltered by a low embankment Mayer, corporal Deifel, and a soldier called Volz crawled towards where a culvert burrowed under the track. One by one they slithered through the shoulder width concrete pipe like migrating eels. First through, scrambling to his feet Mayer spotted a shell crater. Dashed towards it he dived headlong into the shallow depression. Volz was the next to emerge, the two fifty-round ammunition belts slung around his shoulders like a scarf. Zig-zagging across the open ground, he hurled himself into the shallow hole alongside Mayer. Pulling himself clear of the pipe, hampered by the MG-42 Deifel began running towards the two other soldiers. Immediately, a second Russian machine-gun opened fire its opening burst ripping through Deifel's neck and almost decapitating him. Bastards thought Mayer, watching in horror as the lifeless body of the corporal slumped forward onto the ground. The Russian gunner had known about the culvert all along. With the first machine-gun falling silent, led by Schlesser, half a dozen soldiers scrambled to their feet and charged across the track towards its position. Watching their heroic assault, Mayer and Volz opened fire on the second Russian position.

Schlesser and his men were less than halfway across the rubble-strewn ground before the first machine-gun came back to life. The droning of its bullets like a swarm of angry bees. Just a single round struck Schlesser, striking the officer at the top of his Sternum and shattering his Manubrium bone. Strangely, as he began falling towards the ground Schlesser found himself likening the bullet's impact to a violent prod he had once received from a metal-tipped cane. An implement employed by a brutish oaf of an instructor at the military academy he had attended, to focus the attention of any young cadet who he thought might be daydreaming. Sadly for Schlesser, this particular metal-tipped visitor was not interested in whether he was paying attention or not, only in killing him. Watching as the officer stumbled to the ground, firing a burst from his Schmeisser machine pistol towards the Russian gun position Giebeler raced across to him. Dropping down onto one knee he stared anxiously into Schlesser's face. Ah, good old Giebeler thought Schlesser, ever the faithful gun-dog. He tried to smile but because of the pain, all that manifested itself was a grimace.

'Go on Giebeler,' said Schlesser, blood beginning to dribble from the corner of his mouth. And reaching out an arm he handed the soldier a stick-grenade. 'Give the bastards this with my compliments.'

His face etched with concern Giebeler took the grenade from the officer's hand.

'Yes Sir. One for you Hauptmann.'

It's never a good feeling when your gun jams during a battle. This was certainly true for the two Russian soldiers manning the Degtyaryov-27 machine-gun. But for Giebeler it was a sign that God was on his side. Confirmation of this revealing itself to him when the grenade he had just thrown inside the building exploded, destroying both the machine-gun and killing the two soldiers who were manning it. With one machine-gun silenced, seizing the opportunity with Vogt giving him covering fire Mayer ran across to the body of the dead corporal. Retrieving the MG-42 and with no fire coming from the Russian position, Mayer hurriedly retraced his steps. Offering up a sigh of relief when he reached the safety of the shallow crater. Catching his breath, pulling down the gun's bipod Mayer watched as Volz began feeding the ammunition belt into the breach. A pat on the shoulder from Volz and Mayer opened fire. Watching with satisfaction as the high-velocity rounds began chewing away the sill of the window from where the second DP-27 was hidden. Exposed, the Russian gunner's head exploded like a ripened melon under the impact of the bullets. Droplets of brain and bone spraying outwards in a crimson arc. Panic-stricken a second soldier leapt to his feet. Framed in the window, Mayer fired a second burst. Watching as the man's body twitched and jerked like a deranged marionette before dropping out of sight.

With the machine-gun silenced Giebeler and the two remaining soldiers charged towards the gaping hole made by the grenade. Clambering over the pile of fallen bricks, Giebeler entered the building, glancing down at the bodies of the Russian machine-gun crew lying half-buried in the rubble. A second German soldier joined him, both men peering into the gloomy interior for signs of the enemy. Behind them, the remaining soldier clambered in through the hole. But as he pulled himself upright, a shot rang out and with an audible groan, the man dropped onto his knees. Instinctively, Giebeler fired a burst from his machine-pistol into the darkness. With nobody returning fire, signalling his intentions to the other soldier the pair moved deeper into the ruined building.

Easing his finger off the trigger, Mayer rolled away from the MG and peering over the lip of the crater he surveyed what had once been a large apartment block. Although there was a good chance that there would be more Russian soldiers hiding in the ruined building he also knew that he and Volz couldn't stay where they were any longer. And it was then that he spotted Bauer. No more than fifteen yards away, sheltering behind the shattered wall of a concrete cistern. Raising an arm Mayer signalled to him. Watching as Bauer pumped his fist in response. Moments later, with Volz cradling the MG-42 in the crook of his arm spreading out in a line the three soldiers slowly advanced towards the gutted building.

Clambering over the piles of brick rubble they slowly advance into the blackened shell of the building moving cautiously along what appeared to be a central corridor. After a few yards another, much narrower corridor turned off to the right. Gesturing to Volz with a wave of his hand Mayer watched as the soldier ventured into the gloomy passage, his finder resting on the machine-gun's trigger. Even before Volz had disappeared from view, from close by came the unmistakable popping of small arms fire.

Sounds like some of Schlesser's men were still alive then thought Mayer, recognising the sound of Giebeler's Schmeisser firing in short bursts. Proceeding further along the wide corridor they found themselves outside the entrance to a large windowless room. With his inquiring look sanctioned by Mayer's affirming nod, Bauer stepped through the door-less opening. Alert, his rifle resting against his hip he carefully picked his way across the charred floorboards. Surprisingly, amid all the destruction the room's blackened ceiling was still intact. Perhaps if it hadn't been and light had been allowed to flood into the darkened room from above Bauer might have noticed the movement in the basement below. Sadly he didn't and when the Russian soldier hiding in the cellar opened fire with his PPSh-41, it was more a look of surprise than pain which transformed Bauer's face as the bullets slammed into his chest. Rocked by the force of their impact, Bauer staggered back against the wall. Slowly sliding down it as his knees gave way until he was left sitting with his legs stretched out in front, his chin resting on his chest. With the sound of the shots still reverberating through the shell of the building, Mayer appeared in the doorway. From the room below the Russian soldier opened fire again. The bullets from his machine-gun ripping through the floorboards as if they were made of paper. Slinging his rifle over his shoulder, Mayer pulled a grenade from his belt and spotting a gap in the boards he lobbed it into the cellar. Stepping back into the corridor as the explosion ripped the floorboards from their joists, tossing them into the air like the finale to a conjurer's amazing card trick. When the clouds of dust and pieces of floorboard had settled, Mayer re-entered the room. Kneeling down beside Bauer he placed a hand on the man's shoulder. With a supreme effort, Bauer lifted his head, turning it until his eyes could focus on Mayer's face.

'Dear Mother they've got me this time.' The words spoken in little more than a whisper. Mayer slowly nodded his head. They both knew there was nothing Mayer or anybody else could do for him. His wounds were too bad. Fatal.

'You got the bastard,' said Bauer, the words gurgling in his throat. But it wasn't a question. He knew Mayer wouldn't let him down. He had served under quite a few Sergeants in his time but this one was by far the best. The kind of man you wanted on your side when the chips were down. What was it they had called NCOs like him in the Great War? The first among equals. Yes, that was it, the first among equals. It suited Mayer perfectly.

'Bestimmt!' (Definitely) said Mayer watching as the faintest of smiles brightened Bauer's face. Then, in the blink of an eye, it was gone, the man's chin dropping onto his chest and Mayer knew he was dead. Unbuttoning the front of Bauer's blood-soaked coat, Mayer snapped off the perforated section of his identity disc, and together with Bauer's pay book, he pushed it into his pocket. Finally, after ransacking Bauer's greatcoat pockets for any tins of food or ammunition climbing to his feet Mayer walked out into the corridor. With the crunching of his feet on the rubble-strewn floor the only sound, he cautiously inched his way deeper into the interior of the building.

The corridor ended at the entrance to a small room, a study perhaps. Although being devoid of furniture it could just as easily have been somebody's bedroom. Whatever it was or had been all that mattered to Mayer was that the boarded floor was still intact. Overcome with exhaustion, guided by the fading daylight coming in through what had once been a window its charred frame still clinging to the brickwork, removing his helmet he slumped down into a corner. Lost in his thoughts, he brushed a hand over his head stroking the close-cropped hair. A finger subconsciously tracing the outline of the deep scar running across his scalp.

All of them were young. And judging from their distinctive eyes and prominent cheekbones, most were Mongol's. They were dressed in the familiar olive-green uniform of the Russian army and each of them carried a rifle. Drawn up in four ranks, they watched the officer who was striding up and down in front of them. His loud, confident voice extolling the worthiness of their cause. His rhetoric, accompanied by the howling wail of Katyusha rockets hurtling overhead towards the German positions in Stalingrad. With darkness falling and the flash of heavy artillery lighting up the sky, the scene might well have been something Mikhail Doller had conjured up for one of his epic productions. But as these young soldiers were about to discover, this was not a film set. Lined up on the east bank, lying before them was the Volga River its serpentine waters covered by a thick layer of ice. Beyond it screamed the officer, was their enemy. An enemy who had ravaged their beloved Stalingrad and who must be driven out whatever the cost. Ranting on and on; For the Motherland, for their beloved leader. But for the most part, his patriotic overtures were falling on deaf ears. His words blocked out by the fear which was beginning to manifesting itself in the minds of the young soldiers. Creeping into their brains like an unwelcome visitor. Magnified by the realisation of what lay ahead of them.

Stubbing out the butt of his cigarette on the floor, on hands and knees, Mayer crawled across to the window. Shivering involuntarily as the cold air struck his face. Peering out into the night he looked towards the east. It had been freezing hard now for the past five days; sometimes as low as minus 28 degrees and he knew that what they had all been fearing must have finally happened. That the Volga was now a sheet of ice. Hardly daring to contemplate the consequences

Mayer was suddenly distracted as a star shell exploded in the sky overhead, bathing the area below in a brilliant white light.

Although they were not aware of it the regiment of conscripts was already halfway across the river when the night was suddenly transformed into day. At first, they just stood rooted to the spot, staring around them in utter bewilderment. Then from the rear, the dozen or so Commissar's in their distinctive black uniforms began screaming out their orders. 'Move! Go on! It worked at first, the young soldier's nervously advancing. But then the first German shells began falling. Shattering a large section of the ice ahead of them into great slabs and sending spouts of water high into the air. Instantly, panic gripped the young Russian soldiers spreading through their ranks like wildfire as more shells rained down. Then, en masse like a herd of wild animals they turned and began running back towards the east bank. Firing their pistols over the young soldier's heads, even shooting a few as a deterrent the line of Commissars held them back. But as the shelling continued, shattering the ice all around them a collective hysteria gripped the young conscripts. Overwhelmed by the dread of drowning in the icy waters, urged on by the screams and cries of the less fortunate ones, they surged forward. With little hope of stemming the tide of soldiers and finding themselves faced with the prospect of drowning in the Volga, fearing for their lives, the Commissar's turned and raced like madmen for the safety of the shore.

He didn't hear it the first time. But he heard it the second time. A voice calling out in German.

'Is that you Volz?' Mayer called out.

'Yes!' Volz answered. 'Where are you?'

'The small room at the end of the corridor.'

A few moments passed and then the tall gangly figure of Volz, the MG cradled in his arm, appeared in the doorway.

'What's all the fireworks about then?'

'Come and see for yourself,' said Mayer, turning back to the display.

Leaning the MG against the wall, Volz crossed to the window and looked out.

'That's it, lads, give it to them. Blow the Popov bastards to hell.'

With the light from the star shell fading, Mayer crawled back to his corner. Taking a tin of processed meat from his pocket he tossed it across to Volz.

'Thanks,' said Volz catching the tin in both hands.

'Eat up and then we move out,' said Mayer, watching as Volz pulled off his mittens, ripped off the lid of the tin, and begin wolfing down its contents.

'What about Bauer?' Volz asked between mouthfuls.

'Bauer's dead.' Mayer replied as if somebody has just asked him for the time of day.

'Poor bugger. He was a decent sort.'

'They were all decent sorts,' said Mayer angry at the comment. 'Now shut up and eat.'

'What about Hauptmann Schlesser and the others?'

'All dead probably,' said Mayer, watching Volz scooping the meat out with his fingers and stuffing it into his mouth. Finally, after searching the corners for any remaining traces of meat and finding none Volz tossed the tin away.

'Then we had better get back to our old posited eh Sarge?' Volz ventured, wiping his fingers clean on the front of his greatcoat.

'And go back for what' said Mayer bitterly. 'To die of starvation or to freeze to death. Take your pick. Or maybe you'll get lucky and take a bullet.'

'But we can't go on,' Volz replied, not wanting to believe what Mayer had just said.

'Face it,' Mayer replied, 'we've been abandoned. A whole army sacrificed and all for what? All because this God-forsaken place is named after Stalin that's why. If it had been given a different name we would be half-way across Russia by now.'

Volz said nothing, just sat staring down at the floor.

'Come on Volz you're no fool, you know that as well as I do. But we're soldiers. Which means we obey orders. Right?'

'Bollocks to orders,' said Volz angrily.

Mayer stared across at the man. They had come through a lot together thought Mayer, no point in pulling rank on him now even if he wanted to.

'Look,' said Mayer, a more conciliatory tone to his voice, 'Our only hope of getting out of this hell-hole is to be there when Hoth's Panzer's breakthrough.'

'Yeah,' said Volz, unconvinced. 'And what if they don't make it? What then?'

'They'll make it.'

'Hauptmann Schlesser didn't think so,' said Volz, recalling the Hauptmann's conversation with the young Oberleutnant.

'Well maybe he was wrong,' Mayer replied, becoming pissed off with the conversation. 'Either way, he's dead now and were not.'

Volz sat for a moment still staring down at the ground. Only looking up when he heard Mayer climbing to his feet.

'Look,' said Mayer turning towards the doorway, 'either way I'm going on okay? I'd rather take my chances out there that die here like a rat in a trap. You can suit yourself. We each have to look out for ourselves now.' And with that he walked out, the sound of his footsteps echoing along the corridor.

Volz sat for a moment, his head in his hands. Then, the decision made he climbed quickly to his feet, and resting the MG on his shoulder he left the room.

The two soldiers followed the single track through a blighted wilderness of ruined buildings. Past row upon row of naked, windowless brick walls. Each house as fragile as if it had been made from a pack of playing cards. Hollowed out shells that had once been family homes and apartments. Warm inviting places, where good hard-working people had cooked their meals, raised their children and made love. Now nothing more than fire-ravaged caverns whose fate would be decided by the wrecking ball at the end of a crane.

Even though it took a real effort the act of walking kept the blood flowing. It provided the body with some warmth, some protection against the cold. Stopped its icy fingers creeping into your bones and becoming trapped in the marrow like permafrost. Although it had stopped snowing, to Mayer and Volz it hardly seemed like it. The swirling gusts of cold air whipping up the powdered snow and driving it into their exposed faces. At times the lengths of rusting track were visible. Other times it lay hidden, buried beneath the eddying snowdrifts which ebbed and flowed at the behest of the bitter Siberian wind.

Volz spotted them first. Vague shapes outlined against the backdrop of snow. But the more he stared at them the more recognisable the shapes became. It was a row of vehicles. Hard to tell how many, eight, or maybe ten of them at a guess. Turning to Mayer who was lagging a few yards behind, Volz gestured towards them with his outstretched arm. Close to exhaustion, Mayer nodded weakly before dropping onto his knees.

'A bed for the night,' Volz called out, his words carried away on the wind, and energised by the prospect he began striding through the snow towards the abandoned vehicles. Heaving himself onto his feet, Mayer began following after him. Then, after a few paces, he suddenly stopped. Whether it was instinctive or an innate sense of caution but a little voice was telling him that all was not well. Watching Volz approaching one of the lorry's suddenly he knew what it was. Booby-traps!

'Volz!' Mayer screamed as loud as he could. 'Wait!' And with his last reserves of energy, half running, half stumbling he made for the line of vehicles. 'Volz no! Get away!' His voice sounding pathetically weak.

Whether Volz heard him and ignored the warning it made no difference anyway. He already had the door open and was climbing in through the passenger door. The explosion wasn't large but in an instant, it turned the cab into a blazing inferno. Dropping to his knees Mayer watched in horror as the flames licked at the windows with their fiery tongues. Watching helplessly as they devoured Volz's body. Turning his clothing into ash and melting his skin like butter. At least the poor devil was probably killed by the blast thought Mayer, instinctively throwing himself face down into the snow as the MG rounds began going off like firecrackers.

With their voracious appetite sated and nothing left to devour, the flames flickered and died. Leaving nothing but the cabs blackened metal frame and the charred husk of Volz's body, laying curled into the foetal position on the row of exposed springs that had once supported the passenger seat. Dragging himself to his feet, Mayer began walking along the line of vehicles. They were German. Old Opel Blitz trucks with canvas covers. He also noticed that nearly all their cabs had been punctured by large bullet holes. Strafed by a Yak-9 most likely thought Mayer judging by the size of the holes. Its 20-millimetre cannon could inflict that sort of damage. Making his way to the rear of the leading truck, Mayer pulled aside the canvas cover and peered into the gloomy interior. Empty. Whatever it had been carrying was gone. Looted by Russian soldiers no doubt. Probably the same bastards who had booby-trapped the truck that Volz had climbed into. Clambering into the back of the truck, Mayer crawled to the far end, and propping himself up against the wooden planking he carefully removed his gloves. After rubbing some life back into his frozen fingers, undoing the top two buttons of his greatcoat he reached into an inside pocket and pulled out a crumpled packet of Sulima cigarettes. Removing one he clamped it between his chapped lips. Tucked inside the packet was a matchbook, with a picture of a Can-Can dancer, and the name La Vie Parisienne printed on the cover. A souvenir from his time in France. Striking one of the matches, Mayer touched it to the tip of the Turkish cigarette and inhaled a mouthful of tobacco smoke. Savouring its rich aroma as he breathed it out through his half-open mouth. He would stay put until it was dark. It would be good to be out of the weather for a while. Besides, with no railway track to follow anymore, he would do better getting his directions from the stars. And Mayer knew all about the stars. He'd been taught by his father when he was a young boy. The Plough, The Great Bear, Orion's Belt. Where to find them in the night sky, how to recognise them among all the other celestial bodies. How strange he thought that he should need that knowledge now. But glad all the same that his Papa had taught him. It

The Letter

might just save his life. Inhaling a last mouthful of smoke, Mayer stubbed the cigarette out on the floor of the truck. Then removing his helmet, he turned up his collar, and leaning back against the side of the lorry he closed his eyes.

Pulling aside the canvas flap Mayer looked out onto a clear moonlit night. Sheltered from the howling blizzard outside, and with a little warmth having crept back into his body, he had slept well. His toes tingled a little but he took that as a good sign. (The thought of having frostbitten feet terrified him). And jumping down from the back of the lorry, taking his direction from the North Star slinging his rifle over his shoulder Mayer walked away into the swirling snow.

At first, Mayer thought it was the wind playing tricks. But no there it was again and this time there was no mistaking the distinctive sound of a Balalaika. Moving cautiously towards the source, Mayer began hearing the sound of men's voices mingled in with the music. Cossacks. Part of a Russian cavalry regiment no doubt. He could see them now, dancing around a large bonfire. Their rich sonorous voices, lubricated no doubt by generous mouthfuls of vodka in full cry. A Russian folk song probably thought Mayer, sliding away from the scene on his belly. But he had other things on his mind. Where there are Cossack's there are always ponies.

The herd wasn't large. Probably twice as many ponies as there were Cossacks, judging by the number of men dancing around the fire. But that was how it was with these Mongolian horsemen. They liked having two ponies. When one tired they simply mounted the other pony and rode on. There was just one sentry. Mounted on his pony he slowly circled the herd. Once around and then he dismounted. Already a little unsteady on his feet, the man reached inside his thick sheepskin coat and pulled out a bottle. Removing the cork with his tobacco-stained teeth, spitting it out onto the ground he put the lip of the bottle to his mouth and tilted back his head. But it was Mayer's bayonet which found its way into the man's throat, not the fiery liquid. The thick metal blade thrusting into his exposed neck, slicing through muscle and sinew and severing his windpipe. As the Cossack's legs buckled under him soundlessly, Mayer lowered him into the snow. Watching as the man's life-blood permeated the whiteness, staining each crystal a pinkish red as it spread outwards in an ever-expanding circle. Pulling off the dead Cossack's *Ushanka* (fur cap) Mayer removed his helmet and tossed it away into the snow. Better to be warm he thought and a metal helmet is not ideal in freezing weather like this.

Gripping the bridle with one hand, Mayer hauled himself up into the small saddle. Sitting astride the pony, his legs hanging down like a bareback rider he contemplated catching up another mount. Deciding that the risk of spooking the herd was too great, digging his heels into the animal's sides Mayer kicked the small Kazak pony into a walk. He was just a young boy the last time he had ridden a horse. Herr Mecklenburg's old plough horse. Recalling how he had to sit at the base of its neck with a leg on either side because its back was so broad. And how the old mare's bristly hairs had scratched his skin. But he never complained. What glorious summer days they had been. Out in the wheat fields all day; the sound of the threshing machine, the smell of the ripened grain. Watching his older brother Ralph rolling around on the ground with Lotte Rosenmeier and wondering why he would want to wrestle a girl. Where was the fun in that? Little knowing that a few years later he would be doing the very same thing with her younger sister Paula. She had never let him kiss her, he remembered that. She said that if he did she would have a baby. Which was nonsense of course. Even he knew that you had to be married to have a baby. Then at midday, his mother and the other womenfolk would arrive with lunch for everyone, including jugs of beer for the men and lemonade for the boys. A lifetime ago when the world for a young boy was full of endless summers and ice-cold lemonade. Walking the pony until he was well clear of the Cossack camp, reaching down Mayer pulled up each stirrup in turn and looped them around the animal's neck. They were much too short for his legs, so better to put them out the way. Then digging his heels into its flanks, harder this time, the pony broke into a trot.

With an hour seeming like a day, walking alongside the pony when he had the strength to which wasn't often, driven by a determination to survive Mayer trudged on across the windswept steppe. Thankfully the blizzard had abated and warmed by the heat of the pony's body Mayer found himself experiencing a growing mood of optimism. Having given up on the prospect of ever finding Businovka or the soldiers of the 297th who they were meant to join up with there, Mayer knew his only hope, his only chance of survival lay in making contact with Hoth's Panzers. Daunting though the prospect seemed, the thought sustained him. Keeping alive his desire to live. And who knows he might get lucky.

It was just after dawn when they caught up with him. There were twelve of them, riding six abreast of the trail, he had left in the deep snow. Big men with bushy beards, mounted on Kazak ponies their rifles slung across their backs. Their *Shashka* (sabre) hanging from their belts. Mayer had ridden the pony hard during the night, perhaps too hard. It was blowing hard now, with flecks of blood mixed in with the mucus spraying from its nostrils. But still, he urged it on, leaning forward over its neck driving his boots hard into its sides. Ten yards, fifty yards, a hundred yards, and then it stumbled. Recovering, it surged forward again legs pumping. Such a plucky little animal thought Mayer. Then quite suddenly, as if the snow had somehow turned into something more solid, first one of its front legs buckled and then the other and the pony went down. Pitched onto the ground, Mayer scrambled to his feet the rousing cheers of the pursuing Cossacks rending the air. They had him now. Unslinging his rifle, Mayer crawled across to the dying pony its sides heaving as it tried in vain to drag the freezing air into its ruptured lungs. Using the animal as a barricade, Mayer rested his rifle on its saddle. With the five rounds in his Karabiner and two stripper clips, one of which he'd taken from Bauer's coat pocket he had fifteen bullets in total. Enough to make a fight of it. Up ahead of him the Cossacks had formed themselves up into a single line. Sitting patiently astride their ponies, watching and waiting. There were in no hurry. Using the rifle's iron sights, the Karabiner's effective range was about five hundred yards. 'First mistake you bastards,' Mayer said to himself lining up on the Cossack at the centre of the line. At roughly four hundred yards, it was not an easy shot. But he could afford to waste one bullet. If his aim was good and it usually was, even reducing the odds against him by one made taking the shot worthwhile. So he squeezed the trigger. Even before the crack of the Karabiner shattered the silence the Cossack was already falling backwards out of his saddle. Drawing back the bolt, Mayer pushed another round into the breach. But before he had a chance to set his sights on another target, the remaining Cossacks scattered like a flock of wild birds. Wheeling their ponies around and galloping out of range.

It wasn't long before they returned, strung out in two lines twenty yards apart. They were no fools thought Mayer as he watched them kick their ponies into a run. Their battle cries rending the silence as they galloped towards him. Their naked sabres flashing in the air. With the golden orb of the sun rising in the eastern sky as its backdrop. The rays of light spreading out like fingers over the virgin snow; the horsemen charging towards the lone gunman sheltering behind his dying horse, it could have been a scene from a western. But this was not some Hollywood movie. This was warfare refined down to its very essence. Kill or be killed.

Then suddenly out of nowhere came the unmistakable chatter of a Spandau. A pony and rider went down, the animal's neck almost severed by the impact of the bullets. Then another pony was hit. The 7.92 mm rounds peppering its side from flank to shoulder. Each hole equally spaced like a row of buttons on a jacket. Only one of the bullets struck the rider, shattering his kneecap. But of the two his screams were the loudest.

'That's enough Steiner,' said the young officer, shouting to be heard above the noise of the machine-gun. Watching as the remaining Cossacks reined in their pony's and galloped out of range. Reluctantly, the gunner eased his finger off the trigger and the MG-42 fell silent.

Rolling over onto his back, Mayer stared in utter disbelief. They may not be dressed in blue and riding big black horses, with their pennons flying and a bugle sounding the charge. Nevertheless, the half-track ploughing through the snow towards him with clouds of smoke belching from its exhaust was most definitely the cavalry.

'It would seem that you have stirred up a hornet's nest. Yes?' said the young officer, pushing up his snow goggles.

Unable to speak, Mayer pulled himself to his feet and stared up at the young officer. His rank, hidden under the sleeveless fleece jacket he was wearing over his Wehrmacht uniform.

'Are there any more of you?'

'No Sir,' said Mayer finding his tongue.

'So, your lucky day then eh Sergeant?' Said the officer, catching sight of Mayer's left sleeve. 'Climb aboard, I think we have room for one more eh Steiner?'

Steiner looked up and nodded begrudgingly. A bit pissed off that he had not been allowed to continue shooting more of the Cossack bastards. Crossing to the back of the vehicle Mayer climbed in through the open rear door and wedged himself in between two sleeping soldiers. Moments later with the door secured, the half-track's powerful six-cylinder engine roared into life and with its tracks churning up the snow the Sd Kfz 251 raced away. Having accustomed himself to the pitching and rolling of the vehicle, it was then that Mayer became aware that he had something stuck between two of his front teeth. Pulling off a glove, with his thumb and forefinger he removed a small piece of rubber. Wondering how the hell it could have got there, he suddenly remembered Giebeler's joke about the calamari. The sly bastard had obviously cut up the condoms after all and when nobody was looking he'd slipped them into the meal.

Three
Falke Division Rehabilitation Camp
Mid-February 1943

HAVING BEEN TEMPORALLY assigned to the unit from the 16th Motorized Infantry Division which had rescued him. After weeks of fighting a desperate rear-guard action against the Russian Second Army, the front was eventually stabilized by Von Manstein's newly formed Army Group Don. With re-organisation now a priority, together with the remnants of other units decimated by the Russian advance Mayer had been rounded up, loaded onto a lorry, and taken to the camp at Slavyansk.

Mayer looked well. He felt well too. The food was good and there was plenty of it. Even his sunken cheeks had filled out a little. The barber had given him a haircut any convict would be proud of and in place of what the Quartermaster had called rags, he had been issued with a new uniform. Everything from socks to a greatcoat and including two pairs of woollen long-johns. Items of luxury for which Mayer was truly grateful. On his arrival, from first impressions, the camp looked newly constructed and quite substantial. Comprising of four rows of eight single-storey timber buildings, each linked by a central corridor with two larger buildings located on the other side of an area of compacted dirt that served as a parade ground. One housing the kitchen with a seating area where meals were taken. The other a wash house and latrines. Surrounded by a high barbed wire fence, the only access was through a set of gates manned by two sentries. The dirt road leading through them ending alongside the dirt square, the only area which had been cleared of snow.

Distracted by the sound of engines, putting down the greatcoat he was sewing a new insignia onto Mayer walked across to the window. Peered out just as six trucks, the same type he and Volz had stumbled upon, pulled up in a line alongside the parade ground. No sooner had they stopped than their tail-gates were lowered and soldiers began jumping out. More guests thought Mayer, knowing what was coming next. No sooner had the trucks began disgorging their human cargo when an officer, resplendent in his full-length grey overcoat, the red and silver shoulder epaulettes with their single gold pip denoting his rank as that of an *Oberstleutnant* (Lieutenant Colonel) emerged from a wing of the main building. Its importance signified by the large Swastika flag fluttering above the doorway. Accompanied by a harassed-looking NCO he made his way towards the parade ground. Hurrying ahead of the officer the NCO began barking out orders: 'Line up! Line up! And then in an even louder voice. Quickly now! Quickly! Quickly!

After milling around like men trying frantically to evade the clutches of an unwanted partner during a lady's excuse me dance, the soldier's eventually formed up in four straight, perfectly orderly lines. 'Attention!' screamed the NCO and instantly boots came together and chests were pushed out. Each man staring straight ahead, his eyes fixed on some immovable object. Their thoughts focused on the prospect of a bath and a hot meal.

Drawn by the sound of the NCO's bellowing voice, a few

The Letter

of the other men sharing Mayer's barrack-room, putting down the letters or papers they were reading, wandered over to join him at the window. Although most been here for some time and had witnessed what was about to unfold before, it was still proved a source of amusement. The 'Side Show' as they liked to call it always followed the same format, much like the scene from a drama production. First, the stage prop in the form of a low wooden dais appeared. Carried across from the same building by two soldiers and positioned in front of the ranks of motionless men. Then with the two soldiers standing to attention beside it, pausing for a moment to adjust his peaked cap, the officer stepped up onto the small wooden structure. As always, his speech was brief and to the point delivered in a monotone voice and culminating in a vigorous thrust of the left arm in a Nazi salute and the words "Heil Hitler". With his presence no longer required, descending the dais with a nod of the head to the NCO the Oberstleutnant made his way back to the building he had left only a few moments earlier, his highly polished riding boots leaving their impression in the carpet of snow. Relishing his moment of authority, the NCO climbed up onto the dais and began shouting out instructions.

'Right, off with all your clothes! Quickly now I don't have all day.' Adding as an afterthought. 'But keep your boots. There will be no new boots.'

Instantly a great cheer went up from the ranks of soldiers and as instructed they began stripping off their soiled uniforms. Throwing them down onto the ground in front of them. Satisfied that every man was naked, pointing towards the building which housed the wash house the NCO yelled out.

'Dismissed!'

Needing no further encouragement, the ranks of soldiers

immediately disintegrated into an ill-disciplined mob, each man racing towards the wash house as if his very life depended on it.

'Don't worry lads it will all be worth it when you get inside,' Mayer muttered to himself, remembering his own experience of standing under the large showerheads. The feeling of ecstasy as the steaming hot water rained down cleansing every inch of his body. The joy of scrubbing off the layers of filth with a bar of carbolic soap. Washing away the colonies of lice which has found a home in his armpits and crotch. Watching with delight as transformed into a grey scum the insidious creatures disappeared down the drain hole. The simple pleasure of running a razor across your face.

As the last naked backside disappeared through the wash house door, a group of men appeared pushing two large handcarts. *Hiwis,* (Russian prisoners), thin as sticks, their heads shaved their clothing little more than rags. Silently, methodically they began collecting up the discarded clothing and loading it into the carts. Some of the items would be sent back to Germany to be cleaned and repaired for another poor soul to wear. The rest would be burned. After three and a half years of war, providing new uniforms for its soldiers was becoming a luxury the Reich could no longer afford.

Satisfied with his needlework, Mayer looked up as the door to the barrack-room swung open and a young *Obergefreiter* (lance corporal) entered the room. Spotting Mayer the soldier walked up to him.

'Sergeant Mayer?' he asked politely.

Putting the greatcoat down beside him on the bed, Mayer nodded.

'You are to come with me,' said the young NCO, quickly

The Letter

adding, *'Oberst* (Colonel) Frosch wishes to see you immediately.'

Climbing to his feet, buttoning up his uniform jacket as he walked Mayer followed the young orderly out of the room and into the corridor.

The Major's office was located midway between the eight barrack blocks. Recognisable by the brass nameplate screwed to the door, engraved with the word "Commandant". Knocking once, without waiting for a response the young Obergefreiter opened the door.

'I have Sergeant Mayer for you, sir,' he said through the half-open door.

Seated behind a plain wooden desk, Oberst Frosch looked up from the document he was reading, peering at the orderly over his glasses before putting down the sheet of paper.

'Good. Send him in.'

Stepping aside, the orderly gestured for Mayer to enter, closing the door behind him. Although quite spacious the room was sparsely furnished. Apart from the desk and the padded leather chair occupied by Frosch, there were just three uncomfortable-looking wooden chairs and a tall filing cabinet. Firmly secured to one wall was a large corkboard with various maps pinned to it. Hanging on the wall behind the Oberst's desk was a framed portrait of Adolf Hitler. A single window with a rolled-up blackout curtain looked out towards the kitchen block. Approaching the desk, Mayer came to attention and saluted.

'Sergeant Mayer reporting as ordered Herr Oberst,' said Mayer staring over the officer's head at the portrait of The Fuhrer and thinking to himself what an ugly bastard he was. Glancing up from the document he was reading Oberst

Frosch nodded. Then turning his attention back to the document, picking up a gold nib fountain pen he began systematically scoring through some of the words. Afforded the opportunity, surreptitiously Mayer eyed the officer seated in front of him. The first thing he noticed was the red facings denoting a combat unit sewn to his uniform. A proper soldier then thought Mayer, not like the peacock who had performed the welcoming ceremony. Finally, satisfied with his editing with a flourish Oberst Frosch signed his name, and setting down the pen he looked up.

'At ease. You are looking well Sergeant,' said Frosch, smiling.

'Thank you, Herr Oberst. We are well looked after.'

'We do our best, now…'

But before Oberst Frosch could finish his sentence he was interrupted by a man's voice.

'Remarkable! Quite remarkable!'

Taken by surprise, completely unaware that there was anyone else in the room Mayer turned his head towards the man standing in the corner away from the window. An SS Officer judging by the colour of his uniform.

'It would appear that you have led a charmed life Sergeant?' said the man, stepping out into the room.

He was a head taller than Mayer, his slim figure accentuated by an exquisitely tailored field-grey uniform. The right lapel of his jacket was embellished with the lightning bolts of the SS runes. The left with the insignia of his rank, *Hauptsturmfuhrer* (SS Captain). Judging by his facial features he looked to be in his early thirties. He had climbed the ladder quickly Mayer thought to himself. With his pale blue eyes and natural blonde hair swept back from his forehead,

The Letter

he was the perfect embodiment of the Aryan race.

'But what I find strange, puzzling in fact,' said the SS Officer in a cultured voice, 'is where you were found?'

Overcoming his initial surprise, Mayer looked at the man. Was it the SS uniform? For although the officer had been spoken quite calmly, he couldn't help feeling a little unsettled by his presence. He would need to be careful. This one spelled trouble.

'Only you say in your report,' the SS Officer continued, holding up the manila folder he had in his hand. 'That your orders from Division were for your company to leave their position and to proceed to Businovka is that correct?'

'That is correct Herr Hauptsturmfuhrer,' said Mayer, coming to attention.

'And that is what I find so puzzling sergeant,' said the SS Officer, removing a sheet of paper from the folder and holding it up in front of him. 'You see in his report Leutnant Pohlmann of the 16th Motorized Infantry Division. The man who so fortuitously came to your rescue, states that he found you over twenty kilometres to the southwest of Businovka.' With no response forthcoming, returning the sheet of paper to its allotted place in the folder the SS Officer stared hard into Mayer's face. 'Well Sergeant, do you have an explanation for me? Or do I just assume that you are a deserter?'

Mayer stiffened at the sound of the final word. What he wouldn't have given to plant his fist in the arrogant bastard's face. But he knew that anger wasn't going to help him. Stick to the truth he told himself. Just keep calm and tell the bastard the truth.

'With respect Herr Hauptsturmfuhrer you have my report. I have nothing further to add.'

'Ha! You mean this fairy story?' the SS Officer replied mockingly, waving the folder in front of him. 'Do you really expect me to believe that with your officer and men killed that you still attempted to make contact with the 297th Infantry?'

'That was my last order and it was my duty to carry it out.'

'Your duty is to your Fuhrer,' said the SS Officer his voice an octave higher. 'And his order was that you should defend Stalingrad until your last bullet is fired.'

Mayer stared back at him but said nothing.

'But no, instead you chose to run away,' the SS Officer ranted.

'My conscience is clear,' said Mayer, barely able to contain his anger.

'Your conscience is of no interest to me Sergeant,' said the SS Officer dismissively, 'what I wish to know is why you abandoned your brave comrades.'

'I abandoned no one,' said Mayer, infuriated by the accusation. Desperately wanting to scream out the truth. If anybody was abandoned it was us the sixth Army.

'Unfortunately for you Sergeant there are no witnesses to support your story,' said the SS Officer, placing the sheet of paper back into the folder.

'Then perhaps you will take my word as a loyal German soldier Herr Hauptsturmfuhrer?' Mayer replied in a controlled voice.

Although he didn't laugh out loud, the smirk which appeared on the SS Officer's face said enough. Adequately conveying his contempt for Mayer's suggestion.

'I am not in the habit of taking people's word,' the SS

Officer replied pointedly. The smirk, replaced by a deadly serious expression. 'I deal in facts. Proof is what I require, not an assumption that because of your rank I should believe your word.' Slipping the folder under his arm he went on, a more sombre tone to his voice. 'It is my belief sergeant that you deserted your comrades and disobeyed a direct order from your Fuhrer and for that, I can have you shot.'

The officer's words hit Mayer like a hammer blow. But he was not the one who reacted to them. Pushing back his chair Oberst Frosch jumped to his feet.

'And where is your proof Hauptsturmfuhrer,' he demanded angrily. 'Where is the evidence that this soldier was not obeying his commanding officer's last order?'

'What I can prove Oberst,' said the SS Officer, stung by Frosch's words, 'is that when Sergeant Mayer knew there was no hope of carrying out that order, instead of returning to his comrades in Stalingrad, he chose to run away like a coward.'

Frosch smiled. But it was a parody, the warmth never reaching his eyes. 'A coward you say? I have also read Leutnant Pohlmann's report and in it, he states that when his unit came across Sergeant Mayer, that this coward as you call him was killing Cossacks. Something of a contradiction wouldn't you say Hauptsturmfuhrer?'

'That is not the point,' the SS Officers replied, a little unsettled by Frosch's words. 'The truth is …'

'Enough!' shouted Frosch, his anger coming to the boil. 'This business has gone far enough. The whole thing is preposterous. There is no proof. There can never be any proof.'

'But I do have proof,' the SS Officer shouted, outraged by

Frosch's insinuation. I have a report…'

'You have a report Hauptsturmfuhrer from an officer who was in all probability lost himself. And yet based on this you would have a brave soldier shot?'

For a few moments, the two officers stared at each other. Letting a little calmness descend. But Frosch wasn't finished. Walking across to the corkboard he stabbed one of the maps with his finger. 'And as for truth. Here is the only truth you need to concern yourself with. Here is the only truth that matters. Stalingrad is lost. An army of three hundred thousand men. Lost!' Stabbing the map again, 'Manstein's army is in retreat.' Stabbing again with his finger, 'Army Group B is under severe pressure from a Russian offensive. These are the only truth's you should be concerned with Herr Hauptsturmfuhrer, not whether Mayer here is a deserter or not.' Turning away he walked back behind his desk. Gripping the back of his chair with both hands he went on. 'This soldier is now under my command. Therefore I must warn you that should you chose to pursue these accusations against him, you have my solemn word that I will do all in my power to defend him. Is that understood?'

The SS Officer turned away. Staring out through the window, like an actor pausing for effect before delivering his next line. Eventually fully composed, retrieving his cap which he'd placed on the window ledge, he turned and faced Major Frosch.

'As you say Colonel he is one of yours now.' The sarcasm in his voice thinly veiled. 'Let us hope that the men who serve with him in future fare better than those who fought beside him in Stalingrad.' Then, putting on his cap the SS Officer clicked his heels together, thrusting out his left arm as he did so.

The Letter

'Heil Hitler.'

Oberst Frosch raised his left arm in response but said nothing. Formalities over, placing the manila folder on the corner of Frosch's desk with a withering glance towards Mayer the SS Officer stormed out of the room.

'I am grateful Herr Oberst for... For' said Mayer, struggling to find the right thing to say. Holding up a hand Frosch waved his words of thanks away and pulling open a drawer in the desk he dropped the offending folder into it. Pushing it shut he slumped back in his chair.

'I think that is the last we shall hear of that,' said Frosch, with a half-smile. 'As I'm sure our young Hauptsturmfuhrer will soon find he has more pressing matters to attend to.'

At that moment Mayer could have kissed the man. Instead, he just nodded his head. Not so much in agreement with the Oberst. More as a gesture of thanks.

'I believe you have a family Sergeant,' said Frosch, keen to move on to the business at hand.

'Yes Herr Oberst,' Mayer replied, a little surprised by the question.

'And when was the last time you saw them?'

'Six months ago sir.' Give or take a week, it's hard to remember the exact dates.'

Frosch nodded in agreement. 'Yes, it's hard to remember dates in our line of work.' Then, reaching across the desk he picked up a slip of paper. 'Well I have some good news,' he said, handing Mayer the slip of paper. 'I have your pass for fourteen days leave.'

Holding the slip of paper in his fingers, Mayer stared at it in utter disbelief.

'If there is no counter-order it becomes effective in two days.'

'Thank you, Herr Oberst.'

'Frosch's weathered face broke into a smile. It was always good to give out some good news. God knows there was little enough of it going around.

'See the orderly, he will give you your travel details,' said Frosch, reaching for another document from the pile on his desk. 'Enjoy your leave Sergeant.'

From the camp to Uman had taken two precious days. Thankfully for Mayer, he had been allowed to leave Slovyansk the day Oberst Frosch handed him his pass. The young orderly had proved to be a good sort and had stamped his travel permit there and then. Warning him that if there was a counter-order, his leave would still be cancelled. But so far so good and on day three, with the threat of such an order, removed Mayer boarded his second eastbound train. A far different train than the one he had climbed into two days ago. This one was crowded with civilians. Mainly peasant families. With their farms destroyed and their crops burned, with nowhere for them to live they were being transported from the Ukraine to Poland for resettlement. A fresh start. A prosperous new life for them and their children. Acres of rich soil waiting for the plough the Polish Agriculture Official had promised, as he supervised their departure. Promptly disappearing once the train left Slovyansk station. Never to be seen again.

Squashed in among crates of chickens and rabbits, together with about twenty other soldiers who were also headed home on leave for the next two days Mayer endured the stink of their unwashed bodies and the hostile stares of the menfolk. Even when he had offered some biscuits he'd brought with him for the journey to some of the women with young children, they had shied away from him. Clutching the infant tightly in their arms, glaring back at him fearfully as though he were some evil monster. The train was to have taken him and the other soldiers to Vinnytsia where there was a direct line to Lubin and then on to Germany. But instead, still, several miles from the outskirts of the town it was directed off the mainline and into a siding by an Ostbahn official waving a red flag. No reason was given but an hour later it became evident why when belching clouds of black smoke a military train rumbled past like some armoured behemoth. Minutes later a pair of locomotive's, linked together in tandem appeared pulling a long line of flatbed trucks mounted on bogies. Chained securely to each of them was a Mark V Tiger tank, each painted with their distinctive dark wavy camouflage. One of the soldiers with Mayer, an old *Gefreiter* (corporal) confided in him that the tanks were being transported north for an offensive on Kharkov. Wondering how the hell an old Gefreiter came to be privy to such information, Mayer glared back at him.

'I don't give a shit where they're going,' said Mayer his patience wearing thin, 'I just want to get where I'm going. Understood?'

The old Gefreiter smiled through blackened teeth. 'I take it you've not been home for a while then Sarge?'

'You could say that,' said Mayer, seeing the funny side of it.

It was well into the afternoon when Mayer decided to leave the train. The Ostbahn official had never returned and when he had tried to communicate with the crew of the train the engineer and his fireman simply shrugged their shoulders and continued drinking what looked like tea but which was probably something stronger judging by each man's bleary-eyed expression. Pleased that the Sergeant was at least showing some initiative and happy to be getting off the static train, the group of soldiers jumped down from the carriage they had occupied. Falling in behind Mayer and the old Gefreiter who had now attached himself to the sergeant as if he were a long-lost friend, the small group of abandoned soldiers made their way along the track. Stopping at regular intervals for a short rest, after three hours of footslogging just as darkness was descending for no apparent reason the railway line suddenly began curving away from their intended destination of Vinnytsia. Faced with no other option than to keep following the single length of track, it was a very relieved group of soldiers who spotted the cluster of buildings up ahead.

If it was a station it certainly didn't appear to be a very busy one. And if it had a name then somebody had forgotten to put up the sign. The only indication that it was being used at all was seeing a large puddle of water at the base of the circular cast iron water tower. There were just two buildings, both single story one on each side of the track. The only thing that mattered though was seeing the welcoming glow of light emanating from one of the windows. Sadly, the person waiting outside one of the buildings to greet them was not at all welcoming. A mean-looking sod thought Mayer. But then don't they all. It must be a requirement for getting the job in the first place. The *Feldgendarmerie,* (Military policeman) who was the size of the proverbial barn door was dressed in the customary full-length olive green leather coat. His badge of office, a metal gorget hanging on a chain around his neck. Slung over one shoulder was an MP40 Machine pistol and although there was no sign of a motorcycle, a pair of mud-spattered goggles adorned his helmet.

'What's this then? Lost your train have you?' said the MP, sarcastically. Shining the torch he was holding into Mayer's face.

'No it ran out of coal and so we decided to walk,' said Mayer shielding his eyes from the blinding glare of the torch beam.

Sadly, Mayer's levity wasn't appreciated by the MP whose expression quickly returned to its more usual menacing scowl.

'Papers! I'll need to see your papers,' he called out. 'All of you have your papers ready.' Then raising the MP40 to its firing position, 'If you don't have papers,' his face brightening up a little at the prospect, 'then you had better start running now.'

Thankfully, they all produced the necessary paperwork and satisfied that their documents were in order with an undisguised look of disappointment the MP ushered them into the building. Once inside, the room turned out to be very large. There was no furniture of any description, just a pot-bellied stove standing on a concrete plinth in the centre of the room. If there had been beds, then the stove had eaten them. But beds or no beds, this didn't seem to have bothered the hundred or so soldiers stretched out on the dirt-packed floor sleeping like babies. Ah, well thought Mayer, finding a space large enough to accommodate him between two sleeping bodies. It's warm and it's dry and the odour emanating from a hundred sweaty bodies was certainly more preferable than the stink of chicken shit.

Dawn saw the long wooden platform crowded with German soldiers, the tantalising aroma of hot soup floating in the air like an autumn mist. Hovering over its source, an iron cauldron suspended over a gasoline burner, two Babushka's bundled up in coats and shawls ladled the warming liquid into the soldier's mess tins as they filed past. The same Feldgendarmerie was on duty. Bullying the soldiers into line, ably assisted by a fellow MP. The waiting soldiers called them Tweedledum and Tweedledee. Not out loud, of course, that would be asking for trouble. Just whispering the names amongst themselves and giggling like naughty schoolboys.

Its water tank filled to overflowing, the canvas tube still gushing water pulled aside, with a shrill blast on its whistle the locomotive slowly pulled away from the water tower. Hurriedly gulping down the last of the soup, licking their mess tins clean before pushing them into their backpacks, the unruly crowd of soldiers surged forward as the line of coaches and wagons came to a halt alongside the platform.

'Back! Back! Get back you rabble.' Baton's drawn the two MPs strutted up and down the length of the platform. The crowded ranks of soldiers shying away from them as though they carried the plague. Mayer didn't blame them. He had witnessed for himself the authority their rank gave them. Being an officer didn't guarantee immunity either. He had seen the treatment a young Oberleutnant, had received from one of these *Kettenhundes* (chain dogs). The despair in his eyes as he watched his leave pass being torn up in front of him simply because the MP didn't think his uniform was in a fit condition for him to return to the Fatherland. The fact that the dark stain on his tunic which the MP had taken offence to, was from the blood of a wounded soldier he had carried for over two miles to a dressing-station. Or that the holes burned into his trouser leg were made by the red hot fragments of a mortar shell which had just blown off the right arm of his signalman. None of this concerned the MP. All that mattered to him was that good German Volk should be spared the sight of an officer in such an unacceptable state of dress.

'NCOs first,' called out one of the MPs in a voice loud enough to be heard in Berlin.

Mayer and about twelve others who qualified moved to the front and waving his baton the Feldgendarmerie ushered them aboard the carriages. Finding themselves seats by the window, Mayer and the old Gefreiter smiled at each other. Another step nearer home. Outside, finally unleashed by the MPs pushing and shoving like a crowd at a football match the remaining soldiers fought their way onto the carriages. Faced with a barricade of closed doors, the unlucky ones were forced to climb into the window-less freight wagons at the rear of the train. With their hard wooden floor covered in a thin layer of straw and a couple of buckets as a latrine, although they were going home, it was not a journey they were looking forward to very much.

Crowded into the carriage the soldiers finally settled in their seats, a few less fortunate ones having to make do with a space in the aisle. Then with a second blast on its whistle, the ancient PKP Pt 31-64 locomotive began pulling away. Gradually picking up speed as the engineer eased the regulation handle forward. The station slowly fading into the distance with every revolution of its giant wheels. Removing a harmonica from his pocket a soldier began playing the opening refrain to *Der Erika Marsch*. Softly, to begin with, becoming louder as he grew more confident, his fellow soldiers humming along to the tune. Then encouraged by the old Gefreiter's fine baritone voice every soldier in the carriage, including Mayer began singing the words of the song at the top of his voice.

> *Auf der Heide blüht ein kleines Blümelein*
> *Und das heißt:*
> *Erika.*
>
> *Heiß von hunderttausend kleinen Bienelein wird*
> *umschwärmt:*
> *Erika.*

Staring out through the rain-streaked carriage window

Mayer surveyed the seemingly endless panorama of rolling grassland. Mile after mile of it. Just like the prairie in America which he had read about it in the Western adventure books by Zane Grey, borrowed from a friend of his father. Eventually, like most of the other occupants lulled by the hypnotic Clickety-clack of the train's wheels as they passed over the gaps in the rails, Mayer drifted into a deep sleep. Waking after what seemed like minutes rather than hours, Mayer blinked his eyes and peered out through the window. Staring out through the glass into the inky blackness beyond, where land and sky merged into one. The horizon lost somewhere in the darkness. Opposite him, his head lolled to one side snoring away like an old cat the Gefreiter slept on. Reaching a hand into a pocket of his uniform Mayer removed a worn leather wallet. Opening the flap he pulled out a black and white photograph. A picture of his family, their smiling faces gazing up at him. Forcing back the tears which clouded his eyes, Mayer smiled back at them. Not long now my darlings. Not long now and I will be holding you tightly in my arms.

It was early morning when the locomotive pulled into Lubin station its brakes squealing, clouds of white steam billowing from open valves. Deep snow covered the rooves of all the buildings. Only the wide platforms were free of it, while bright winter sunshine belied the freezing temperature outside. No sooner had the screeching of metal on metal subsided and the locomotive shuddered to a halt when a male voice boomed out over the P.A. system.

'Attention! Attention! Everyone off the train. Everyone must leave the train.'

Obediently, collars turned up packs slung over their shoulders the soldiers climbed down from the carriages. No sooner had they formed up in two long ranks when a door to one of the buildings opened and an NCO, his portly

The Letter

figure enveloped in a long greatcoat emerged. After pacing up and down the line of soldiers as though he were carrying out an inspection, he bellowed out.

'Attention!' Waiting while the ranks of soldiers reluctantly brought their heels together. 'Pay attention. Everyone is to go to the station hall at the end of the platform,' he said, pointing towards the building in question. 'Quickly now. Move along.'

With a few mutterings of discontent, collectively the two lines of disconsolate soldiers turned to their left and slowly made their way along the platform. The portly NCO striding along beside them, berating those who he thought were dragging their heels. Given that the majority of the station building bore a certain elegance, with their ornate brickwork and arched windows. The so-called station hall appeared drab and out of place. Quite an ugly building in fact. Its low brick walls and oval roof giving it the appearance of an aircraft-hanger. Certainly not a building you would expect to find at such an important provincial railway station as Lubin. Even its two doors set into the end wall were oversize. Certainly wide enough to accommodate a C-2 Storch with its's wings folded. Standing guard outside them were four burly MPs. Each with a snarling Alsatian on a short leash. Something wasn't right though Mayer as he approached the so-called station hall. But what troubled him more was seeing the locomotive which had transported them across the Ukraine being uncoupled.

Filled with apprehension, the soldiers filed into the brightly lit building. Taking heart when they were greeted by a bevvy of young Polish girls dressed in traditional costumes handing out cups of ersatz coffee and small cakes smeared with a topping of jam. With the last soldiers finally herded inside the two enormous doors were slammed shut.

'For you brave soldier,' said the pretty young Polish girl in perfect German, handing Mayer a cup of coffee and a cake.

'Thank you Fraulein,' said Mayer before moving deeper into the cavernous building hemmed in on all sides by his fellow soldiers. At the far end of the hall was a raised wooden platform with a central podium. Maybe we're to be treated to a concert thought Mayer, spotting the microphone. Perhaps Mimi Thoma has been asked to entertain them by singing *Lieber Soldat*? (Dear soldier).

Given the odds of this happening were probably one in a million, just like the uncoupling of the locomotive the presence of the microphone was not a good omen. Moments later, three German Officers ascended the set of steps at the rear of the wooden platform, each taking their pre-arranged positions on the podium. Instantly the babble of voices subsided and in a matter of moments there was complete silence. Standing in front of the microphone with the two other officers on either side of him like a pair of bookends, the senior of the three officers, an Oberst, tapped the microphone with a finger. The two large speakers, suspended above his head on chains, crackling in response. Whether or not this was intended as a signal, but immediately like some choreographed dance sequence, a line of grim-faced MPs began making their way from opposite wings of the platform. Meeting in the middle, like a bizarre chorus line they turned to face their audience.

'Soldiers of the Reich.' the officer began, his lips pressed up against the mouthpiece. 'Today we are faced with difficult times.'

Immediately, a feeling of unease rippled through the packed ranks of soldiers.

'And at this moment it is necessary for us all to put our duty to the Fuhrer and the Fatherland before our own needs.'

'What's this you're telling us?' Someone in the crowd called out angrily.

Ignoring the question the officer continued with his dialogue.

'It falls to me to tell you that all leave is cancelled and that you are to return to your units.'

Instantly, cries of disbelief echoed through the building as the enormity of his words dawned on the assembled soldiers.

'This is not right,' a voice screamed out. 'You can't do this to us,' another soldier yelled out.

'We must all …' the officer began saying before his words were drowned out by a collective chanting of: 'No! No! No!' from the angry soldiers.

Raising his voice the officer yelled into the microphone, 'We must all make this sacrifice. We must all make a supreme effort to achieve a final victory for the German people. Nothing,' he went on a hint of hysteria in his voice. 'Nothing must stand in the way of our nation's destiny to destroy the Bolsheviks.' With beads of sweat running down from his forehead the officer stepped away from the microphone and immediately, *The Deusches Marsche* (German march) blared out from the two speakers. Behind them, the doors to the building were pulled open and forced back by the line of MPs, slowly but surely the crowd of soldiers were shepherded out of the building.

The carriages they had climbed out of such a short time ago were standing just as they had left them. The only difference this time was that the locomotive which had carried them across the Ukraine to Lubin was now coupled to the end carriage. Waiting patiently to take them back to war. Drained of their anger and discontent, the downcast soldiers so cruelly stripped of their leave filed past the row of tables that had been set up along the platform. Helping themselves to their consolation prizes; a sheepskin overvest, a box of tinned food, a pair of woollen gloves, before climbed back aboard the train. As he walked past the line of watching MPs, a deterrent against anyone thinking of deserting, one of them called out to Mayer.

'Bad luck aye?' the MP said, the note of sympathy in his voice sounding quite genuine.

Mayer nodded his agreement, then gripping the side of the door he hauled himself into the carriage. There was a war to be won he told himself, even though in his heart he knew it was already lost. The hard part was going to be staying alive until it was over.

Four
An Area West of the Narew River – NE Poland
Late October 1944

WITH A FEELING of exquisite pleasure, Major Eismann watched the jet of steaming amber liquid burning a hole in the layer of freshly fallen snow. Then with his bladder finally emptied, after the obligatory shake he returned his "handy little gadget," his grandmother's euphemism for the male member, to the warmth of his trousers. Boys had it easy when it came to taking a pee she was always telling him. Where girls had to go to the bother of pulling down their *Schlupfer's* (knickers) a boy simply opened his trousers and took out his handy little gadget. The memory, bringing a smile to his weathered face. Turning away from the urine-stained snow he looked back along the row of parked vehicles and at the line of soldiers standing beside them, each taking the opportunity to relieve themselves.

'Quickly now we don't have all day,' Eismann shouted.

Obediently, buttoning up their flies the soldiers began making their way back to their respective vehicles. All baring one.

'That means you too Toepfer.'

'It's his cock Herr Major,' a soldier replied. 'It's so small he's having trouble finding it.'

Blushing like a schoolboy at the remark and the accompanying bout of amused laughter, sticking up a middle digit and giving his tormentor a one-finger salute Toepfer quickly made his way back to the truck which had been his home for the past six months.

Winter was coming early thought Eismann glancing up at the leaden overcast sky. But at least the sudden change in the weather was keeping the Russian Yak's grounded and he was thankful for that. Making his way back to the waiting *Kubelwagen* (scout car) as he passed the half-track at the head of the column he called out to the man standing beside the driver.

'We must be near Rozan don't you think Mayer?' His breath vaporising in the freezing air.

'Yes, Herr Major. A little to the south maybe but we must be close.'

Mayer had certainly aged. But then two year's war can do that to a person. The gaunt features and sunken cheeks had returned, covered in a pepper-pot stubble. He'd also lost weight. They all had. But given the type of war they had been fighting for the past twenty months, it came as no surprise. Attack and retreat. Attack and retreat. Tank battles and skirmishes too many to remember. Too costly to forget. And now, low on fuel and with their ammunition almost depleted they were retreating once more.

'Well as the cloud cover is good we'll take a chance,' said Eismann. 'If we don't find fuel soon we're done for anyway.' With his words hanging in the air, he jumped in beside the driver, and with its wheels fighting for traction engine roaring, the Kubelwagen headed out across the snow-covered steppe.

The Letter

'They're well dug in but they are ours I think,' Eismann said, removing the field glasses from around his neck and handing them to Mayer. 'At least their guns are pointing in the right direction.'

Taking the field glasses, Mayer scanned the rising ground ahead of them. 'Either that or the Popov's are so drunk they don't know east from west Major.'

'Ha!' Laughed Eismann, 'That could be our secret weapon. Instead of dropping bombs, the Luftwaffe can drop crates of Schnapps and the war will be over by Christmas.'

Smiling, Mayer lowered the field glasses.

'And another Iron Cross for you Herr Major,' said Mayer, handing back the glasses.

'One for each of us Sergeant. A whole chest full. Why not.' Patting the front of his sleeveless fleece vest as he spoke. Then looking down at the man crouched in front of a radio transmitter he said in a more sober voice, 'See if you can raise them on short wave Voller. I don't want them mistaking us for Ivan's.'

'Yes Herr Major,' Voller replied, clamping a pair of earphones over both ears and turning one of the radio transmitters dials to the required frequency. Satisfied, holding the hand mic to his mouth pressing down the button on the side he began speaking. *Panzergruppe* (Panzer Group) Valhalla calling. I repeat Panzer Group Valhalla calling. Acknowledge over.'

After waiting for a minute or so, reaching out a hand Voller adjusted the setting. 'Panzer Group Valhalla calling. I repeat Panzer Group Valhalla calling. Acknowledge over.' Almost immediately Voller's earphones crackled with static. Gently tweaking the dial he listened again. Unconsciously nodding his head as the static died away, and the sound of a man's voice permeated his earphones.

'Panzer Group Valhalla understood. Out.' Lowering the hand mic he looked up at Eismann. 'They're sending a vehicle to escort us through their minefield Herr Major.'

'How considerate of them, 'said Eismann, relieving Mayer of the field glasses. 'Let's hope they also have some fuel for us eh?'

Mayer smiled. 'Two miracles in one day is too much to hope for Herr Major?'

'Don't be so pessimistic Mayer,' said Eismann training his binoculars on the German position. 'We must all be positive, it is the only way to victory,' he said enthusiastically, watching as an open-topped scout car zigzagged its way towards them at speed.

Slithering to a halt inches from the front of Mayer's half-track a youthful-looking officer jumped out of the scout car. Instantly coming to attention and throwing up his arm in a salute.

'Oberleutnant Heitz Sir. You gave us quite a shock Herr Major,' said the young officer, struggling to contain his excitement.

Smiling down on the young Oberleutnant, Eismann returned his salute.

'A pleasant one I hope Oberleutnant?'

'Most definitely Herr Major,' Heitz replied, his broad face breaking into a beaming smile.

'Good!' said Eismann. 'Now this minefield of yours, can my Panzers get through?'

'Yes Herr Major, if they follow my tracks they will be quite safe.'

'Very well then,' said Eismann jumping down from the half-track. 'Lead the way. But slowly now you understand. I want no accidents.'

Throwing up his arm again, Oberleutnant Heitz climbed back into the scout car.

'See them through sergeant and make sure they are well spaced,' Eismann shouted up to Mayer. Then climbing into his Kubelwagen he ordered the driver to take him down the line of parked vehicles. Shouting out to the men as he passed.

'Keep in the tracks of the vehicle in front. No short cuts remember?' And let's hear you sing. Let them know that Panzergruppe Valhalla is here. Show them who we are.'

Cries of *Jawohl, Mein Herr!* Greeted his words and as the Kubelwagen turned around and raced to the front of the convoy, behind him the words of the *Panzerlied* began ringing out.

> *Ob's stürmt oder schneit,*
> *ob die Sonne uns lacht,*
> *Der Tag glühend heiß,*
> *oder eiskalt die Nacht,*
> *Bestaubt sind die Gesichter,*
> *Doch froh ist unser Sinn,*
> *Ist unser Sinn;*
> *Es braust unser Panzer,*
> *Im Sturmwind dahin*

With Major Eismann's Kubelwagen leading, the remnants of Panzergruppe Valhalla snaked their way through the German minefield. A little over eighteen months ago the small battle force had comprised of thirty vehicles and almost four hundred and fifty men. Now the numbers were much smaller. Eleven vehicles, twelve if you counted the Kubelwagen, and one hundred and eighty-eight men. Three of them were seriously wounded. Of the original fifteen tanks, one Panther and three Panzer IV's had survived. Together with five Kfz 251 half-tracks and two Opel Blitz trucks. Both of which, having run out of petrol was being towed by two of the Panzers. Once through the minefield, Eismann began running his experienced eyes over the German fortifications. Set into the natural contours of the low hillside and connected by a network of reinforced trenches, the bunkers and gun emplacements were well constructed. Behind them, scattered along the edge of a spruce forest were a dozen or so timber-framed huts with thatched rooves. As a defensive position, it had a lot going for it thought Eismann and the fact that it was protected by a minefield was an added bonus.

'They look like bloody choir boys,' shouted Voller, trying to make himself heard above the cheering voices of the hundreds of young soldiers swarming around the slow-moving convoy. Their angelic faces wreathed in smiles as they gazed up at the grim-faced panzer grenadiers riding on board the Panzers and half-tracks rumbling past them. Yes thought Mayer, not bothering to answer. Another generation for the meat grinder to get its teeth into.

Climbing out of the Kubelwagen, Eismann removed his fleece vest. Throwing it onto the passenger seat, he straightened his black wrap-over tunic and walked across to where Oberleutnant Heitz was waiting for him outside one of the huts. Pushing the door open, the young officer stepped back and ducking to avoid knocking his field cap off on the door lintel Eismann entered what had once been the home of a Ukrainian peasant. Thankfully, with there being no ceiling the major was able to straighten up to his full height before taking in his surroundings. There was just one room, its dirt floor covered in a layer of straw. Pushed up against one wall was a pine table, with a cot covered in a grey army blanket shoved up against the opposite wall. With its only window covered by a crude wooden shutter, the only source of light emanated from an oil lamp suspended from a central beam. While a small kerosene stove provided the room with a modicum of warmth. Standing with his back to it, the bottom of his full-length greatcoat and knee-length riding boots splattered with mud was a tall, elderly German officer. Stepping into the centre of the room, throwing his left arm up in a salute the Panzer officer introduced himself.

'Major Eismann. Panzergruppe Valhalla, 60th Panzer Grenadier Division.'

Expressionless, the officer stared back at him. Then as though suddenly becoming aware of Eismann's presence, he pulled his lips back into the semblance of a smile.

'Good day to you Major. I am Oberst Broder. The commanding officer of the 427th Infantry Regiment' said the officer, holding out his hand. 'You and your men are a welcome sight.'

'Not as welcome as we are to find you, Oberst,' said Eismann, shaking the man's hand. 'A few more miles and I fear my vehicles would have been out of fuel. And regrettably, my men have got out of the habit of walking,' he added, smiling.

'Then I must disappoint you,' said Broder, the smile disappearing from his face. 'I don't have any fuel for you Major.'

'You have no gasoline?' said Eismann stunned by Broder's words.

'We are an Infantry Regiment major. So it shouldn't come as a surprise. Besides,' he continued before Eismann could respond. 'Even if I did, I would not let you have any.'

'I don't understand you, colonel.'

'It's quite simple Major. As of now, I am placing you and your men under my command.'

'I must protest Oberst,' said Eismann, Broder's words striking him like a hammer blow.

'Protest all you want major. The truth is that I outrank you and therefore you will obey my orders. Is that understood?'

Speechless, Eisman simply stared back at him.

'You must understand Major,' Broder continued, a more benign tone to his voice, 'the situation we are all faced with is a grave one. And no doubt if our roles were reversed, you would do the same yourself. Am I right?'

Eismann remained silent.

'My orders are to defend this position at all cost,' said Broder, a flush coming to his cheeks. 'And I will obey them. However as you may have seen, most of my regiment are raw recruits. So I fear the cost will be a very high one. But!' he said, curling his right hand into a fist and slamming it in the palm of his left hand, 'with your tanks and men there is a good chance we can succeed.'

'I understand your dilemma, Herr Oberst,' said Eismann, trying to put up a fight while at the same time knowing how futile it was. After all the other man held all the aces. 'And I sympathise. But I too have my orders and they do not include using my Panzers in a defensive role.'

Broder allowed himself the smallest of self-satisfied smiles before calling the Panzer officers bluff. 'And without fuel, what other use is there for them? None.' He said, answering his own question. 'No Major I think you must accept the situation and make the best of it. Yes?'

'Very well Herr Oberst,' said Eismann, trying to sound

The Letter

magnanimous in defeat, 'as you say I have little choice in the matter.'

'That's the spirit major,' said Broder cheerfully, I know it may seem that my good luck is your bad fortune but such is war. Then crossing to the table, he picked up a half-empty bottle of Schnapps, 'Now come let us put this animosity behind us and drink a toast to the Fuhrer.'

'Perhaps another time Oberst,' replied Eismann curtly, 'I should like to speak to my men first and then if I may look over your position?'

Unscrewing the cap on the bottle Broder proceeded to fill a tin cup with the clear distilled spirit. His hand shaking quite noticeably.

'By all means. I am sure my adjutant Oberleutnant Heitz will be only too pleased to show off his handy work to you,' he said, putting the cup to his lips and downing the fiery liquid in a single swallow.

Standing off to one side, Oberleutnant Heitz watched with a certain admiration as the men of the Panzer group relaxed around their vehicles. Smoking and chatting, with the occasional burst of laughter when someone came out with a ribald comment. Then seeing Major Eismann leaving the hut and striding towards him, he jumped to attention. Nodding his acknowledgement, Eismann walked past the young officer and displaying admirable agility he climbed effortlessly up onto the front of the nearest Panzer. Silenced by his appearance, all heads turned towards him. If the officer's facial expression was anything to go by thought Mayer, then the news they were about to get was not going to be good.

'I won't beat around the bush,' said Eismann in a loud, clear voice. 'It seems there is no fuel for us. So until division gets around to sending us a tanker, we will be staying here.'

Although in the main a philosophical bunch, the officer's words still caused a few disgruntled expressions to appear on many of the grenadier's faces.

'Look,' Eismann went on, trying to inject some levity to the proceedings, 'I know it's not the news you wanted to hear and you know I share in your disappointment. But at least for now, you will be sleeping with a roof over your heads and somebody else to do the cooking.'

Indifference was probably as good a word as any at describing the men of the Panzergruppe Valhalla's reaction. They had all had a hard time of things and this for each of them was a shitty outcome.

'I have spoken with Oberst Broder the commander here and while he is in overall command, you will still take your orders from me. Understood?' Pleased by the murmurs of approval, Eismann continued. Now you have seen for yourselves that most of his soldiers are recruits.'

'We did notice Herr Major,' Voller called out. 'Still, at least we won't have to share our razor blades, I doubt any of them even need to shave.'

Sensing a lightening in his men's mood, Eismann replied in a jocular fashion.

'Then hopefully I can expect some freshly shaved faces among you tomorrow then eh?' Smiling at the laughter which followed. 'But what I will expect from you,' he went on, a more serious tone to his voice, 'is that you take them under your wing. Show them what it takes to be a good soldier. You all know as well as I do that it won't be long before Ivan comes calling, so they will need your support just as we will need theirs.'

'Are we expected to wipe their bums for them too Herr Major?' said Voller, clearly the comedian of the bunch.

The Letter

But before Eismann could respond, Obergefreiter Linden a tough-looking, no-nonsense NCO shouted out. A mocking tone to his voice.

'You'd like that eh Voller? All those nice young arses to stick your sausage into.' His caustic comment, greeted by roars of laughter from the other soldiers.

With the men clearly in a better mood, Eismann jumped down from the Panzer, and accompanied by Oberleutnant Heitz and Sergeant Mayer, he headed towards the line of gun emplacements.

With a measured stride, walking parallel to the row of trenches Major Eismann began his inspection of the fortified position. His eyes searching everywhere. Nothing was missed. Reaching the final gun emplacement and noting how well the PaK 40 had been sited he turned to face Oberleutnant Heitz.

'You have done well Oberleutnant. I commend you on your fine work, said Eismann, the sincerity in his words quite apparent.

'Thank you, Herr Major,' the young officer replied, clearly delighted by Eismann's comments.

'Now to business,' said Eismann, planting his feet apart, hands clasped behind his back. 'Are there any other officers besides yourself?'

'Yes Herr Major, Leutnant Schaeffler. He is in the infirmary,' pointing across to one of the larger huts. 'Some of the men have come down with dysentery.'

'Is he a doctor?'

'Not a qualified doctor Herr Major but he was studying at a medical college in Frankfurt. Before he was called up I mean.'

'How long? One year, two years?'

'Two years I believe Major,' said Heitz with a degree of uncertainty. Schaeffler had told him once but for the life of him, he couldn't remember how long he'd said.

'Good. Long enough to know his way around the human body then, said Eismann, plainly cheered by the news. 'When we have finished here, tell him I have three wounded men who need his attention.'

Yes, Herr Major.

'So Oberletnant some numbers for me.' How many men do you have?'

'In total, including those who are … including those who have diarrhoea there are three hundred and twelve Herr Major,' said the young officer, confident of his figures.

'Munitions?'

'Each soldier carries 100 rounds with another 100 rounds in reserve. For our three MG's we have 80 boxes of ammunition.

'Five belts in each?'

'Yes sir,' said Heitz 'they are all full boxes.'

Eismann nodded. Well, at least they were well-armed. Always a comforting thought.

'And your PaK's?'

'Fifty shells for each gun Herr Major, 30 AP and 20 HE.'

'Your quartermaster is a very generous man Oberleutnant,' said Eismann, smiling. 'A relative of yours perhaps?'

Not knowing quite how he should respond, Heitz simply smiled at the major's witticism.

'Final question. Have you laid all your mines?'

The Letter

'We have a few left Major but not many.'

'Good. Have them laid where we came through.' Then seeing the questioning look on the young officer's face. 'Sadly Oberleutnant Heitz there will be no more cavalry riding to the rescue. The only people coming from that direction now will be Popov's out for blood.'

Mayer grimaced. Don't spare the poor lad will you, you cruel-hearted bugger he thought to himself. Watching the colour drain from Heitz's face.

'Don't worry Oberleutnant we'll be ready for them,' said Mayer, trying his best to lift the young officer's sagging spirits.

With no further need of him, Eismann turned towards Heitz. 'Thank you Oberleutnant that will be all for now,' bowing slightly at the waist to acknowledge his thanks.

'Very good Herr Major.' And throwing up his arm in a salute Heitz turned and with his shoulders pulled back he walked away.

'Well Mayer,' said Eismann, watching the young officer striding towards the hut housing the infirmary, 'no more hit and run for a while. For now, we must stand and fight.'

Reaching into a coat pocket Mayer removed a small metal flask. Unscrewing the cap he handed it to Eismann.

'It will make a change' said Mayer, watching as Eismann put the flask to his lips. 'Pity they're such a green bunch.'

'Oh we'll lick them into shape,' Eismann replied, running the back of his hand across his lips. 'Nothing like a baptism of fire to show them what war is all about,' he said, handing the flask to Mayer. Watching through pale blue eyes as the sergeant took a long swig.

'Use what fuel we have left for my Panther and Voller's half-track, then get them tucked back in the trees. The other Panzers can guard the flanks,' said Eismann, concerning himself with the final details.

'And the half-tracks?'

'Put them next to their PaK's but don't dig them in. If by some miracle fuel arrives I don't want to waste time digging them out.' Then as an afterthought. 'Oh and get Linden to elevate the mountings on a couple of the MG's. It will give us some air cover if the weather turns against us'

'And the men?'

'See they are issued with ammo and then spread them out along the line.'

'They'll like it better if they could stick together major.'

'No doubt they would sergeant,' Eismann replied with a half-smile. But we must give these young fellows some backbone.'

He was right of course thought Mayer, so no point in arguing. What was it they said about eggs and baskets? Well, whatever it was maybe there was some truth in it.

'Also,' said Eismann looking across to a reinforced rectangular trench positioned behind one of the bunkers, home to two Granatwerfer 34 mortars and their three-man crews, 'have their mortars moved farther back towards the trees. They are too exposed where they are.'

Mayer nodded. 'Should I get Voller to try making contact with division?'

'Why not?' said Eismann before turning and walking towards the infirmary. 'We should at least make an effort to tell them what has become of us.'

Everywhere there was the buzz of activity. The roaring of

Panzer and half-track engines as they manoeuvred into position. Clouds of black smoke belching from the exhaust of Eismann's Panther as its driver backed it in amongst the trees, crushing any it encountered like matchsticks. With the three wounded grenadiers gently lowered onto stretchers and carried to the infirmary, the last of the Panzergruppe's rations were moved to the hut which had been converted into a field kitchen. Then, heaving and shoving a dozen soldiers pushed the two empty trucks into cover at the edge of the wood. Removed from the hive of activity, his instructions carried out, Mayer and another soldier, an MG-42 balanced on his shoulder and carrying an ammunition box made their way towards one of the bunkers dug into the hillside. Approached by a flight of steps reinforced with short lengths of timber hammered upright into the ground, the bunker opened out into a space approximately twelve feet square. Just high enough to accommodate Mayer's six-foot frame, the roof was constructed of lengths of closely packed logs laid vertically from one side of the bunker to the other. Covered over by layers of compacted earth. The uneven dirt floor, trampled flat by soldier's boots was already puddled in places where water had seeped up through the ground. At the front, supported by wooden frames two narrow gun slits looked out across the minefield. Peering out through one of them, manned by a young soldier was an MG-42. Three more soldiers, teenagers too by the look of them, squatted in a corner warming themselves around a kerosene stove. After allowing his eyes to get accustomed to the gloomy interior, Mayer stood for a moment taking in his surroundings. Not at all pleased by what he was confronted by, he bellowed out.

'On your feet. Quickly now! You too.' Glaring at the soldier slouched beside the machine-gun.

Scrambling to their feet the four young soldiers hurriedly formed themselves into a line.

'Right who's in charge?' said Mayer, running his eyes over the four privates.

'I am Sergeant,' said the one standing on the far end, trembling in his boots.

'Name?' Mayer asked, moving along the line of terrified youngsters until he was opposite the soldier who had spoken out. A tall, strapping eighteen-year-old with a face ravaged by acne.

'Kohlar Sergeant. Private Kohlar,' his voice an octave or two higher than normal.

'And what are you lot doing skulking away down here? Well?' said Mayer.

'We have been relieved from duty Sergeant,' said Kohlar, desperately wanting to pull his head back to escape the smell of Mayer's vodka-infused breath.

'On whose orders?'

'Leutnant Schaeffler Sergeant. We have been on duty in the infirmary,' said Kohlar, his voice a little more normal.

'I see,' said Mayer. Feeling a little more sympathetic towards the four youngsters. It can't have been pleasant dealing with bed-pans full of shit all night.

'Well gentlemen,' Mayer went on, allowing his expression to soften a little, 'while you might be happy living like Troglodytes in this hole of yours. Grenadier Schmitt and I are used to more comfortable surroundings. Isn't that so Schmitt?

Schmitt sanctioned the statement with a broad smile. Revealing a mouth with more gaps than teeth.

'So, some improvements are in order' and turning on his heels Mayer walked towards the steps. Calling over his shoulder. 'All of you follow me.'

With his backside precariously balanced on an ammunition box, hovering over the large oval tin sitting on top of the kerosene stove like a witch over a cauldron Schmitt slowly stirred its glutinous contents. Squatted in a half-circle opposite him, Kohlar and the three other young soldiers their mess tins clutched in their hands watched mesmerised. After a final stir, Schmitt lifted the improvised spoon to his lips and licked.

'Ah! Delicious, just like my old mutti used to make.'

Encouraged, the four young privates held out their mess tins in anticipation.

'Patience now my little vultures,' said Schmitt, lisping slightly due to the lack of incisors, 'don't worry there's plenty to go around.' Ladling out equal helpings of the delicious smelling broth into each soldier's mess tin. Calling out when he caught sight of Mayer entering the bunker. 'Better come and eat Sarge before these greedy young bastards scoff the lot.'

Pushing two of the MG's ammo boxes together Mayer seated himself, accepting the brimming mess tin Schmitt handed to him with a nodded thanks. They had done well he thought to himself as he swallowed a mouthful of Schmitt's aromatic concoction. The roof was now supported by eight upright timber props. A thick layer of freshly cut spruce branches covered the floor and a curtain of sacking covered both the gun slits. Now it was just a case of waiting. For some a time for reflection. For others, a time to contemplate the inevitability of what was to come and the hope that it didn't include a visit from the Grim Reaper.

Mayer heard it first. The sound filtering in through the gun slits. Cries of Urra! Urra! Urra! Chanted over and over like a mantra. Growing steadily louder. Now Schmitt heard it too and climbing to his feet he walked across to one of the gun slits. Pulled aside the sacking he peered out, his eyes focusing on the seemingly endless mass of advancing Russian infantry.

'The Popov's have arrived,' he said. Calmly sticking the unlit cigarette between his lips. 'Right, on your feet,' shouted Mayer, prodding the sleeping soldiers with the toe of his boot.

From outside the shrill blast of a whistle pierced the silence, followed by the sound of Oberleutnant Heitz's voice yelling out orders. With both of the MG-42's resting on their tripods, kneeling behind their respective guns Mayer and Schmitt peered out through the gun slits. After the previous evening's meal, Mayer had ordered the four young soldiers to remove the five ammunition belts from six of the boxes. After demonstrating what he wanted, he set them to work linking all five of the fifty round belts together. It was an old trick that had now become standard practice. A way of giving a longer period of continuous fire without changing belts. Positioning themselves to the right of each MG, acting as loaders Kohlar and another young soldier began feeding the first extended ammunition belts into the gun's feed-block.

From outside, the cries of the advancing Russian infantry grew steadily louder and louder.

'Shouldn't we open fire Sergeant?' asked Kohlar, anxiously.

'No, not yet. Let's see how the bastards like your minefield first eh?'

No sooner had Mayer spoken when the air outside was filled with the sound of exploding mines as the leading ranks of Russian soldiers entered the killing field. Had he not seen it before, like Kohlar and the other young soldiers even Mayer wouldn't have believed what he was witnessing either. Men with their legs blown off at the knee, being tossed into the air like rag dolls. Screams reserved for the slaughterhouse resounding across the battlefield. Yet, seemingly oblivious to the carnage still they came on. Hovering behind them, their exhausts belching smoke a squadron of Russian tanks roared up and down like caged animals. Cynical bastards thought Mayer watching the twenty of so T-34's. They knew what they were doing. Then, as the Russian soldiers who had survived the minefield charged forward the German MG's opened up. Inside the bunker the noise was deafening as Mayer and Schmitt, firing in short bursts joined in. The empty cases cascading onto the dirt floor. Crouching at the back of the bunker, the remaining two soldiers pressed their backs against the dirt wall and clamped their hands over their ears.

Pistol in hand Eismann jogged along the line of the defences shouting encouragement to the gunners. Stopping, he lifted his field glasses and surveyed the expanse of open ground. Everywhere he looked the minefield, pockmarked by the craters left by the exploding mines was littered with the bodies of hundreds of Russian soldiers. Some dead, most alive. Men with their lower bodies missing dragging themselves over the ground like human slugs leaving a trail of blood and entrails behind them in the snow. Severed limbs and mangled pieces of flesh strewn on the ground like discarded offal in an abattoir. Tearing away his eyes from the slaughter Eismann focused his gaze on the Russian tanks. Several of which, growing impatient had unwittingly ventured into the range of the German anti-tank guns.

'Very well Oberleutnant,' he said turning towards Heitz,

'time for your PaK crews to show us how good they are.'

'Yes Sir Herr Major,' Heitz replied excitedly.

'Each gun to select a separate target you understand?' said Eismann, 'And use AP rounds. Their T-34's are tough nuts to crack.'

Sprinting like a one hundred metre Olympic contender, Heitz moved from one PaK position to another issuing Eismann's orders. With an efficiency he found quite surprising, Eismann watched in admiration when in a matter of minutes the first PaK began firing. Swiftly followed by the three remaining anti-tank guns.

'That's it, lads.' Eismann shouted out like an excited schoolboy. 'Pour it into them.'

At first, it appeared as though the Russian tank had just stopped. But then flames appeared. Flicking out through the hatch cover and the driver's window like a lizard's tongue tasting the air. Seconds later and an explosion ripped through the T-34, hurling its turret up into the air like a spinning top. A great rousing cheer rippled along the line of defenders. Growing louder as a second tank was hit and erupted into a fireball incinerating its four-man crew in the ensuing inferno. Now it was the turn of the three Panzer IVs to prove their worth. With their turret guns horizontal, they began firing round after round of HE shells into the advancing ranks of infantry. The exploding missiles throwing up great fountains of earth. Murderous fragments of shrapnel embedding themselves into the bodies of the Russian soldiers. Maiming and killing with impunity. Then, joining in like some orchestral accompaniment, the MG-34's mounted on two of the Panzerpgruppe's half-tracks opened up. Their chattering staccato bursts music to the ears of the defending soldiers. Their murderous firepower scything down the few

The Letter

remaining Russian soldiers who had survived the minefield. Eventually, unable to withstand the onslaught, ignoring the vitriolic cries of the officers those Russian soldiers who were able to, turned and fled. Tramping over the mutilated bodies of their dead and dying comrades, splashing through the pools of blood, the soles of their boots slipping on lumps of flesh and intestines in a desperate attempt to save their own lives.

'Cease firing! Cease firing!' Eismann screamed out as he watched the fleeing soldiers.

Further along the line of defenders, Heitz echoed his words. 'Cease firing! Cease firing!'

It was over. At least for now.

No sooner had the two MG's fallen silent when filled with a mixture of joy and relief Kohlar and the other loader began cheering.

'First round to us, said Mayer, pausing for a moment before adding 'But they'll be back.'

Deflated by the sergeant's words, the two young soldier's euphoria died away. Falling silent, they began busying themselves by loading another belt into each of the MG's before scooping up handfuls of spent casings and dropping them into one of the ammunition boxes. Eventually, unable to suppress the question any longer Kohlar looked up at Mayer.

'Why did they do that Sergeant? Why did they just charge into our minefield like that?'

'Well,' said Mayer, resting his back against the wall of the bunker and stretching out his legs. 'The first thing you need to understand about Russians is that they have no regard for human life.

Not your life. Not even their own.'

Kohlar stared back at him. Still unable to comprehend why anyone, even a Russian soldier would run headlong into a minefield. It was beyond belief that anyone except a madman would do such a thing.

Mayer smiled wearily, 'Do you know what a Muzhik is?'

'No,' said Kohlar, slightly puzzled by the question.

'He's a Russian peasant. A person of such low intelligence that even the cow he keeps in his barn has more sense than he does. Well,' pausing for a moment to put the lit cigarette Schmitt had handed him between his lips, 'the Russian army is full of them.' Pausing to drag a mouthful of smoke down into his lungs. 'Un-trained, many of them un-armed they use them as cannon fodder.' Glancing over at the gun slit. 'After all, why risk sacrificing your tanks when a few hundred muzhiks can clear a minefield for you?'

Shocked and strangely depressed by Mayer's explanation, Kohlar just nodded his head.

'Hey! Come on stop looking so fucking glum' said Schmitt retrieving a bottle containing a clear liquid which certainly wasn't water from his pack and unscrewing the cap, 'Let's drink to our victory.' Taking a swig before tossing the bottle to Mayer.

Leaving the hut occupied by Oberst Broder, Eismann and Heitz walked together towards the gun emplacements. Out of earshot Eismann stopped and turned towards the young Oberleutnant.

'How long has he been like that?'

'I am not sure I understand you, Herr Major.' Heitz replied. A little shocked by the directness of the question.

'The drinking, when did it begin?'

Heitz stiffened his shoulders but said nothing.

'Come now it's a simple enough question.'

'The Oberst has not been well Herr Major,' said Heitz, a slight inflexion in his voice. 'You must understand…' The words drying up in his throat.

'Your loyalty does you credit Oberleutnant,' said Eismann, 'but I am not interested in your platitudes.' A hard edge to his voice. 'And what of the men, are they aware of his condition?'

'No Herr Major, they have only been told that he is unwell.'

'Ah well, that at least is something to be thankful for.'

After the brief exchange, the two men stood facing each other in silence. One deep in thought. The other wondering what he would be asked next.

'Very well,' said Eismann, finally reaching a decision, 'we will say no more on the subject but as of now I am in total command here do you understand?'

'Yes, Herr Major.'

'Good,' said Eismann, keen to dismiss the matter and move on. 'Tomorrow things will be more difficult for us. Without the protection of the minefield, our task will be harder. But your men performed well today and this will give them confidence.' Pleased when a faint smile appeared on Heitz's face. 'And confidence does wonders for morale. You see this?' Said Eismann, fingering the Iron Cross First Class suspended on a ribbon around his neck. 'For me it just a piece of metal. But for my men it has meaning. It is a symbol of bravery, of what a single person can do when he is fighting for the Fatherland and it is good for them to see me wearing it. Do you understand?'

'Yes Herr Major,' said Heitz, his eyes fixed on the black,

silver-edged medal with the swastika at its centre.

'Always remember Heitz without moral an army is just a rabble. You must never underestimate its value. It can mean the difference between victory and defeat.'

'Thank you, Major, I will remember your words.'

'Well,' Eismann continued, we have done all we can. The men are well fed and they have their orders so let us hope they sleep well. If the weather remains the same then we will not have their Yaks to contend with. So if you are a praying man Oberleutnant, tonight you should pray for bad weather. Yes?'

Heitz smiled, whether he was a praying man or not he was not saying. But if he was he would most definitely be praying for bad weather.

'Then I wish you a good night's rest.' And with that Eismann turned and walked away.

Darkness descended with the speed of a guillotine. The drab grey sky replaced by an inky blackness, studded by millions of bright stars. Unable to sleep, Eismann strolled along the ridge enjoying the solitude, the crunching of his boots on the crystalized snow the only sound. The faint glow of an oil lamp emanating from the infirmary window the only sign of light. Apart from the ten or so soldiers who had lost control over their bowel movements, there had been only one casualty from the day's battle. A loader manning one of the PaKs, slow in withdrawing his hand, had lost two fingers when the gun's breach slammed shut. Turning up his collar against the chill of the night air Eismann walked on until he reached the Panzer guarding the left flank of the fortified position. With his broad back pressed against the cold steel of the tank's tracks, reaching into a pocket he removed a packet of cigarettes and a gold-plated lighter. Slowly tracing the outline of the finely engraved monogram on its side with his fingertip. It had been a fortieth birthday present from his late wife. A cherished memento of the happy life they had shared. Clamping a cigarette between his lips he thumbed the lighter, its bright orange and yellow flame illuminating his tired face. From a nearby bunker, the sound of someone playing the harmonica drifted like marsh gas on the cold, clear air. Then a soldier took up the tune. Humming it at first. Then singing the words in a deep sonorous voice.

> *Vor der Kaserne*
> *Vor dem grossen Tor*
> *Stand eine Laterne*
> *Und steht sie noch davor*
> *So woll'n wir uns da wieder seh'n*
> *Bei der Laterne wollen wir steh'n Wie einst Lili Marleen.*

Normally a person with little time for sentimentality, moved by this impromptu rendition of a song so dear to German soldiers, gripping the lighter tightly in his fist Eismann gazed up to the heavens. If ever there was a time for weeping and wailing at the sheer absurdity of it all, it was now.

Although the first shell landed a dozen feet in front of the bunker, the shock waves were enough to wake Mayer and his small band of soldiers from their troubled sleep. The sound of the explosion ensuring that they stayed awake.

'Artillery,' said Mayer confidently. 'They mean to soften us up a bit this time.'

'Howitzers. Probably their ML-20's, Schmitt replied calmly while lighting up a cigarette.

'Looks like we're in for a pounding,' blowing the smoke out through his nostrils.

'Right you lot, helmets on,' Mayer called out as two more explosions shattered the silence. 'And get up against the back wall. Quickly now!'

Shaken from their stupor by his words, Kohlar and the three other young soldiers did as they were ordered. Cowering in the semi-darkness, two of them with their hands already clamped over their ears. The second "straddling" shot exploded in the treeline beside the infirmary. The Russian gunners had their range now. Moments later all along the narrow ridge artillery shells began pounding the German position, each detonation throwing up the earth like impatient spring bulbs bursting forth into the sunlight. A PaK takes a direct hit. The bodies of the gun crew and their weapon tossed into the air. Falling back down to earth moments later as unrecognisable pieces of flesh and metal. Soldiers who hadn't been assigned to a bunker, huddled together in the trenches dirt raining down on them. Oblivious to the shelling Eismann moved up and down the line of bunkers. Yelling out orders and shouting words of encouragement. Stopping for a moment to whisper meaningless words of reassurance in the ear of a dying soldier crying out for his mother. A half-track and two of the huts were next to be hit, instantly bursting into flames. Soldiers, engulfed by the inferno, their uniforms ablaze shrieking in terror as the fire consumed them. Heitz and a dozen other soldiers carrying ammunition boxes moved from bunker to bunker distributing their precious cargo. At the far end of the German fortification, the Panzer which Eismann had been leaning against just hours earlier was also in flames. Its turret tilted over at an angle, the twisted gun barrel drooping down towards the ground like an elephant's trunk.

First one, then a second shell exploded above the bunker dislodging two of the props and causing the roof to sag

The Letter

ominously. Fearing that the whole thing would collapse and bury them alive, each grabbing a wooden prop Mayer and Schmitt struggled to push them upright.

'Well don't just stand there,' Mayer called out through gritted teeth, 'lend a bloody hand.'

Shocked into action, Kohlar and another young soldier rushed to their aid and wedging their shoulders against the posts, heaving with all their might the four soldiers pushed the props back into position. Panting from the bout of exertion, no sooner had Schmitt's helper stepped back towards the gun slits when a shell exploded immediately in front of the bunker. The blast ripping away the sacking and hurtling soil and clods of earth through the exposed openings. At first, despite the ringing in their ears, everything seemed normal. No damage was done. But then the young soldier screamed. Just once. He wouldn't scream a second time because the piece of shrapnel from the exploding shell had sliced across his throat with the precision of a surgeon's scalpel, severing his windpipe. Instantly, a fountain of blood sprayed outwards its bright red droplets falling like gentle summer rain on everything and everybody it touched. The teardrops of a dying heart. Mayer was the first to react. Throwing an arm around the young soldier's waist, he clamped a hand over the wound. Feeling the flow of blood pushing against his palm. Forcing its way through his fingers. Gently lowering the dying soldier onto the ground he cradled his head in the crook of his arm. There was still a flicker of life in his eyes, so Mayer smiled. But then it too died and all that was left was the warmth of the blood on his hand. Huddled in a corner one of the other soldiers began crying. Schmitt glared at him and he looked away, wiping the back of a hand across his eyes, ashamed for showing such weakness.

Then, as though a switch had been flicked the shelling stopped and silence descended. A silence so complete that it made them all think they had suddenly gone deaf. But then they heard it. The chanting of a thousand voices. Urra! Urra! Urra!

'What was his name?' Mayer asked, oblivious to the sound.

Surprised by the question, it took Kohlar two or three seconds before he answered. 'Hochstetler Sergeant. Michael Hochstetler.'

Carefully removing his arm, Mayer lowered the dead soldier's head onto the spruce covered floor. Then getting to his feet, accepting the strip of sacking Schmitt had torn down from the gun slit he began wiping the young soldier's blood from his hand. 'Do you hear that?' The question directed at the three young soldiers standing in line, like The Three Wise Monkeys, in front of him. 'Well, now we have a debt to repay. A debt we owe to young Hochstetler here who has given his life for the Fatherland. The bastards who killed him want to kill us too. Remember that. Also, remember that they want to kill your mother and father and our brother and your sister and only we can stop them. 'Never forget that.' His sermon delivered, throwing down the blood-soaked sacking with Kohlar a step behind him Mayer walked across to the MG. Brushing away the dirt from its barrel he pulled the butt into his shoulder. Dropping to his knees beside him, Schmitt did the same.

'Come on you Muzhik bastards. Come and meet your maker,' bellowed Schmitt, squeezing the MG's trigger. The rhythmic chattering of the Spandau and the tinkling of the shell casings as they cascaded onto the floor music to his ears.

In the aftermath of the shelling, the bodies of German soldiers were laying everywhere. Some dead. Others wishing they were. With a medical kit hanging from his shoulder, Leutnant Schaeffler moved from body to body. Helping those he could. Passing by those he couldn't.

To the rear of one of the bunkers, a trench had caved in burying its occupants. Digging with their bare hands a squad of soldiers, spurred on by the hope that some might still be alive worked frantically to free their trapped comrades. Almost all of the huts were in flames. Smoke from the fires drifting upwards into the embrace of a pitiless sky. Only a few vehicles and guns had escaped from the devastation caused by the bombardment. Thankfully, two of Heitz's PaK's had survived and three of the Panzergruppes tanks, including Major Eismann's Panther. Out of the five half-tracks, only Voller's and Linden's were serviceable. Of the others, one had taken a direct hit reducing it to a lump of scrap metal. Another, with its shattered track laying on the ground like a discarded snakeskin, was immobile. There was better news for the third Kfz 251 for although its front wheels had been destroyed by an exploding shell, its MG-34 was undamaged. Thanks to Major Eisammn there was also good news for the crews manning the two mortars. The trench they had been so reluctant to vacate, having been swallowed up by a huge shell crater.

With its engine roaring and clouds of black smoke pouring from its exhaust, Eismann's Panther burst free from the closely packed trees. Tearing up the earth with its wide metal tracks. Slowing as it passed one of the surviving PaK's, Eismann leaned over the side of the cupola and shouted out.

'Tell your gunners to save their shells for their tanks. Is that understood? Leave their Infantry to the machine-gunners and your mortar's.'

'Yes Herr Major,' said Heitz, shouting to be heard over the din of the engine.

'Good man Heitz, do your best,' Eismann replied, using his cupped hands as a megaphone. 'But if things go badly pull your men out understood. Don't sacrifice yourselves. Live to fight another day. Yes?'

But before Heitz could reply, Eismann disappeared like a rabbit down a hole, the cupola's hatch cover closing over him with a resounding clang. With the grinding of gears and the two Panzer IV's in close attendance, the small squadron of tanks lumbered forward, their wide caterpillar tracks churning up the ground.

Confident that the artillery barrage had knocked out most of the German's heavy weapons and gun emplacements, like the incoming tide ranks of Russian infantry strung out in long lines advanced across the exposed minefield. Only this time they had support. Scattered in amongst them were upwards of fifteen tanks, all T-34's. With little to fear from mines, they rumbled forward across the open ground. But at a thousand yards they were well within the range of the two PaK's and in the space of a few minutes, two of the T-34's fell victim to a HE shell. Each one bursting into flames as the deadly missiles pierced their armour and exploded. Raising Eismann's field glasses, a parting gift from the Panzergruppe commander Heitz scanned the lines of advancing enemy. Identifying another target he yelled out instructions to the PaK's gun crew before turning his attention to the trio of German tanks. Watching with admiration as like medieval knights at a jousting tournament they rumbled towards the onrushing hoard of Russian soldiers and their escort of T-34's. Spaced some fifty feet apart with Eismann's Panther in the centre, acting in unison the two Panzer's halted. Their turrets slowly traversing as each gunner searched for a target. The crash of their 75-millimetre guns echoing across the battlefield when a suitable victim was found.

Crouching in their trenches the young German soldiers cheered with unrestrained delight when three more T-34's burst into flames. Plumes of inky black smoke billowing up into the frosty air. Swiftly identifying the danger posed by the Panzers, nine of the surviving T-34's turned and raced to engage them, smoke and flames erupting from their gun muzzles. But with inexperienced crews and a bumpy, uneven terrain to contend with, their chances of actually hitting one of the three Mark IVs was remote.

Sadly for the Russian tank commanders, the opposite could be said for Eismann's little force. All of his tank crews were battle-hardened, experienced veterans and firing from a static position, although at a moving target, each bright orange muzzle flash from their turret guns spelling disaster for a Russian tank. The first T-34 to be hit suddenly slewing to one side as the shell struck its road wheels, sending it zigzagging into the line of infantry, its severed track flailing the air like the tail of an enraged dragon. The second and third T-34's were struck almost simultaneously. The first erupting in a huge fireball when the armour-piercing shell punched a hole in its side, rupturing its fuel tank. The second coming to a halt when the shell from Eismann's Panther penetrated its turret. Its warhead ricocheting around inside, decapitating its commander and dismembering the bodies of the other three crew members, leaving the walls of the tank covered in a bloody paste.

Firing in short bursts, without a flicker of emotion Mayer and Schmitt watched as their relentless firepower and the exploding mortar shells decimated the advancing infantry. The expanse of open ground in front of them turning into a human abattoir. Yet still, they came on. A seemingly endless wave of foot-soldiers. For a second time, Mayer unlatched the MG's vented casing and gripping the overheated barrel with a piece of rag, he pulled it out and threw it onto the floor. Taking the replacement barrel from Kohlar, sliding it into place he closed the casing and resumed firing. The whole exercise taking less than a minute. But despite the carnage, the leading ranks of Russian soldiers were now returning fire. Those equipped with a DP-27 machine-gun throwing themselves onto the ground and shielded by a barricade made of dead bodies, opening fire on the German trenches and bunkers. Now it was becoming a fair fight thought Mayer as incoming rounds thudded against the outside wall of the bunker.

A few minutes later as the last ammunition belt finished feeding its rounds into the MG, Mayer released his grip on the trigger.

'That was the last belt Sergeant,' said Kohlar. 'We have no more ammunition.'

'Ah well,' said Mayer, and pulling back the breach handle he removed the MG's bolt. Slipping it into his coat pocket, he pushed aside the disarmed weapon and climbed to his feet. 'Right time to go,' and picking up his machine-pistol he looked across at Schmitt. 'Come on Schmitt let's get out of here.'

'You go on Sarge,' said Schmitt, looking across at Mayer. 'I've still got some ammo left. Be a shame to waste it'

The two men stared at one another and what passed between them didn't need expressing in words. It was simply an understanding between two soldiers who had fought together side by side for the past twenty months. An unquestionable acceptance of a comrade's wishes.

'Suit yourself,' said Mayer, his voice as emotionless as the expression on his face. Then turning to Schmitt's loader. 'Come on lad no point in you staying.'

'No! Said the young soldier, a hint of defiance in his voice. 'My place is here with grenadier Schmitt.'

'Don't be such a bloody fool, Schmitt can manage without you,' Mayer replied a note of anger in his voice. 'Now come with us, that's an order.'

Schmitt's loader stared back defiantly but didn't move.

'Come on Karl,' said Kohlar reaching out and taking hold of the young soldier's arm.

Karl slapped his hand away. 'No! I am staying.'

Seeing it was a hopeless cause, reluctantly Kohlar turned away and followed Mayer and the other young soldier out of the bunker. Behind him, the MG began its song of death once more. Accompanied by Schmitt singing as loud as he could in his distinctive Brandenburgisch voice.

> *Auf der Heide blüht ein kleines Blümelein*
> *Und das heißt:*
> *Erika.*
>
> *Heiß von hunderttausend kleinen Bienelein wird*
> *umschwärmt:*
> *Erika.*

Emerging from the bunker Mayer paused for a moment. Quickly taking in the scene. Assessing all the possibilities. All along the line of the German defences soldiers were retreating. Urged on by Heitz's bellowing voice.

'Pull back! Pull back!

Earlier, Heitz had witnessed the arrival of yet more T-34's. At least twenty of them. Half had gone to the aid of their comrades locked in battle with Eisemann's Panzers. The others racing at top speed towards the German position. With just a few shells remaining for the two PaK's and the impending threat posed by the approaching T-34's, deciding that it was futile to fight on after spiking the two guns Heitz ordered a withdrawal. Live to fight another day as Eismann had said so succinctly. A further reason if one were needed, was seeing two of the three German tanks suddenly turned into burning hulks. One from the concentrated fire of the Russian T-34's. The other sabotaged by its crew. Without neither ammunition nor fuel, they had abandoned their tank and were now clinging on like bare-back riders to the outside of Eismann's Panther as it frantically sought to evade the attentions of the T-34's as they closed in for the kill.

'Follow me!' Mayer shouted running towards the treeline.

The three soldiers had hardly covered half the distance when with its engine revving, Voller's half-track suddenly burst out from the woods. Without a moment's hesitation, Kohlar and the other soldier turned and raced towards it.

'No!' Yelled Mayer. 'Run for the trees.'

Ignoring the sergeant's advice the young soldier continued towards the half-track. But Kohlar stopped. Caught in two minds he looked back towards Mayer. Then deciding that his best chance of survival lay with the sergeant he began running back towards him. As he did so two Russian soldiers appeared on top of one of the German bunkers. Spotting Kohlar they raised their rifles and fired. Watching as Kohlar stumbled and dropped to his knees, shooting from the hip Mayer fired a burst from his machine pistol. Hit by the volley one of the soldiers staggered backwards and slumped to the ground. Witnessing the fate of his comrade, as Mayer opened fire again the second soldier threw himself headlong into one of the German trenches. Apparently unharmed Kohlar climbed to his feet, smiling in gratitude as Mayer grabbed him by the arm and dragged him off towards the safety of the trees. Desperate to escape the hoard of advancing Russian infantry more German soldiers began running towards the half-track. Pushing and shoving each other aside in a frantic effort to scramble aboard the slow-moving vehicle. With the synchromesh transmission squealing in protest Voller slammed the half-track into gear and with a roar from the powerful six-cylinder engine, the vehicle lurched forward, quickly gathering speed.

Like some monster rising from the deep, the T-34 climbed up the sloping side of the German bunker. Reaching the point of equilibrium with a final surge of power the tank tilted forward, its tracks crashing onto the roof of the bunker. Standing with his head and shoulders visible above the cupola, the Russian tank commander spotted the half-track and immediately, shouted into his microphone. With its caterpillar tracks churning up the earth the T-34 surged forward, its turret slowly traversing as the gunner hunted for his target. Voller could see the T-34 through the driver's narrow aperture. He even heard the detonation of its 76.2 mm tank gun. Saw the bright orange muzzle flash. But nothing more. Like the superbly engineered Maybach HL42 petrol engine, which took the full impact of the shell, he had ceased to exist. At least in human form and even though parts of him were recognisable sadly not even God could reassemble them. Lumbering forward, determined to extinguish all signs of life the T-34 smashed into the side of the half-track the impact turning the vehicle over onto its side. Then with its engine spitting and roaring the tank rolled over the stricken vehicle, crushing it as though it were a tin can together with all the poor souls trapped inside.

Half running, half walking spurred on by the diminishing sound of battle behind them Mayer and Kohlar moved deeper into the forest. Eventually, with the young soldier too exhausted to go on Mayer called a halt. Breathing hard both men dropped to their knees. It was pointless continuing, for while there was still daylight above the dense canopy of trees, beneath it there was only a gathering darkness.

'We'll rest for a while,' said Mayer, catching his breath. 'I doubt the Popov's will bother coming after us. They've probably had enough for today.'

'I've left my rifle behind Sergeant.'

A faint smile touched Mayer's face.

'Don't worry lad. I'll tell the MPs you broke it cracking open an Ivan's skull.'

Lapsing into silence, with their backs resting against the trunk of a tree, for several minutes both soldiers reflected on the day's events.

'Do you think Karl and grenadier Schmitt got away?' Said Kohlar, voicing the question which had been nagging him.

'Who knows?' said Mayer with a slight shrug of the shoulders. 'They might have got lucky.'

'They were brave to stay behind.'

'They were bloody fools, both of them. Now shut up and get some rest.'

'Karl wasn't a fool, he was a good soldier.' Kohler replied angrily.

Staring into Kholar's face Mayer watched as the boy's anger drained away. Cursing the brusqueness of his reply.

'No, you're right. He was a good soldier,' said Mayer hoping to atone for his harsh words. 'A brave lad.' Before adding. 'But he still should have come with us.'

Kholar nodded. 'Yes, I wish he had obeyed your orders and Schmitt too.'

The Letter

'It was different for Schmitt.'

'Why?'

Mayer pondered for a moment. Unsure whether he should answer the question or not. Eventually, he decided that he may as well know. Schmitt wouldn't have minded.

'Schmitt wanted to die.'

As he expected, Kholar was shocked by the answer.

'Why would he want to die, Sergeant? Surely nobody wants to die?'

'He had his reasons,' said Mayer, hoping that would put an end to the conversation.

'I don't understand. What reason could there be that would make him want to die?'

Like a dog with a bloody bone, this one thought Mayer.

'Because he had just received news from home,' said Mayer, telling him that his wife and his two young sons were dead. Killed in a bombing raid.'

Stunned by the revelation, hanging his head Kohlar stared down at the ground.

'So you see, there is always a reason for not wanting to go on living. Even for a tough old sod like Schmitt.'

But Kohlar wasn't listening, he had fallen asleep even before Mayer had finished speaking.

Removing a crumpled cigarette packet from his pocket Mayer removed one of his three remaining smoke's. Then, settling back against the trunk of the tree, thumbing his lighter into life he dragged in a mouthful of smoke, the tip of the cigarette glowing like a firefly in the darkness.

Waking with a start, instinctively Mayer pulled back the

sleeve of his greatcoat, and even though he had been without a watch for as long as he could remember he still found himself staring down at his wrist in search of the time. Consoled by the fact that being able to see his wrist probably meant it was morning Mayer climbed to his feet. Thankfully there was enough light to determine which direction to take. Without it, surrounded by a dense forest you could easily find yourself going around in circles. It was then that he noticed that Kohlar had forsaken the support of the tree trunk and was lying stretched out on the ground. With his helmet removed, his features relaxed he looked even younger. Walking over to him, Mayer prodded the young soldier with the toes of his boot.

'Come on wake up, it's time we were going.'

But Kohler didn't stir. Kneeling beside him, even before he touched the young soldier's face with his fingers Mayer knew that he was dead. Turning the body over his gaze was immediately drawn to the dark stain on the ground. The bullet from the Russian's gun had done its work after all. Poor bugger thought Mayer, he probably wasn't even aware that he was slowly bleeding to death. In one sense it was a good way to go. There was no pain, just a sense of drifting into a deep sleep. Turning Kohlar over onto his back, Mayer unbuttoned the dead soldier's greatcoat, and freeing his identity tag he snapped it in half. Then, reaching into a jacket pocket he removed his pay-book from a breast pocket. Opening it he began reading. Name; Wilhelm Kohlar. Date of birth; 27/2/1925. Trade or profession; student. Place of birth; Lippstadt, Westphalia; Status; unmarried. Actions fought; Eastern campaign; 30/11/42. Rzhev-Vyazma; 19/1/43 to 15/3/43. Fallen on the / /19... Buried at ... As for the last two entries, well firstly Mayer had no idea of the date or where they were. Secondly, he didn't possess a pen or a pencil. Convincing

The Letter

himself that he would attend to these later he pushed the pay-book and the identity tag into his pocket. Right now he had more pressing matters to attend to. Like saving his own life. He thought about searching through the young soldier's pockets but what would be the point? Even if he found letters from Kohlar's loved ones; his mother or a girlfriend perhaps. Or maybe some photographs. What was he going to do with them anyway?

With sufficient light slanting through the crowded trees for Mayer to get his bearings, with a last lingering look at Kohlar's prostrate body he turned away. Leaving a fallen comrade unburied was a terrible thing to have to do. You just had to keep reminding yourself that it was only a corpse, an empty shell and that the person it once was had gone. Hopefully, if the Russians found him they might possess enough humanity to bury his body. One soldier doing unto another as it were. If it were Partisans, that would be a very different matter. Something which he didn't like to contemplate. With a deep hatred of all German soldiers regardless of whether they were SS or not, they would take great pleasure in stripping off every item of clothing and mutilate Kohlar's body. Pushing the thought from his mind and the memory of all the others he was leaving behind, their fates unknown; Eismann, Voller, Linden, Schmitt even young Toepfer, Mayer walked away. Who knows perhaps nobody will find him and he will lay here undisturbed in his forest graveyard forever. But even as the thought crossed his mind Mayer knew there was little hope of that happening. Even if humans didn't find his body the wild animals certainly would.

Five

Regrouping Area West of Rozan – NE Poland
Early November 1944

AT FIRST, THEY began emerging from the forest in ones and twos. Then in small groups. Then larger groups. All eventually merging like strands of hair being plaited into a braid. A trickle of weary men their haggard faces etched with despair. The trickle becoming a stream. The stream turning into a river. A river of retreating German soldiers flowing westward. A defensive front two hundred miles wide had collapsed. Overrun by an unstoppable Russian offensive and this was the result. Regiments reduced to a dozen men. Divisions decimated. The remnants of an army in full retreat. Tanks and vehicles starved of fuel for their engines abandoned. A narrow strip of land, a corridor of hope clogged by exhausted, demoralised men and the few machines of war which they had managed to salvage. Its rain-sodden surface, churned up by the tracks of the Panzers quickly turned into a muddy morass by the seemingly endless procession of overloaded vehicles and the boots of footslogging soldiers. But this wasn't just mud. Mud was something which you got on your boots when you were gardening. Mud was something naughty children made pies with. No this was a veritable quagmire created by the tramping of countless feet and the hooves of horses. The constant churning of tyres and metal tracks. A living entity that dragged the weak to their knees and sucked the wheels of the trucks ever deeper into the mire.

Mayer had got lucky. In a show of comradeship, two panzer grenadiers had hauled him up onto the running board of the Blitz truck they had been sharing. It was a precarious perch for the three of them on the narrow strip of metal but it was better than walking. Later that day as they were driving through a large village its burned-out houses abandoned except for a few stray dogs, they passed a shrine housing a statue of the crucified Christ. Hanging around the figure's neck was a crude placard with the words *Gott Hilf Uns* (God help us) crudely painted on it. Ever the cynic Mayer smiled to himself. Given that it had been soldiers like themselves who had nailed his only son to the cross in the first place, pushing a spear into his side for good measure. It seemed highly unlikely that any help would be coming from that quarter. Even a merciful God was not that forgiving. After driving for an hour, up ahead of them things appeared to be becoming more organised. Dejected crowds of soldiers were being herded together into a single column and vehicles marshalled into designated areas. Not long afterwards, Mayer saw why. Parked by the side of the road were six Zundapp-Russland sidecars each of them looking like they had been dipped in chocolate. Their owners, recognisable by the distinctive gorget's worn around their necks, were a dozen MPs. Each of them exercising his authority with a blast on his whistle and a gesturing arm. Say what you like about them thought Mayer as the driver of their Opel Blitz was ordered to join a line of trucks, but somehow the bastards were always able to create order out of chaos.

Ordered down from the truck, Mayer and the two panzer grenadiers together with the vehicle's other occupants were shepherded towards a slow-moving column of soldiers. Each man clutching his pay book, eager to join those already enjoying a hot meal at the field kitchen. Off to one side in an area reserved for tanks and self-propelled guns their crew's, fuel cans in hand queued patiently alongside a tanker. Towards the head of the column, positioned like a rock in the middle of a stream a burly MP began dividing the flow of soldiers into three orderly rows. At first, Mayer thought he was segregating NCOs from other ranks. Or weeding out soldiers from special units like his own perhaps. But as it turned out he was merely carrying out the duties of an usher. Funnelling soldiers, regardless of rank or status in a slow but steady flow towards a table where another MP carefully scrutinised each soldier's pay book. With frustrations mounting, an old veteran his gaunt unshaven face half-covered by a bloodstained bandage began mouthing his opinions to anybody within earshot.

'What a bloody mess Eh? They say the whole front has collapsed.'

Taking offence at the soldier's remarks, a young soldier, his Arian features highlighted by straw-coloured hair called back at him.

'How dare you say such things? The Fuhrer warned us that there would be setbacks but that we must use them to strengthen our resolve.'

The veteran looked across at him. Noting the twin lightning bolts denoting an SS division on the young soldier's lapel. Obviously from a Jager Division, he thought.

'Ah so this is to strengthen our resolve is it?' He replied, his voice laced with sarcasm. 'Look around you lad, a few more of these bloody setbacks as you call them,' emphasising the

The Letter

word "setbacks" 'and we'll be fighting these Bolshevik bastards on the streets of Berlin. What would you're beloved Fuhrer have to say then Eh?'

Enraged, the young SS soldier shouted back at him.

'How dare you speak of your Fuhrer in this way…'

But before he could finish his rebuke, the burly MP bellowed out in a loud voice.

'Quiet back there! No more talking.'

Obediently the two soldiers fell silent.

Like an Emperor inspecting his troops, his bony hands gripping the top of the Kubelwagens windshield the officer surveyed the lines of soldiers. Middle-aged with a thin face and sunken eyes, his Wehrmacht uniform was covered by a blood-stained white coat. Reaching out a hand he tapped the driver's shoulder and instantly the vehicle stopped.

'You there! Sergeant!' He called out loudly.

Mayer stiffened. Then without really wanting to, he turned his head.

'Yes, you Sergeant. What is your name and your unit?'

'Mayer Sir. Panzergruppe Valhalla, 60th Panzer Grenadier Division.'

'Where are the other men from your unit?'

'All missing or dead sir,' said Mayer, resisting the temptation to add that they were probably all in Valhalla. The officer didn't look the humorous type so the irony would have been wasted on him anyway.

'I see.' The officer replied his expression unchanged. It was an answer he was hearing so often that it had lost all significance. His mind immune to the horror conjured up by the words. 'Well in that case you can be of help.'

Not quite certain what the officer's intentions were. Mayer simply stared back at him.

'Well get in… Quickly now I don't have all day.'

Pushing his way through the line of soldiers Mayer climbed aboard the scout car. Hanging on with both hands as the driver slammed his foot on the accelerator, sending the Kubelwagen racing away, mud spraying up from its rear wheels. Weaving through the log-jam of vehicles. Passing a field kitchen busy dispensing hot food to the growing queue of hungry soldiers, the scout car eventually pulled up outside a large single-story brick building with a tiled roof. Painted in large letters along one wall was the word "*Krankenstation*" (Infirmary).

'Come with me.' Shouted the officer and jumping down from the vehicle, walking with long purposeful strides he made his way towards the door set into the end wall. Following the officer into the building, Mayer's nostrils were immediately assaulted by a smell of rotting fruit. Only it wasn't of course, it was the cloying odour of putrefied flesh. Instinctively covering his nose with his hand he gazed about him. The conditions were appalling, the scene before him more like a Charnel house than a hospital. There were hardly any beds, just a few canvas cots. The majority of the wounded laid out on the floor or a filthy mattress if they were lucky. Several orderlies wearing white coats over their uniform scurried around like worker ants administering what little medication they had or simply quenching the insatiable thirst of the dying. After exchanging words with one of the orderlies, the medical officer walked towards a set of double doors, and pushing them open he stepped outside.

Now that was a surprise though Mayer as he followed the officer outside. A railway line. Well more a railhead really, a single track with a set of buffers at one end. But what

The Letter

surprised him more than anything was seeing the old pre-war PKP Class Ok22 locomotive and the long line of wagons coupled up to it.

'Tomorrow,' the officer began, his strides lengthening. 'I will begin evacuating the wounded. Your job sergeant will be to ensure that there are no unwanted passengers. This is my train and it is for the wounded only. Do you understand?'

'Yes Sir.'

'Good. Those men are your guards,' pointing towards a group of soldiers warming themselves around a brazier. 'They are hand-picked by me and they know why they are here. You can billet them in that hut over by the infirmary for the night. Do you have any questions?'

'No Sir.'

'Excellent.' And with a final look towards the locomotive, the medical officer began walking back to the infirmary building. Calling out over his shoulder. 'You can get some food from the Infirmary kitchen. But don't be greedy, there is not much of it to go around.'

'Thank you, Sir,' Mayer replied. But the officer was already striding away. So whether he heard or not Mayer couldn't be sure. Not that he cared, the important thing was that he wasn't going to have to go hungry tonight and that was all that mattered.

At midnight, Mayer and another soldier, having enjoyed a hot meal relieved the two sentries guarding the line of wagons and stationing themselves on either side of the track, they began patrolling the line of wagons. With a full moon floating above him in an ink-black sky and a silence so deep it made the noise of his boots crunching on the clinkers beside the track sound like he was walking on broken glass, Mayer felt the trauma of the past few days ebbing away. Sadly, the mood wasn't to last, to the east the faint glow lighting up the night sky like a distant firework display reminding him that the war was never far away.

Lost in his thoughts Mayer wouldn't have given the wagon a second glance if it hadn't been for the metal padlock. The fact that it was attached to what looked like a door only serving to increase his curiosity. Intrigued, pulling out his bayonet he slipped the blade into the padlock's U-shaped shackle, and exerting downward pressure he forced it open. After a quick glance along the line of wagons, removing the padlock from the iron staple, and using the hasp as a handle Mayer pulled open the narrow door and peered inside. From what he could tell the compartment, which was barely a yard wide, was a kind of tool store. Hanging from metal hooks screwed into the wooden bulkhead which partitioned it off from the rest of the wagon were lengths of chain, with items of railway paraphernalia; crowbars, sledgehammers, and metal spikes covering much of the floor. His curiosity satisfied Mayer closed the door, and replacing the padlock he resumed his patrol.

He wasn't sure why he had left it unlocked. But that little voice inside his head had seemed to think it was a good idea, and he wasn't about to start ignoring it now. It could mean the difference between life and death.

At first, light, watched by Mayer and the seven other soldiers the orderlies began loading the wounded onto the waiting wagons. Stretcher cases first. Then the walking wounded. Eager to be underway, leaning out of his cab the elderly engineer watched anxiously as the lines of wounded soldiers were ferried onto the line of coupled wagons. Behind him, bathed in an orange glow his fireman continued shovelling more coal into the open jaws of the firebox.

The Letter

It was the soldier standing next to Mayer who heard it first and tilting back his head he looked upwards. "Shit!" That was all he said but it was enough to get Mayer's attention and staring up into the ever-brightening sky he saw it too. A Russian Polikarpov Po-2 spotter plane. Dropping to a height of two thousand feet it began circling above the regrouping area like a buzzard looking for carrion. The droning of its engine magnified by the silence. Seconds later, flinging open the door to the infirmary the medical officer dashed outside, his eyes scanning the sky overhead.

'One of Ivan's spotter planes. We must be in range of their artillery,' said Mayer hurrying towards him.

After nodding his head in response the officer turned away and began running back towards the infirmary. Even before he reached the doorway, all across the regrouping area thousands of eyes were staring up at the solitary aircraft. Then a gun opened fire. An 8.8 cm. Its long slender muzzle pointing skywards. Seconds later a black smudge appeared in the sky just yards from the spotter plane. A great cheer going up from the watching soldiers as the Po-2 immediately banked steeply and veered away. Quickly gaining height it turned eastwards and in a matter of minutes, it was out of sight.

There was an urgency to things now. The medical officer, mindful of Mayer's warning moving along the line of stretcher-bearers urging them to hurry before dashing across to the locomotive.

'Are you ready to leave?' he shouted up at the engineer in Polish.

'Yes we are ready,' the engineer replied, nodding his head vigorously while wiping his oily hands on the front of his soiled overalls.

'Good. Wait for my signal.'

Meanwhile, in the confines of the regrouping area gripped by a sense of unease hundreds of soldiers began milling around like a herd of wild animals before the arrival of an impending storm. And then the first shell landed. Quickly followed by a second. Both falling on the perimeter of the area. Their explosions gouging out deep craters in the ground and filling the air around them with clumps of earth and deadly shards of shrapnel. At first, the calming rhetoric of their officers and the shrill blasts of the MPs' whistles were enough to maintain order. But as the salvo increased and the barrage began creeping towards them like some insidious beast, pandemonium broke out among the soldiers. Soon shells were falling from the heavens like rain. The ground trembling as though it were in the throes of an earthquake. Men and machines devoured with impunity. A generator was hit, its severed power cables thrashing around like beheaded snakes. Then the fuel depot received a direct hit, hundreds of barrels of petrol exploding in a giant fireball. Tanks and trucks hurled into the air like toys. Their wheels and metal tracks transformed into lethal missiles. Terror-stricken, in groups of ten and twenty, to begin with, and then in their hundreds; seeing the train as their only hope of survival, soldiers began streaming towards the railhead. Initially, the cordon formed by Mayer and the seven soldiers held firm. The medical officer screaming out to the fear-crazed soldiers; 'Go back! Go back! This train is for the wounded only.'

But his words had little effect and slowly the cordon was forced back. Even when Mayer began firing his machine pistol over their heads, still they surged forward. Eventually, through sheer weight of numbers the cordon was pushed back and en masse the terrified soldiers raced towards the line of freight wagons. Barging aside the orderlies and trampling over the wounded in a desperate attempt to secure their ticket to safety. Horrified, the medical officer turned, and waving his arms wildly above his head he ran towards the locomotive. Taking the officer's frantic gesturing as a signal, with a prolonged blast on the train's whistle the engineer pushed on the regulator lever and with clouds of black smoke billowing from its funnel the locomotive began slowly pulling away.

As the line of wagons inched their way forward a shell landed on the infirmary, the explosion reducing the building to a pile of brick rubble and filling the air with a choking cloud of dust. Fighting his way through the fear crazed mob Mayer made for the railway track. Survival meant getting on that train and he meant to survive. Crossing over the rails, hidden from the crowd of soldiers each clamouring to board the slow-moving wagons, Mayer began running, lengthening his stride as the speed of the locomotive increased. Reaching the wagon with the small compartment, stretching out an arm Mayer grabbed the padlock with his hand and yanked it open. Freeing it from its staple he pulled open the door and throwing in his machine-pistol he scrambled inside. Taking a moment to catch his breath, reaching out to close the door Mayer spotted one of the guards running alongside the railway line towards him.

'Come on! Come on!' Mayer yelled at him.

And then a shell exploded beside the track, the force of the shock wave threatening to derail the line of wagons. Mercifully, with wheels and rail maintaining contact clinging onto the door, Mayer looked back along the track. But the man wasn't there anymore. Just a thin veil of dust floating in the air.

He waited until the train was well underway before jettisoning most of the tools and lengths of chain. Pushing them through the narrow opening with his feet. Having cleared enough space to move around in and with sufficient daylight filtering in through the chinks in the wood to see by Mayer set about removing one of the two horizontal planks of wood from the crudely made door. Working as quietly as he could, using one of the rail spikes as an improvised crowbar little by little he prized it away, the rusty nails groaning in protest. With enough of it freed, pushing hard on one of the vertical planks he squeezed his other arm through the opening and taking hold of the hasp with his fingers he slipped it back over the staple. Retracting his arm, with the padlock gripped in his hand Mayer repeated the process. This time looping the open end of the padlock's U bar through the eye of the staple, pushing on it until he felt the locking mechanism engage. Having successfully locked himself into the compartment Mayer gently hammered the plank back into place. Pleased with his work, removing his helmet he stretched himself out full length on the floor his hands folded behind his head. Where the train was going and what he would do when it arrived didn't concern him unduly. For now, he was safe and that was enough.

Twice the locomotive was diverted off the line and into a siding, giving way to a train travelling in the other direction. Everything moving east had priority. An endless procession of men and supplies feeding the war's insatiable appetite. The third time was different and altogether more ominous. Although he was blind to what was going on outside the confines of his self-imposed prison, the sound of dogs barking, and a harsh voice shouting out orders soon alerted Mayer to the danger. The train was about to be searched and helpless as a baby all he could do was to pray that he wasn't discovered. Well not quite helpless, there was always his faithful Schmeisser and the three magazines stuffed into his greatcoat pocket.

It was an SS officer who had ordered the train into the

siding. And it was on his orders that the dozen or so SS soldiers began searching the train, wagon by wagon. Sliding open the heavy double doors, their torches probing the semi-darkness. They knew who they were looking and they were easy enough to identify. If you weren't laying on a stretcher or swathed in bloodstained bandages then you were a deserter. It was as simple as that. Moving back as far as he could, hoping that even if they opened the door he wouldn't be seen in the gloomy interior Mayer waited. His eyes fixed on the narrow door. The Schmeisser gripped firmly in his hands. He wasn't concerned at all by the presence of the dogs. The cloying smell of decaying flesh was so overpowering that their sense of smell was about as much use as a husband with a cold trying to decide which perfume he should buy for his wife. But what if one of the soldiers became intrigued by the locked door? What if he tried it and the lock opened. Could he really kill a fellow German soldier? It was a question Mayer hoped he would never have to answer. But one thing he was sure of, whatever happened he was not going back. Then, alerted by the sound of approaching footsteps Mayer tensed. His heart rate increasing when they stopped directly outside.

Just as it had with Mayer, the padlock caught the eye of the *SS Rottenfuhrer* (SS Corporal) patrolling the other side of the train. And just like Mayer he reached out a hand and taking hold of the padlock he pulled on it. Thankfully for both of them, the padlock remained shut. With the sound of the NCO's footsteps growing fainter, from the other side of the train a second SS Rottenfuhrer began shouting. 'Out! Out! All of you get out!' Sheepishly, one by one the soldiers he was shouting at jumped down from the wagons. Prodded into two lines by the barrels of the SS soldier's rifles, they stood awaiting their fate. Most hung their heads and looked down at the ground. A few braver ones stared back defiantly at their grim-faced guards and the slathering

Alsatians tugging on their leashes. Unhurried, the SS Officer immaculately dressed in a full-length leather overcoat, his highly polished black leather boots gleaming in the weak sunlight, climbed out of the Steiner. With measured strides, he walked across to the lines of detainees. There were eighteen of them in total. All unarmed and hatless except for four, two who were still wearing their helmets and two others with field caps on their heads. With contempt for those standing before him oozing out of every pour, the SS Officer slowly paraded up and down the lines of soldiers.

'You are all deserters. Traitors to your Fuhrer and the Fatherland and as such you will be severely punished.' His words laced with malice.

'No! No! Called out one of the men in an anguished voice 'It was escape or die. We had no choice.' Sobbing, 'What were we supposed to do?'

The officer stared at the soldier with eyes as cold as a fish. He could have reminded him that true German soldiers stand and fight. They don't hide away among their wounded comrades like cringing cowards. But instead, he chose to say nothing. After all, the man would be dead in a few minutes so why even bother answering him. Then like a captain choosing players for his team, pointing at each soldier with the short baton he was carrying in his gloved hand the SS Officer began making his selection. Each decision condemning eight of them to death.

Selection over ten of the soldiers, noticeably the younger once were led away to a waiting truck. Resigned to their fate, unable to control his bladder one of the remaining soldiers began urinating. The tell-tale stain spreading down the inside of his trouser legs. Another began sobbing, his shoulders trembling uncontrollably. Had Mayer been able to witness the scene he might have recognised one of the condemned men. True his cheeks were even more sunken, his eyes a little more deep-set. But he was as erect as ever, his narrow shoulders pulled back as though he were on parade. Perhaps if he had started singing, hearing the sound of the man's deep baritone voice might have jogged Mayer's memory. Reminding him of their journey to Lubin together. But then when you are about to be executed; and the old Gefreiter knew that this was what was about to happen, bursting into song was probably the last thing on your mind. There was a part of him though that wanted to speak out. To scream at the injustice of it all. But he knew that he would be wasting his breath. It was quite obvious that the SS bastard had already made his mind up and that was that.

With his presence no longer required the SS Officer climbed into the Steiner and after gesturing to the locomotives engineer that he may proceed, he settled back in his seat as the scout car pulled away. It wasn't that he was squeamish. Heaven forbid. Or that he saw such punishment as a waste of good soldiers. No regrettable as these actions were he was an advocate of the necessity for them. Examples must be made as a deterrent to others. The two Rottenfuhrer's were well aware of what must be done. The pair had done it many times before. He sometimes thought they rather enjoyed it. The truck driver on the other hand, eager to spare himself the gruesome spectacle was only too happy to leave. Yanking on the gearstick he pushed his foot down hard on the accelerator pedal and with a glance in the wing mirror, he pulled away, following in the wake of the departing Steiner. While they may have escaped death, life for the truck's ten other occupant's wasn't exactly looking rosy. Their penalty for attempting to desert would mean spending at least the next eighteen months in a Punishment Battalion. Eighteen long months of being treated worse than a prisoner of war. Their uniform's stripped of all regimental insignia, collar badges, and shoulder-titles. Their entitlement to mail restricted. Associating with other soldiers strictly forbidden. Assigned to tasks so horrific that even the prospect of death seemed strangely comforting. Removing dead soldiers, or what was left of them from the battlefield and burying their mutilated bodies in makeshift graves. Interring those poor souls who hadn't survived the surgeon's knife in the casualty clearing stations, together with their amputated limbs. Carrying away live mines from the paths the units of sappers had cleared through the Russian minefields. Tasks that perfectly defined the word punishment. But all that lay ahead of them. At least they were alive and that was something to be thankful for.

Slowly the locomotive pulled away, the tightening of the couplings sending a judder through the line of wagons. Sighing with relief, bending his knees Mayer slumped down into a sitting position, his legs stretched out in front. It had been a close call but they were underway again and he was safe. Then he heard it. Muffled a little by the noise of the locomotive as it picked up speed. The unmistakable 'chattering' of machine-pistols. A reminder if he needed one of just how lucky he had been. Banishing the thought from his mind, turning up his greatcoat collar he stuffed his hands into his pockets and closed his eyes. From beyond the wooden partition, the cries of the wounded began again: Water! Water! The same pitiful request over and over. But as the miles rolled past and the hours ticked by their anguished cries grew less and less. Some falling silent because they no longer needed it. Others finally realising that even if there was water, there was nobody there who could give it to them anyway. Eventually, lulled by the gentle rocking of the wagon, cocooned in the darkness of his wooden cell Mayer finally succumbed to sleep. An escape from the madness, no matter how brief or how fitful was always welcome.

Six

Potsdam
Mid-November 1944

MAYER HAD NO way of telling what time it was. He only knew that it was dark outside. And although his body ached and his stomach rumbled from want of food, the fact that it wasn't broad daylight was what mattered. On arriving at its destination the train had been kept waiting outside the station like an uninvited guest at a party for over an hour before finally being allocated a platform. Thankfully, it wasn't long before the reception committee arrived. Made up of nurses and stretcher-bearers, with caring hands and whispered words of comfort they immediately began removing the injured from the crowded wagons. Many of the nurses themselves were worn out from the countless days of caring for the sick and injured in a city constantly pulverised by Allied bombs. Even their once-crisp blue and white uniforms were now crumpled and stained. But concealing their fatigue behind a smiling face they began helping the walking wounded down onto the platform and escorting them to the waiting line of trucks and ambulances. Working in pairs the stretcher-bearers, many of them just teenage boys with Red Cross armbands stitched to their jackets began removing the more seriously wounded. Sadly for many, rather than being a chariot of hope transporting them to salvation the train had taken on the role of a hearse. Some would argue that at least they had been brought home to the Fatherland and that their final resting place would be on German soil. But to the poor soul laying on the stretcher, his face covered by a grey army blanket this was a poor reward. All he had wanted was to return to Germany alive not to be buried there.

Blind to this hive of activity, privy only to the pitiful cries for water and the moaning of those in pain, crouched in his self-imposed prison Mayer waited. Finally, the last stretcher was removed and the sound of shuffling feet ebbed away. The groans of the suffering and the voices of the stretcher-bearers giving way to silence. Once the wounded had been removed he had expected the empty wagons to be shunted into a siding. A quiet backwater somewhere among the train sheds and workshops. But instead, abandoned by their locomotive they remained where they were and presumably would do so until morning. Which didn't suit Mayer one little bit.

Having had ample time to reflect on his predicament, the one conclusion Mayer had reached was that giving himself up was not an option. The memory of those poor devils being executed by the SS had convinced him of that. To them, he was now a deserter. Not something he had ever envisaged or wanted but the truth was like it or not that's what he had become. Strangely, by accepting the fact unpleasant though it was it focused his mind. Gave him a purpose. The war was lost. At least in the east, it was. Nothing could halt the Russian juggernaut no matter how bravely they fought. No matter how many good men were sacrificed. He also suspected that it would be the same in the west, the might of the Allied armies would surely prove too great. Too powerful to resist. So all that was left was for him to go home to his family. How he would manage it he wasn't sure. But at least the first step was relatively easy. Getting off the train.

The Letter

The plank of wood came away easier this time the rusty nails offering little resistance. Pulling aside the vertical plank he had previously loosened, pushing his arm through the gap Mayer wedged the end of the spike into the padlock's shackle and forced it open. Slipping the padlock out from the staple, freeing the hasp he slowly eased the door open just wide enough for him to peer outside. Greeted by the sight of a deserted platform, with his Schmeisser gripped in his hand Mayer jumped down from the wagon. Relieved that his legs hadn't stiffened up after their enforced period of confinement he weighed up his options. Thankfully, the few surviving lights hanging from what remained of the glassless, iron canopy had been extinguished. So deciding that leaving the station was probably his best option Mayer began walking towards the far end of the deserted platform. Reaching the last of the freight wagons he jumped down onto the track and with enough light to make out the silhouettes of buildings, using the sleepers as stepping stones he made his way towards what he hoped would be a good hiding place.

It was debatable who was the more surprised. Mayer or the two sentries standing in the shadowy entrance to one of the railway sheds enjoying an illicit smoke. But whoever it was, it didn't matter. What mattered more was who would be the first to react? Fortunately for Mayer, it was him, and right now being given a head start in a race you couldn't afford to lose was a Godsend. To their credit, it didn't take the two sentries long before they realised what was happening.

'Hey you stop!' shouted one, throwing his unfinished cigarette onto the ground.

Knowing that shouting wasn't likely to have much effect, his partner in crime was already giving chase. Without knowing where he was running to, Mayer knew his only chance to escape was by putting as much distance as he could between himself and the two sentries in the hope that they would give up the chase. Summoning his last reserves of strength, hurdling the ribbon of tracks which branched out from the station like outstretched fingers with an agility born from desperation he raced away. Behind him, he heard one of the sentries cursing the darkness. Better that than the crack of a rifle thought Mayer, it seemed his pursuers were more interested in catching him rather than killing him. Then up-ahead revealed through a break in the clouds he saw what appeared to be the shadowy outline of houses. Their rooves and walls silhouetted against the night sky. Spurred on by the hope that they might provide a hiding place he began running towards them. Hurdling the last set of rails Mayer found himself confronted by a low brick wall and the welcoming sight of a row of terraced houses. Spotting a chink of light in one of the downstairs windows, gasping in a mouthful of air Mayer scrambled over the wall and staggered towards it. Positioned to the left of the offending window was a door. Praying that it wouldn't be locked, Mayer grabbed hold of the handle turned it, and pushed.

The next thing Mayer knew he was standing inside what he instinctively knew was a kitchen. Slamming the door shut, reaching up for the bolt he dragged it across and bolted the door. Transfixed, with her back to the stove the old woman stared across at him. The look on her face a mixture of surprise and terror. Mayer stared back at her, praying she wouldn't drop the large earthenware dish she was holding. He wanted to say something reassuring but before he could form the words a fist slammed against the outside of the door, quickly followed by a man's voice bellowing out; 'Open up! Open up! It wasn't a request.

Oddly enough it was the door leading from the hallway into the kitchen which opened. Taken by surprise Mayer

The Letter

instinctively raised his machine pistol and aimed it at the man framed in the doorway. A big broad-shouldered man wearing a pair of dark blue overalls the shoulder straps hanging down like braces. Un-smiling he looked across at Mayer, his eyes moving from the sergeant's face down to the Schmeisser pointed at his chest. Judging by his facial features he was about the same age as the woman. An interesting face. Possibly a handsome one once. That was until someone had broken his nose. Then quite suddenly, gesturing for Mayer to follow him the man turned around and disappeared. Without a second thought, Mayer hurried across the room and into the hallway. By then the man was halfway up the flight of stairs. After beckoning again he continued up the narrow staircase, taking two steps at a time. Slinging the Schmeisser over his shoulder, Mayer followed.

'Come on hurry up! Open the door.' The same man's voice but more agitated now.

'Patience! I'm coming, I'm coming.' The old lady called out, as she pulled back the heavy bolt. Stepping aside as the two sentries came bursting into the room.

'Where is he?' Shouted the older of the two sentries, not at all happy to be gallivanting about in the dark. 'I know he came in here we saw your door open. So don't lie.'

'It was my husband,' said the old woman, fearful of revealing the truth.

'Doesn't he know there's a curfew?' The sentry shouted back at her.

'He… He works on the railway. He is an engineer.' She blurted out.

The man glared at her. Clearly not happy that she had a plausible excuse. 'Search downstairs,' he said to the other sentry before striding into the hallway. 'I'll check upstairs.'

Reaching the first floor, his finger on the rifle's trigger one by one the older sentry opened each of the three doors fronting the small landing. The glow from the gas lamp on the wall providing just enough light for him to see inside them. Behind the first door was a small, simply furnished bedroom. Filling most of the available space was a faded armchair, a single metal framed bed, and a table with a three-legged stool pushed under it. Certainly nowhere for a man to hide. On the other hand, the next room, which was undoubtedly the couple bedroom was packed with furniture and clearly lived in. Pushed up against one wall was a glass-fronted double wardrobe topped by a gilded bronze ormolu. Against another was a tall chest of drawers and squeezed into one corner was a small table, home to a group of framed black and white family photographs. Dominating the room and taking up most of the available space was an enormous double bed with an impressive hand-carved headboard. After looking inside the wardrobe, failing in his attempt to lift the heavy bed the sentry dropped onto one knee and peered under it, wondering as he did so how they had managed to get the bloody thing up the narrow stairs in the first place. The final door belonged to the bathroom which contained nothing more surprising than a porcelain washbasin with a set of brass taps, a hot water geyser an enamelled bath, and a WC. Due to the boarded-up window, the second-floor bedroom at the front of the house was so gloomy it was difficult to see very much. From what little light there was, it seemed the room wasn't being used for anything other than storage. There were several rolls of carpet propped up against one wall and piled up in the middle of the floor, stacked one on top of the other were at least a dozen large cardboard boxes. What could be seen were a pair of wooden trunks, each of them covered in stickers; New York. London. Paris.

Someone had done a bit of travelling, thought the sentry, reading the place names on the stickers.

By the time he entered the other second-floor room the old man had taken of his shirt and his boots. Perched on the side of the unmade double bed, one sock on the other half off, he looked up at the armed soldier and smiled.

'What's this then, come to tuck me up have you?'

The sentry scowled at him. Not at all amused.

'Your old lady tells me that you're an engineer? Been on a late run then have we coming home at this hour?'

'I'm not at liberty to say I'm afraid. By order of the Fuhrer himself. But you are welcome to ask Herr Schweiger the station supervisor if you like.'

Cheeky bugger thought the sentry. All the same these bloody Reichsbahn lot. Think they run the country.

'Right, lift up the bed.'

The old man stared at him but didn't move.

'Come on I haven't got all night.'

'It's heavy, you'll need to give me a hand.' The old man replied pulling off his sock.

'You look strong enough to me old man. Now get on with it. I've had enough of trying to lift beds for one night.'

Not wishing to push his luck, bending at the waist and gripping the side of the bed with both hands, the old man straightened up. Lifting it effortlessly off the floor. Lowering it down again when the sentry had finished inspecting underneath it. Satisfied, without saying another word the sentry turned and left the room. The sound of his heavy footsteps fading as he descended the stairs.

Unaware of the events being played out inside with his legs

splayed, feet firmly planted in the overhanging metal guttering his back, and hands pressed against the sloping tiled roof, Mayer gazed up at the moonless sky. Having placed his life in the hands of a total stranger, all he could do now was to pray he had done the right thing.

'They have gone Otto. They have gone.' The old woman called up the stairs.

Grateful for the news, putting his socks and boots back on the old man crossed to the window. Drawing back the flowered curtain, he pulled it open and leaning out he gestured for Mayer to come back inside. Nervously, with his hands glued to the tiles, the machine-pistol hanging around his neck shuffling his feet along the guttering Mayer edged his way towards the open window. Reaching his goal, heaving a sigh of relief he clambered over the sill and dropped down into the bedroom. Closing the window and pulling the curtain, without saying a word the old man walked towards the bedroom door and together the two men descended the stairs.

When they re-entered the kitchen the old woman was still standing in the same spot. Her hands down by her side, the earthenware dish she had been holding now resting on the stove. Walking over to her the old man placed a reassuring arm around her shoulders. Hard though it was to comprehend, no matter how surreal the events of the last few minutes may have seemed, looking across at the old couple Mayer knew that they had just saved his life.

'Thank you,' said Mayer. And although he meant it from the bottom of his heart, no matter how sincere somehow the two words seemed pathetically inadequate.

'You must go!' Said the old man in a firm voice. 'We will say nothing, you have my word.'

He was right of course thought Mayer but first, he had a

The Letter

question.

'Yes don't worry I will be on my way. Just tell me one thing, where am I?'

'You don't know where you are?' Said the old man, shocked by the revelation. 'How is that possible?'

'There were no signs at the station.'

'No,' said the old man a little apologetically, taken down and burned long ago.' But what about your ticket or whatever it is they give you, didn't it have a destination?'

'The train I was on didn't require one,' Mayer replied with a half-smile.

The old man frowned. And then the penny dropped.

'Where you were on the hospital train? The one which came in earlier?'

'I was,' said Mayer.

'Are you wounded?'

'Sadly no,' said Mayer. 'If I was I would be tucked up in a nice warm hospital bed.'

The old man's face hardened.

'So if you are not wounded why were you on the train?'

'Trying to save my life. Trying to live a little longer,' said Mayer.

Stunned by the soldier's admission, the old man looked Mayer in the eyes.

'And is that why those two were looking for you because you are a deserter?' The measure of disgust he felt evident in his tone of voice.

'Yes I'm a deserter,' Mayer spat back at him. 'But not by

choice so don't judge me, old man. I am not a coward but I don't intend to be a martyr and if that means being called a deserter so be it, my conscience is clear.'

Stunned into silence by Mayer's angry outburst the old man stared into the soldier's emaciated, un-shaven face.

'If what you say is true,' said the old man, desperately wanting to believe him, 'and you boarded the train to save your life then surely if you gave yourself up and explained the circumstances then …'

'Perhaps to survive would be a more honest way of putting it,' said Mayer interrupting him.

'After all, it is only God who could say whether I would have died or not. But the odds were not good. Either way, I doubt they would have believed me.'

'But you are an NCO,' the old man replied. 'A sergeant.' Pointing at the badge of rank on Mayer's greatcoat sleeve, 'surely that must count for something?'

Mayer didn't think he had a laugh left in him. But surprisingly one came from somewhere. Short, slightly humorous, and laced with a touch of sarcasm.

'This,' said Mayer, pointing the patch on his sleeve, 'means nothing. No, they would have just handed me over to the SS, and believe me they are not very good listeners. A bullet to the head is all they understand.'

'You must be hungry?' Said the old woman quite matter-of-factly. Quite unconcerned by the conversation the two men were having.

It was hard to tell who was the more surprised. Her husband or Mayer.

Surprised or not Mayer was quick to respond. 'Yes that's true.' he said, remembering the bowl of horse-meat soup

The Letter

and half a slice of bread he had eaten two days ago. With very little before and nothing since. 'Whatever you can spare I would be grateful for. I imagine finding food will be hard.'

'Nonsense!' said the old woman, a pronounced firmness to her voice. 'You must stay and have supper with us.' Staring at her husband as if daring him to challenge her decision.

'Yes … Yes you are right mother, you must eat with us. Come sit at the table,' said the old man pointing to a chair.

Mayer hesitated, his head turning towards the door.

'Don't worry I bolted the door when they left,' said the old woman smiling.

Needing no more persuading, after taking off his helmet and unslinging the Schmeisser, hanging them on the back of the chair Mayer seated himself at the table.

'Besides,' said the old man, making conversation while his wife ladled the contents of a large copper pan into three bowls, 'while you're eating it will give those two bloodhounds time to go back to their kennel.'

'You're both very kind. Especially after the ordeal, I've put you through.'

The old man smiled and shrugged his shoulders.

'Nonsense! It's nice to have a little excitement at our age isn't that right mother?'

It was a simple supper; a watery fish soup to begin with followed by boiled sausage and a few potatoes covered in grated cheese, but Mayer couldn't remember when he had last enjoyed a better meal. Well, maybe the officer's pet Doberman he'd eaten with young Neubauer. After clearing away the dinner plates the old woman returned to the table carrying a beautiful, hand-painted Dresden coffee pot and began pouring the contents into three blue and white cups each with a matching saucer. With the aroma of coffee in his nostrils and the cloying warmth of the kitchen, Mayer began thinking he was in paradise.

'It's real coffee,' said the old woman, watching as Mayer put the cup to his lips. 'A little luxury.'

Mayer smiled back at her. The whole experience was so surreal he was beginning to think that perhaps he had fallen asleep and the whole thing was just a dream.

'There's a black market at the Tiergarten and a few lumps of coal will buy you most things,' said the old man tapping the side of his nose with a forefinger. 'Even real coffee.'

'It's wonderful. Truly delicious.' Mayer replied, brought back to earth by the comment.

And then in deference to the coffee, the three of them lapsed into silence.

'So Sergeant if you can't give yourself up what will you do?' asked the old man, placing his cup in the saucer.

'There is only one thing I can do,' Mayer replied, 'I must go home to my family.'

'So you have a family?'

'Yes. Why does that surprise you?'

A little embarrassed by the question, the old man shrugged his shoulders.

'I have a photograph if you would like to see,' said Mayer, reaching into his tunic pocket and taking out his wallet. 'Of course, they are older now ... Except for my wife of course!' and removing the black and white photograph he handed it to the old man.

Smiling at this simple endearment, moving closer to her

husband the old woman gazed down at the picture of Mayer's family.

'You have a son,' said the old man. It wasn't so much a question as a statement of fact.

'Yes, his name is Wolfgang. He must be ten now,' said Mayer a little disconcerted that he couldn't remember his son's age.

'We also had a son. Ernst.'

At the sound of the name, the old woman reached out and placed a hand on her husband's shoulder. Squeezing it gently with her fingers.

'Now all we have is a letter. A letter telling us that our beloved son died a hero's death fighting for the Fuhrer and the Fatherland.'

Mayer watched as the man clenched his huge hand into a fist. Rage and sorrow fusing into a single, all-consuming emotion. Hatred.

'A lousy piece of paper for a life,' said the old man angrily. 'He was our late blessing and that madman has murdered him.'

Then just as quickly the rage drained away until all that was left was a look of sadness in the man's eyes.

Taking the photograph from the old man's fingers Mayer returned it to his wallet and pushing back the chair he climbed to his feet.

'I am truly sorry for your loss,' he said buttoning up his greatcoat. 'Now I must go. And with that Mayer walking across to the door. Reaching up for the bolt he hesitated for a moment and then lowering his arm he turned and faced the old couple. 'I will never forget your kindness. I hope one day I can repay you.'

The old man waited until Mayer was reaching up to un-bolt the door before climbing to his feet.

'Since you wished to know, you are in Potsdam.

Lowering his arm once more, Mayer turned to face the old man.

'I thought it might be Berlin,' said Mayer. 'One of my men was from Brandenburg and he had an accent like yours.'

'Pooh! A common lot,' said the old man, expressing his disdain at the comparison.

'Maybe,' said Mayer, but he was a good soldier.'

'So! Now you know where you are, is it far to your home?'

'Far enough. But I'm used to walking, the Eastern Front has seen to that.'

'Yes but what of the dangers?'

'I'll take my chances.'

Getting up from his chair the old man walked across to where Mayer was standing.

'It's won't be easy out there you know. And what will happen if you are stopped? You have no papers. No travel documents. Nothing.'

'I'll travel at night so hopefully, that won't be a problem.' Mayer replied, hoping that would put an end to the conversation.

'And how will you know where you are going? It's hard to find your way in the dark.'

'I don't need a compass to find my way old man,' said Mayer, becoming a little agitated.

'Of course, you could always follow a railway line,' said the old man, as if the idea had just popped into his head.

Mayer looked at him but said nothing.

'A line going south perhaps?'

'So you are a detective now?'

'No. Not a detective but you are not the only one here who can recognise an accent.'

Willy old bugger thought Mayer before replying.

'Perhaps, but better for you both if you don't know. You understand that don't you?' A note of warning in his voice.

'What if I said I could help you?' said the old man brushing aside Mayer's concern. 'What would you say to that?'

'I would say that you have both done enough for me already and every minute I stay it becomes more dangerous for you.'

As though prompted by Mayer's words, getting up from the table the old lady walked across to her husband and taking hold of his hand she looked up at him and smiled.

'We have nothing to fear,' said the old man, squeezing his wife's hand. Herr Hitler and his accursed war have already destroyed our lives' said the old man. 'But you still have your family and when this madness is over Germany will need you. She will need men like you to make her strong again. So please, you must let us help you.'

Moved by the old man's words, for the briefest of moments Mayer was drawn towards the beacon of hope they were offering him. But then reality quickly doused its flames.

'I am grateful for your offer truly I am but ...'

'But you are thinking how can this old man help me eh?'

'Look,' said Mayer growing increasingly impatient. 'I appreciate your kindness but I need to be on my way. I've got a long walk ahead of me.'

'What if I said I could get you a ride instead?'

If he had meant to shock Mayer he certainly succeeded. But the remark also angered him and stepping back Mayer raised his Schmeisser.

'Don't test my patience old man.'

'No please!' The old woman cried out, clearly terrified. 'He can do it. My Otto is a *Lokfuhrer* (engine driver).'

Stunned by the revelation, Mayer instinctively lowered the machine-pistol.

'My God! You're a train driver?'

'A bit of good luck eh Sergeant?' said the old man, a broad smile masking his relief. It was no fun looking down the barrel of Schmeisser especially at his age.

Speechless, Mayer just stood and stared at him. If he was dreaming it was certainly a dream he didn't want to awaken from.

'My! My!' Said the old woman, freeing her hand. 'All this excitement has quite tired me out. I must go up to my bed.'

'Yes you go up mother,' said the old man, kissing her lovingly on the forehead. 'I'll be along shortly.'

'Very well but don't be too long.' And without another word she removed her apron and after hanging it on the back of a chair, she walked out of the kitchen.

'Time for a toast to our new adventure,' said the old man when she was gone and crossing to a cupboard he removed a half-full bottle of Schnapps and two glasses.

Setting the pair of cut glass tumblers on the table, unscrewing the cap he poured a generous measure of the spirit into each of them. Handing one to Mayer he raised his glass into the air.

The Letter

'Prost!'

'Prost!' Mayer replied, putting the glass to his lips and downing its contents in one gulp. Shuddering slightly as the liquid burned its way down his throat.

'Right,' said the old man placing his glass on the table, 'plenty of time to talk tomorrow. Yes?'

'Now we must find you somewhere to sleep. Ah but first I must do something.' And with that, the old man picked up the bottle of Schnapps, and wetting a forefinger he began rubbing it over a small pencil mark on the label. Satisfied that it had been erased, standing the bottle on the table he removed a pencil stub from his pocket. Bending forward, his head at eye level with the bottle, he carefully pencilled a line on the label similar to the one he had just rubbed out. Making sure that it corresponded exactly with the surface of the liquid inside. 'She thinks I hadn't noticed her little trick,' he said, returning the pencil to his pocket. Impressed by the man's ingenuity, Mayer quickly spotted its obvious flaw.

'Yes, but if you keep drinking one day she is bound to notice.'

'Ah but not if I keep topping it up.' The old man replied, a broad smile on his face.

Mayer found himself wanting to laugh out loud but somehow he managed to keep his level of amusement down to a smile. The devious old bugger had thought of everything.

'Tomas my fireman brings me a flask now and then. So it works perfectly. My dear wife is none the wiser and I can enjoy a glass of Schnapps whenever I please. It is how a good marriage should work. Yes?'

Mayer shrugged his shoulders. How could he argue with

the man's logic?

Rinsing both glasses under the tap and drying them with a tea towel, the old man returned them to the cupboard along with the bottle of Schnapps.

'I'll just see to the fire and then I'll take you up to your room.'

'No please, I can sleep here,' said Mayer. 'The chair looks comfortable enough.'

'Nonsense! You must sleep in a bed. I'll bet it's been a while since you had that luxury eh?'

Mayer grinned. In all honesty, he couldn't recall the last time himself. But whenever it was Hannah had been lying beside him. Crossing to the fireplace the old man picked up a poker and began raking out the ashes from between the ribs of the cast iron fire basket. Satisfied, removing a few lumps of coal from a copper bucket standing in the hearth he carefully placed them on top of the glowing embers. It was obviously part of his nightly ritual thought Mayer, watching as the old man finished banking up the fire for the night before placing a fireguard in front of the open grate.

'She likes a warm kitchen in the morning,' he said by way of an explanation. Then turning off the light, followed by Mayer he made his way into the hall.

'This was our Ernst's room,' said the old man, striking a match and lighting the candle perched on a ledge just inside the door. 'Sorry about the candle but light bulbs are hard to come by these days.'

'The kitchen would have been fine. You didn't need to go to this trouble.'

'Nonsense! It's no trouble. Besides, it's good to have the room used again. It's a good bed,' said the old man prodding the mattress with his outstretched fingers.

'A luxury for me,' said Mayer.

'So time for introductions I think,' said the old man holding out his hand. 'My name is Otto Neusch.'

'Mayer. Franz Mayer.'

'I am pleased to make your acquaintance Franz Mayer,' said Otto, exchanging a warm handshake. 'The bathroom is just across the landing. Sleep for as long as you like. I won't be here in the morning but my wife will take good care of you.' And with formalities over, wishing Mayer a good night's sleep he turned away and walked out of the room.

With a quick look around the Spartan room, crossing to the window Mayer stared out into the darkness, amazed at how still and quiet it was. But then he heard it. The unmistakable sound of aircraft, the steady droning of their engines growing louder. Bombers thought Mayer. So he hadn't quite escaped the war then.

'Not our turn tonight thank God.'

Instinctively Mayer turned around to find Otto standing behind him.

'Too far to the north. Pankow perhaps or maybe Reinickendorf. They stay clear of Charlottenburg these days, the *Flakturm* (flak tower) in the Tiergarten sees to that.'

No sooner had he finished speaking when the searchlights positioned on top of the Zoo tower came to life. Their powerful beams of light piercing the night sky, each seeking a potential target for the anti-aircraft guns positioned alongside them.

'Sleep well.' And with that Otto was gone.

Turning away from the window, ignoring the bed Mayer settling into the small armchair and stretching out his legs, with the Schmeisser cradled in his arms like a tired child he quickly fell into a deep sleep.

Waking with a start Mayer immediately looked around the bedroom. The bright sunlight pouring in through the small curtain-less window giving new life to its faded wallpaper. His first thought was that he must be dreaming but then he remembered the events of the previous night. Easing himself out of the armchair, throwing the machine pistol onto the bed followed by his greatcoat, he stretched some life back into his body. It was then that he suddenly realised he needed to pee and quickly crossing the narrow landing, with the tantalising aroma of fresh coffee wafting up from the kitchen he pushed open the bathroom door.

She had thought of everything. There placed side by side on the glass shelf above the washbasin were a shaving bowl, a shaving brush, a cut-throat razor, a tin of Solidox toothpowder, and a bone-handled toothbrush. Hanging from the hook on the back of the door was a shirt, a pair of trousers, and a pair of underpants. Neatly folded on the toilet seat was a towel. Best of all though was the bath-full of hot water, the steam rising off the surface like a lake on a frosty morning. Quickly stripping off his filthy clothing Mayer crossed to the toilet. Removing the towel he lifted the seat and aiming for the small pool of water he began relieving himself. Amazed at just how civilised it felt to be pissing into a porcelain bowl and not a hole in the ground. Suitably relieved, reaching up to flush the toilet Mayer was surprised by someone tapping on the door. Followed almost immediately by the sound of Frau Neusch's voice.

'Put your clothes out on the landing.'

'Thank you,' Mayer called back.

Waiting until he was sure she had returned downstairs, opening the door Mayer deposited his soiled clothing in a pile on the floor. It shamed him to do it but given that her husband was a train driver he didn't imagine Frau Neusch would be too horrified by their condition. Crossing to the bath, Mayer slowly lowered his body into the water. Feeling its warmth permeating his skin and seeping into his bones. After allowing himself a few moments of indulgence, retrieving the scrubbing brush and block of carbolic soap which Frau Neusch had left, he began scrubbing his body. The brushes stiff bristles peeling away the accumulated layers of grime with ease. Scouring his skin until it was almost raw.

Looking up as Mayer entered the kitchen, putting her hand to her mouth Frau Neusch choked back the cry which was about to leave her lips. Her eyes filling with tears.

'I'm sorry,' she said, struggling to compose herself. 'It was just seeing you in Ernst's clothes that was all.'

Unsure of what to do or say Mayer just stood there. Initially, he had thought that the clothes might be too small for him. But actually, they were quite a good fit. The trousers were a little on the short side and he had had trouble buttoning up the shirt. But apart from that, he looked quite presentable. Though hidden from sight, best of all was the luxury of clean underpants. He hadn't bothered putting his boots back on and the simple pleasure of walking around barefooted was wonderful.

'Are you hungry?' It was a silly question but just asking it was enough to stem the tide of sadness that threatened to overwhelm her. 'It's just bread and jam I'm afraid. But there is plenty of coffee.'

'I feel guilty eating your food.'

'Nonsense. Besides the jam is homemade. I hope you like

blackberries?'

Mayer smiled 'My favourite.'

'There is a bush growing up against our wall. Otto threatened to dig it up but I wouldn't let him,' she said with a pleased smile. And now of course he is delighted that he didn't.'

As Frau Neusch set about applying a thick coating of jam to a slice of bread, Mayer quickly glanced around the room. Hanging on the back of the kitchen door, his mud-caked greatcoat had been brushed until it looked almost as good as new. The row of tarnished buttons, restored to their former glory by Frau Neusch's metal polish and a good rub with a duster. The remainder of his clothes all freshly washed, were drying on a wooden clothes-horse in front of the fire.

'There now sit and enjoy your breakfast while I go and do some tidying,' said Frau Neusch putting a plate of jam and bread and a steaming cup of coffee on the table in front of him before disappearing into the hall. Looking to make sure that the door was bolted, pulling out a chair Mayer seated himself at the table and began tucking into the meal. The jam was delicious. The coffee tasted even better. Luxuries he could only have dreamed about a few days ago.

When Frau Neusch returned with Mayer's wet towel draped over her arm, he was standing at the sink washing up the cup and plate.

'Ah, I can see you were a good husband and didn't always leave washing the pots to your wife.'

'She was always very strict with me,' said Mayer, smiling to conceal the lie. In truth, he couldn't remember ever doing the washing up. Not that he was ever going to admit to it.

'The jam was delicious Frau Neusch.'

It was the first time that he had used her name and hearing it brought a smile to her face.

'Can I ask one more favour of you? Does your husband have some oil? Or perhaps some grease I can use?'

'Yes, I'm sure he has some somewhere. But first, you must go back upstairs. Herr Schweiger the station superintendent sometimes comes to the house' Adding quite innocently. 'Even when Otto is not here.'

Amused by her unfortunate choice of words; hinting at a clandestine relationship between herself and the superintendent, Mayer found himself smirking. Instantly, Frau Neusch's cheeks flushed with colour.

'Such thoughts indeed' she said indignantly, waving a finger at him. Whilst inwardly a little flattered by the implication. 'What I meant was that he would find it strange if the door were bolted.' Adding for good measure, 'And he has a very suspicious nature.'

She was right of course thought Mayer, becoming complacent was not only foolish but it was also dangerous. And not just for him he reminded himself. Suitably reprimanded, putting down his cup Mayer crossed to the kitchen door and lifting his greatcoat off the hook he left the room.

'It's Otto's toolbox,' said Frau Neusch, a little out of breath after carrying the heavy wooden box upstairs. 'If he has any oil it will be in there,' she added, slipping the wide leather carrying strap off her shoulder and placing the toolbox on the small table.

'I'm very grateful,' said Mayer.

'There is probably a tin of black polish too.' She said, looking across at the pair of boots on the floor beside the armchair.

'Yes they do look pretty bad don't they?' said Mayer, casting a guilty look at his care-worn footwear.

'Well, I will leave you to your cleaning then.' And with that, she was gone.

After rummaging around in the toolbox, Mayer found what he was looking for. A small 'Aladdin's lamp' oil can. Thankfully with some oil in it. Folding his greatcoat inside out, draping it across the table Mayer picked up the MP 40, and with practised ease, he began dismantling it. The barrel first, then the bolt and firing mechanism placing them onto the lining of his coat. Squirted a few drops of oil onto the piece of rag which the can had been wrapped in, he began wiping it over the exposed metal. Rubbing it over each part as though he were caressing a woman's skin. Satisfied, after re-assembling the weapon he propped it up against the chair and turned his attention to the boots. Aware that the polish was probably as difficult to come by as the coffee, collecting a small amount onto a corner of the oil rag he began working it into the dry, cracked leather. Aiding the lubrication process now and then by adding copious amounts of saliva.

With his boots now restored to something like their old selves, Mayer was beginning to feel like a new man. His body was scrubbed from head to toe, his face freshly shaved and his mouth no longer tasted like a dung-box. On top of which he was now wearing clean underwear and a freshly washed and iron uniform. But as he stood gazing out through the second-floor bedroom at the back of the house, he knew that while his appearance may have changed his circumstances hadn't. He was still a deserter. Still a man on the run. Yet despite this somehow against all the odds, he had found help and this had given him hope. A belief that things would work out. Forget your faith and charity, if he was ever going to carry a banner it would have the word hope emblazoned on it.

Not like some thought Mayer, reflecting on the brand of religious dogma employed by the padre's attached to the 6th Army. Standing, bible in hand before their open-air congregation of bare-headed soldiers on the eve of battle, eulogising about death and sacrifice. No mention of God being their Lord and Protector. Nothing inspirational like "The sword of the Lord is in the hand of the righteous". No words of hope. Just the same old depressing clap-trap. Not that their sermons ever had any real effect. There were a few perhaps who listened and believed but in reality, each soldier would eventually say a prayer of his own. Commune with God in his own words. Although not a religious man Mayer had always offered up a prayer. Simply on the basis that if God was listening it never hurt to have him on your side.

Pushing such thoughts from his mind Mayer surveyed the landscape in front of him. The station and the marshalling yard had certainly taken a pounding. Nothing on the apocalyptic scale of Stalingrad; nothing could eclipse that, but terrible enough nevertheless. Despite all the damage caused by the round-the-clock bombing raids, it was still a functioning station. Even as he watched a pair of shunting engines were busy at work ferrying empty freight wagons into the rows of sidings or undamaged engine sheds. And at one of the platforms, a newly arrived locomotive waited patiently while scores of soldiers, many of them wounded were evacuated from its carriages. Everywhere, watched over by armed soldiers large gangs of men, prisoners of war judging by their thin emaciated bodies and ragged clothing worked feverishly filling in the huge bomb craters and replacing lengths of buckled track. Turning away Mayer made his way back to the small bedroom, pausing for a moment on the landing as the voice of Frau Neusch and another woman emanated from the kitchen below. Picturing the two women chatting over a cup of coffee perhaps, he walked into the bedroom. Closing the door behind him, with a self-satisfied look at the freshly oiled MP 40 and the pair of polished boots he stretched out on the narrow bed and closed his eyes.

It wasn't a noise that woke him but the smell of cooking. Unable to resist the enticing aroma wafting up from the kitchen, pulling on his boots Mayer made his way downstairs.

Standing with his back to the fire, a pipe clamped between his teeth Otto Neusch glanced across when the door opened. Smiling when Mayer walked into the kitchen.

'My! My! Who have we here then?' he said, removing the pipe from his mouth. 'Quite a handsome fellow under all those whiskers eh mother?'

Mayer grinned sheepishly.

'Your wife left me your razor. I hope you didn't mind?'

'Not at all,' said Otto waving a hand dismissively. 'You're welcome to use it. It's good and sharp eh? Dovo only used the finest Solingen steel for their blades.'

'Well if nobody is hungry?'

Before she could say another word, all thoughts of razors quickly forgotten both men hurried across to the table.

'It smells delicious,' said Mayer, pulling back a chair.

'Rabbit stew,' said Frau Neusch proudly, setting down the large earthenware pot on the table. 'Frau Bachmann kindly gave me one that her husband had caught. He has a small allotment behind the engine sheds and the rabbits can't resist his greens. I sometimes think,' she went on, wrapping her hand in a corner of her apron and removing the lid.'

That's the only reason he grows them because I have never had any vegetables from him.'

'Yes, they are good people. Good neighbours,' said Otto, choosing to ignore his wife's observation concerning Herr Bachmann and his vegetables. Much more interested in the contents of the pot; diced pieces of lean meat and thick slices of potato floating in a rich brown gravy, its diaphanous surface dotted with toasted croutons.

'A meal fit for a King,' said Otto, picking up a large spoon and ladling the stew into three empty bowls.

'And a Queen,' said Mayer, looking across at Frau Neusch and smiling.

For the next few minutes, nobody spoke, each absorbed in their meal. The first to finish, Mayer refused the offer of a second helping. Not out of politeness but simply because he didn't think his stomach could accommodate any more. Besides which, not being accustomed to such rich food he was well aware of the consequences of overindulging and it was not a pleasant thought. So with the meal concluded and enough leftover for lunch tomorrow, albeit a less indulgent one Frau Neusch returned the pot to the stove. After clearing away the bowls and with his wife happy to see to the washing up, Otto turned to Mayer.

'Come I have something to show you.'

Thanking Frau Neusch for the wonderful meal, Mayer climbed to his feet, and together the two men left the room.

On entering Ernst's bedroom Otto pulled the small table away from the wall. Instructing Mayer to position himself at the opposite end, on his command they lifted the table, and turning it upside down they lowered it onto the floor. Running diagonally across the underside of the table was a wooden baton a few inches wide, secured to the frame by a screw at each end. Retrieving a screwdriver from his toolbox, without a word Otto set about removing both screws. Once this was done, using the blade of the screwdriver as a lever he then prised away the wooden panel which had been held in place by the baton. It wasn't the fact that the table contained a hidden compartment that surprised Mayer, just what was inside it. A neatly folded blanket! There had to be more to it than that surely? Aware of what Mayer must be thinking, without wishing to prolong the suspense, taking hold of a corner of the blanket Otto pulled it back and revealed the true contents. Radios! Exactly how many it was difficult to say, because from what Mayer could tell they all appeared to be in pieces.

'Quite a treasure trove eh?' said Otto. 'This was our Ernst's little hobby.'

Too flabbergasted to speak, Mayer just stood staring down at the jumbled collection of radio parts. Everything from Bakelite panels, tuning dials, batteries, tubes of different shapes and sizes, lengths of insulation wire, rectifiers. A veritable radio jigsaw puzzle.

'Quite a collection,' said Mayer overcoming his initial surprise. 'Do any of them work?'

'Ah!' said Otto, stroking his chin with his finger and thumb. 'A very good question. 'I am sure some of them do, or rather they did. The one which Ernst built certainly worked.'

'So why have they all been dismantled and hidden away?'

'At first, it was to keep them safe until Ernst returned,' said Otto, seating himself on the bed. 'Now I suppose it's just out of sentiment. I should get rid of them. After all what use are they to an old train driver eh?'

'So they are all radios that your son had built?' said Mayer nodding towards the up-turned table.

'Yes. Ernst loved radios. Even from an early age. I remember we had a *Volksempfanger* (People's receiver) but I could never get on with it. Ernst said I wasn't tuning it properly. Said I was too heavy-handed. Which was probably true. Anyway soon after he began collecting old parts from radio's people had thrown away or didn't use any more. And as you can see my Ernst built up quite a collection.' Waving a hand towards the table. 'He would spend hours up here tinkering as I called it. Then one day he comes into the kitchen with a big smile on his face, carrying what I thought was another *Volksempfanger*. "Ah! But this one is different Papa." 'He said.' "Come let me show you." 'So his mother and I followed him up to his room and watched as he plugged in the radio.' Pointing to the empty light fitting with its twin connector, hanging down from the ceiling 'Then taking the end of a wire coming in through the window he pushes it into the back somewhere twiddles the dial and the next thing we know the room is filled with the sound of music.'

Mayer frowned.

'Ah!' said Otto, grinning, 'I know what you are thinking? So what is so special about that?

Any *Volksempfanger* can receive music it is not forbidden. Herr Goebbels even encouraged it. Wagner and Bach; good German music. But not jazz music.' The grin widening into a smile. 'Not jazz music from America.'

Intrigued, Mayer lowered himself into the armchair.

'So suddenly there we were sitting in this very room listening to Dizzy Gillespie playing Sunlight Serenade on his trumpet. It was amazing.'

'I take it that the radio Ernst had built was not just an

ordinary *Volkssempfanger* then?'

'No, you are right. Ernst had made what he called a "modification" Ha! I don't remember all the technical jargon just that as well as receiving long and medium wave Ernst's radio could also receive short wave signals.'

'Which is forbidden of course.'

'Yes of course. But that was half the fun.'

Mayer smiled. Amused by the thought of the Neusch family sitting up in this small bedroom together listening to illicit radio programmes.'

'Each evening we would listen to programmes from all around the world. It was wonderful. We even listened in to the BBC European Service. Ernst had learned a little English at school so he would translate for us. The news was not always good to hear but at least we knew the truth. We knew how things really were.'

'So why did you stop?'

'A stroke of bad luck really,' said Otto, recalling the reason. 'My wife bumped into a neighbour one day and she told her that somebody had spotted a *Funkabwer* (Listening service) van on Am Stellwerk. She was so frightened that we would be discovered and that Ernst would be sent away to one of the camps we were hearing about, that she begged us to stop.'

'Yes but surely ...'

'I know what you are going to say,' said Otto interrupting. 'But even when Ernst explained that they were only after people who were transmitting she wouldn't listen. She said what we were doing was wrong and that we must stop. And so we did. A month later Ernst received his call-up papers and that's when we decided to hide his radios away. To keep them safe until he returned home.'

Mayer looked across at the old man, his head down, shoulders slumped. Those last few words had taken their toll.

'Well for what it's worth,' said Mayer, attempting to lighten the mood 'If it were up to me I would keep them.'

'You would?' said Otto, a little taken aback by Mayer's admission.

'Yes, I would.'

'So you don't think I should get rid of them then?'

'Certainly not! We men are far too quick at throwing things out. And you have my wife's word on that,' said Mayer with a broad smile. 'Besides one day you might find a use for them.'

'Very well then Sergeant I will follow your orders.'

With the blanket replaced and the panel and baton secured, standing the table back onto its legs Mayer and Otto pushed it back against the wall.

'Time for a glass of Schnapps I think,' said Otto.

Mayer nodded. Why not, it had been a good day for all concerned.

The bombers returned that night. The droning of their engines filling the night sky. Away to the north again, there must be something, some factory perhaps which they are keen on destroying thought Mayer peering out the window. A bright moonlit night. What the crews of the Lancaster and the B-17 Flying Fortresses called "a bomber's moon". I suppose you could also call it a flak gunner's moon too as it gave them enough light to see their target without the aid of their side-kick, the searchlight. Then right on cue, the four powerful 12.8 cm guns on top of the Zoo Flak tower opened up. The "crump, crump, crump" as they fired their shells into the sky as regular as a heartbeat. Earlier that day Mayer had decided that he would be leaving tomorrow night. It was becoming too dangerous for him to stay. He had almost been discovered that very afternoon when quite unexpectedly Frau Bachmann had suddenly appeared at the back door. Thankfully, by diving under the kitchen table and hiding there like a child who's afraid of the *Butzemann* (Bogeyman), he wasn't seen. Both he and Frau Neusch had laughed about it after she had left. Mainly from relief but also because as it turned out the reason for her visit was to bring Frau Neusch some leeks from her husband's vegetable plot.

Following the railway line south seemed his best option. And if he walked at night, hiding out during the day it was probably the safest thing too. Hopefully, Herr Neusch would put him on the right track. So with a plan of sorts in his head, Mayer stretched out on the single bed and with the rhythmic thumping of the flak guns acting as a lullaby, praying that the moon didn't return for an encore the following night, he drifted off to sleep.

She hadn't expected him home this early so Frau Neusch was taken a little by surprise when her husband suddenly walked in through the kitchen door.

'Is everything alright Otto?'

'Couldn't be better mother. Couldn't be better,' he replied cheerfully, putting his *Deutsche Reichsbahn* billycan with its embossed blue circular emblem, onto the table.

'But why are you home so early?'

'All in good time,' said Otto, slipping off the satchel which was weighing down his shoulder. 'So where is our guest?'

The Letter

Before Frau Neusch had time to answer, right on cue Mayer walked in from the hall.

'Don't look so worried the pair of you,' said Otto, walking across to the fireplace and emptying the contents of the satchel, a dozen large lumps of coal into the brass coal bucket.

'Don't worry he will eventually get around to telling us,' said Frau Neusch, puffing out her cheeks and crossing her arms across her ample bosom. 'He just likes infuriating people.'

'Now! Now! Mother don't nag me, said Otto, who had picked up the poker and was prodding some life into the fire. 'I have some news. Some good news.'

Frau Neusch stared at him but said nothing.

Admitting defeat, putting down the poker Herr Neusch turned to face his expectant audience.

'Well it seems Herr Bachmann's rabbit had a lucky foot,' said Otto, smiling at the puzzled look on both their faces. 'Because I have just been given a run to *Munchen* (Munich) tonight.'

'My God! Exclaimed Mayer.' Suddenly realising what this meant. 'And can you get me on it?'

'I think it can be arranged,' said Otto with a half-smile. 'But you will have to ride in one of the wagons.'

'I'll ride on the roof if I have to.'

'In this weather? Ha! You would freeze to death in minutes,' scoffed Otto.

'Maybe not then,' said Mayer not relishing the prospect of dying from exposure.

'But Herr Schweiger promised not to send you on another of those runs,' said Frau Neusch, a note of anguish in her voice.

'It's an emergency mother. Old Habicht is unwell and there is nobody else.'

'But he promised,' said Frau Neusch, tears welling up in her eyes. 'After what happened last time, he promised.'

Yes! Yes I know,' said Otto walking over and putting a comforting arm around her. 'But there is no one else. I have to do it.'

Frau Neusch looked at him, concern turning to despair.

'What if something should happen to you? What would I do?' And then the dam burst and the tears began trickling down her cheeks.

'Now! Now! You mustn't take on so. Nothing is going to happen to me. This is God's work.

He has sent Franz to us and now he has found a way for me to take him home.'

Finding some reassurance in what he had said, pulling a small lace handkerchief from her apron pocket Frau Neusch began dabbing at her eyes. He was right of course, her Otto was always right about these things. She wasn't going to tell him that of course. Better to keep such things to oneself. The last thing she wanted was a conceited husband.

'You will need a clean shirt.' and with that, she turned away and walked out of the kitchen.

As the door closed behind her Mayer turned to face Otto.

'What is she talking about?'

'Oh it's nothing,' said Otto dismissively.

But Mayer wasn't finished.

'It didn't look like that to me. I mean to make your wife cry like that. And what did she mean about the last time?'

Without answering, Otto walked across to the cupboard where he kept the bottle of Schnapps. Removing it, together with two glasses he crossed to the table.

'Come sit down,' and unscrewing the bottle he filled both glasses to the brim.

'It happened last year,' said Otto, swigging down a mouthful of Schnapps. 'If we had left on time everything would have been fine. But we were late and that was that. It was a run to *Nurnberg* (Nuremberg), six maybe seven hours at the most. We were doing well, still, plenty of darkness left but then we got pulled into a siding. No reason was given. Anyway by the time we were allowed back on the mainline it was dawn. And that's when he found us. Pausing, Otto took another swig from his glass. 'Tomas, my fireman thinks it was a Hurricane. I'm not sure, I was too busy doing other things. Like shitting my pants'

'So you were strafed?'

'Ah yes, that's the word I was looking for. Strafed! Such a little word to describe something so frightening. Luckily for us, his shooting was not so good and he just hit some of the wagons. By the time he came around again, I had slowed the engine down, so Tomas and I jumped off and ran for our lives. Good job for us that we did because he did better the second time and my dear old DB-38 was blown sky-high.'

'And this is why she worries? She thinks perhaps it could happen again.'

'Yes, but isn't that what wives do? Worry. It must be the same for your wife? My God, it must be even worse for her.'

Mayer didn't answer him. It was not a door in his mind

which he opened very often.

'But,' said Otto, downing the last mouthful of schnapps from his glass, 'as it is not likely that lightning will strike twice, it must be looked upon it as a golden opportunity.' With that said, opening a table drawer he removed a used envelope and a pencil. Turning the envelope address side down onto the table, he began drawing a diagram. 'We are here,' said Otto, drawing a circle, 'and this is *Nurnberg*.' Drawing another circle about two inches away and connecting the two with a straight line.' As we are a freight train they will send us around the main station until we rejoin the mainline again about here.' Making a cross, Otto continuing the pencil line down from the second circle. 'After about an hour we will reach the junction to *Regensburg*,' said Otto drawing a second line. 'The good news for you is that just before we reach it there is a steep incline.' His face breaking into a broad smile.

'Why good news for me? Said Mayer, knowing he was going to regret asking the question.

'Because my friend that is when you will be jumping off the train. And better to be doing it when we are travelling at ten miles an hour than thirty. Yes?'

Mayer grinned back at him. Whether it was to hide the fact that he had been more concerned about where he was getting off the train than how he would be getting off it. Or simply to disguise the fact that he was terrified by the thought of actually jumping from a moving train. It was hard to tell.

'Well you didn't image I would be stopping did you?' said Otto, stifling the urge to burst out laughing. 'For that kind of service, you needed to be on a passenger train.' And at that, he did begin laughing. The sound loud enough for it to be heard in the couple's bedroom, where Frau Neusch

The Letter

was so startled by it that she almost banging her head against the wardrobe door. Stony-faced, Mayer waited patiently while Herr Neusch fought to bring his laughter under control. Which he was finding hard to do because of the even funnier quips waiting in the wings. Such as; "Perhaps if he had signed on as a *Fallschirmjager* (Paratrooper) then maybe he wouldn't be feeling so bad about it." Or "Just land on your head and you will be okay." Eventually, with his composure restored Otto returned to his map.

'Follow the line to *Regensburg* for maybe eight or ten miles until you reach the branch line to *Amberg*,' said Otto, drawing another line. 'There you must decide which one you choose to follow to reach *Hohenburg*. You know the area so I will leave it up to you. Yes?'

Swigging back the last of his schnapps Mayer nodded. It seemed like a workable plan.

'Good!' Said Otto, screwing the cap back on the bottle. 'Now I must go and get some sleep. We leave after supper, okay?'

'What about the bottle?'

'Ah, we will leave it this time. My wife is not silly, she will know we have had a drink together.' Otto replied, pushing back his chair. 'Get some rest now, we don't want you falling asleep on the train and ending up in *Munchen*.' (Munich)

Getting up from the table, without thinking Mayer picked up the envelope and pushed it into his jacket pocket.

It was an emotional farewell. But one without tears. For Frau Neusch, these would come later when both men had gone. Three people thrown together by chance or fate depending on which one you believed in, standing in a small kitchen in Potsdam. Mayer had spoken his words of gratitude. The pleasure in hearing them evident on the faces of his saviours. But for them, the real joy came from what they were doing. They were saving a life. They were robbing the war of another victim. Their beloved Ernst was lost to them but at least they had saved someone. They had saved the life of Franz Mayer.

Knowing that the most dangerous part of the journey was getting Mayer onto the train, Otto decided on a bold approach. They would simply make their way to the engine sheds together. A German soldier about to go on duty and an engineer joining his train. Walking along together, passing the time of day. What could be more natural than that? Closing the back gate behind them, after crossing the main tracks leading into the station the pair made their way along a cinder path towards the marshalling yard. After a hundred yards or so, positioned against the end wall of a building, Mayer spotted the distinctive outline of a sentry-box.

'Shit!' This was the last thing he wanted.

Thankfully, as Mayer was soon to discover, there was nothing to worry about. The sentry on duty, who on first appearances looked old enough to be someone's grandfather had no intention of leaving the relative warmth of his box to challenge anybody. Settling instead for a simple nod of the head as the pair walked past. Clear of their only obstacle with Otto leading, skirting around the huge cleaning pits and bunkers piled with heaps of coal they eventually reached the corner of the main engine shed.

'Wait here Franz while I go and see which wagons are ours.'

And with that Otto slipped away into the gathering darkness. Taking a deep breath Mayer leaned up against the wall of the building. So far so good. And then the sirens began wailing. It seemed that Potsdam was not going to be so lucky tonight.

At first, there was nothing. A false alarm thought Mayer. It was always possible. But then the ominous droning of the Lancaster's Rolls-Royce Merlin engines filled the night sky. No, it wasn't a false alarm. This time Charlottenburg and Reinickendorf were safe. Tonight it was Potsdam's turn to endure the nightmare which was about to be unleashed on them.

'Come! Said Otto, suddenly appearing out of nowhere. 'This way, quickly now.'

With just enough light to see where they were putting their feet, they began running along the single length of track. Eventually, panting for breath they found themselves confronted by a line of coupled goods wagons. Approaching the one nearest to them, Otto reached up and grabbing the lever he unhooked one of the doors.

'Right in you get,' he said, sliding it open.

Without a word Mayer climbed up into the wagon, squeezing himself into the narrow space between the two large wooden crates which filled the wagon.

'I won't lock it, then you can just slide it open from inside. Okay?'

Mayer nodded.

'And remember. Keep awake!' And with that Otto began closing the heavy door. No sooner was it shut when Mayer was suddenly thrown against the side of the crate. Mercifully the violent jolt was not the result of a near-miss by a bomb but the arrival of the shunting engine. Collecting what its driver hoped would be his last job for the night. Having heard the sirens he had taken the precaution of closing up his firebox door, no point in making a bomb aimer's life any easier. But it was just a precaution. With carpet bombing, your life was in God's hands. So better to get the hell out of the way just in case you were in his bad books. On the other side of the tracks, it seemed the elderly sentry had the same idea, and abandoning his sentry-box he began running towards the station's air-raid shelter. Given the choice between warmth and safety, warmth came a poor second.

Enclosed within the soot-blackened walls of the cavernous engine shed were six lengths of track, separated down the centre by a large workshop area crammed with benches and lathes. Above it, a girder supported a one-man crane with a jib giving it access to both sets of tracks. Suspended from the wide arching roof, covered by ceramic domed shades were two rows of lights. The milky glow from their pear-shaped bulbs illuminating everything below them. Even at this hour, the place was a hive of activity with dozens of men in dirty overalls swarming over the three locomotives brought in to be serviced or repaired. Pierced by flashes of iridescent light from acetylene torches, the acrid air was filled with the crackling of welding rods and the clanging of wheel-tappers hammers. On the far track a fourth engine, steam venting from its valve gear and wisps of white smoke rising from its chimney waited patiently to begin its night's work.

Hauling himself up into the engine's cab, taking a moment to catch his breath before hanging his billycan on one of the levers Otto plonked his backside into the small metal driver's seat.

'Ah! What better place to be on a cold night eh Tomas?'

'Better yet if I had a Stein of cold beer.' Tomas replied, shutting the firebox door with the end of his shovel. A reed of a man with rounded shoulders and a slightly lop-sided face, he had been Otto's fireman for the past fifteen years and his friend since they were at school together.

Otto nodded, running his eyes over the array of gauges. Tapping one or two with the end of a finger as if questioning the position of their needle.

'Did you hear the sirens?'

'Yes. But where are the bombs?' said Tomas, watching as Otto went through his usual routine.

'Perhaps they just came to frighten us,' said Otto, shrugging his shoulders.

'Or maybe like us they have a Herr Schweiger in charge and he forgot to give them any bombs?' Said Tomas, wiping the perspiration from his forehead with a grubby rag.

Otto laughed. Tomas always had an answer for everything. Not always a good one. But usually a humorous one.

'You are late Neusch!'

Speak of the devil thought Otto peering down at the man standing beside the track below him. A middle-aged man with a portly figure, wearing a long black topcoat with twin rows of gold buttons. Its collar and epaulettes embellished with the insignia of the *Deutsche Reichsbahn* (German railway). The peak of the cap he was wearing was so highly polished Otto swore you could have used it as a shaving mirror. Tucked tightly under his right arm was a clipboard.

'Apologies Herr Schweiger I was just checking our rolling-stock.'

'That!' said the supervisor, with more than a hint of annoyance in his voice, 'is none of your concern.'

'She's an old engine,' said Otto, patting the side of the cab with his hand. 'I wanted to be sure she could manage the load.'

'Old or not, the ability of a German locomotive to carry

out what is required of it should never be in doubt.' Schweiger replied defiantly. 'Surely an engineer like you should know that?'

'I am reassured by your optimism Herr *Stationsleiter* '(Station manager) said Otto, quietly amused by the fact that the locomotive in question had been built in Poland.

'Good!' Said Herr Schweiger. 'Now are you ready to leave?'

'Definitely!'

'Then I wish you a safe journey.' And with that he turned away, cursing the man's insolence under his breath as he strode across towards the workshop area. One day he would go too far and then the joke would be on him.

Flight Lieutenant Jimmy Lambert was not a happy man and he wanted the world to know it. The trouble was the only person within earshot was his navigator. A Polish Sergeant called Wojciechowski whose English vocabulary was so limited that the idea of ranting on about it to him seemed pretty pointless. Any form of meaningful conversation was difficult, but they got by somehow. The raid had been an unmitigated disaster. God knows why it was aborted but it was. I mean it wasn't as if they couldn't find the thing. With all its searchlights combing the night sky the tower was lit up like a bloody Christmas tree for Christ's sake. But instead of turning left over Potsdam and flying towards the Tiergarten flak tower, flight after flight of Lancaster's ended up dropping their bomb loads into the Harvel. Tons of bombs dropped into a sodding lake. Unbelievable! If that wasn't bad enough, to make matters worse not a single Foche-Wulf 190 showed up either so he couldn't even make a kill. Now here he was returning to his *ALG* (advance landing ground) in Melsbroek after a nine hundred-mile round trip with nothing to show for it but a numb backside.

But then through a break in the cloud cover, he spotted

something out of the corner of his eye. And even though it was still the middle of the night, things suddenly began looking a whole lot brighter for Jimmy. But before getting too excited, just to make absolutely certain, dipping the left-wing of his de Havilland Mosquito he took another look. Right, first time Jimmy my boy he said to himself. It was a bloody train.

Tomas didn't have time to identify this particular aircraft because the first he knew of its existence was when he saw the bright orange gun-flashes. Followed instantly by the impact of the Mosquito's 20 mm cannon shells tearing through the roof of two of the wagons.

'God in heaven!' Cried Tomas, rushing across to the other side of the cab and peering up into the night sky. But there was nothing to be seen. Just the sound of the aircraft's engines as it disappeared into the darkness.

'The bastard will be back,' screamed Tomas.

But Otto wasn't listening. His mind was on other things. Like saving their skins. He had travelled this stretch of track enough times to know that not far ahead there was a tunnel. And all that mattered now was reaching it in before the bloody plane came back.

'Shit!' Said Jimmy pulling on the control lever and bringing the Mosquito around in a wide arc, annoyed with himself for over-shooting the target. 'I'll get you next time.'

Sitting beside him, Sergeant Wojciechowski's broad, expressionless face broke into a smile. Well, at least his Polish friend looked like he was enjoying himself thought Jimmy. He hoped so anyway because this was the only excitement he would be getting.

Surprisingly, even though the splinter of wood had buried itself deep into his upper arm there wasn't very much blood. There was more when he pulled it out though. Gritting his teeth as the pain surged down the length of his arm. Watching as the rivulets of blood trickled out from the sleeve of his greatcoat and dripped onto the floor of the wagon. Bending his elbow across his chest, resting his back against the crate Mayer stared up at what was left of the roof. Just a couple of feet lower and his body would have been as mangled as the top of the crate which had kindly donated the shard of wood. It was then that he suddenly realised the train was travelling faster. Much faster in fact. Why he wasn't quite sure. He had yet to hear of a train outrunning an aircraft. Especially a night-fighter which was what he assumed had just attacked them. But good for you Otto for at least giving it a try.

After gaining height Jimmy brought the aircraft around in a wide loop, banking sharply when he was directly above the railway line. With the manoeuvre completed, gripping the throttle lever Jimmy pushed it forward, feeling the sudden surge of power as the Mosquito's twin Merlin engines responded. Ahead of him, away in the distance he could just see the faint orange glow of the train's firebox shining like a beacon in the night. A beacon certainly but not one of hope. More like a marker. A nice target for Jimmy to aim at.

Like a man possessed, Tomas, shovelled more coal into the furnace. While perched on his seat, the regulator lever tightly gripped in his huge fist Otto silently urged the locomotive to give him all the speed it had. Man and machine in a race for survival.

With the twin ribbons of steel directly below him unrolling like a reel of film, easing the Mosquito's nose down slightly Jimmy gradually reduced altitude. No cock-ups this time Jimmy lad he told himself, his forefinger hovering over the firing button of the four Hispano cannons. Moments later, despite the line of wagons being obscured by the clouds of white smoke pouring from the locomotive chimney, at a range of two thousand yards Jimmy opened fire.

Torn from their bed of sleepers by the impact of the cannon shells, the buckled and twisted lengths of track littered the ground like decapitated snakes. The trail of destruction creeping forward inexpiably towards the rear of the train. But no sooner were the 20 mm rounds ripping into the end wagon, shredding its timbers into matchwood when to Jimmy's horror up ahead the locomotive suddenly disappeared. A tunnel. The bloody train was entering a tunnel. Horrified, instinctively Jimmy pulled back on the control column and praying he hadn't left it too late he pushing open the throttle. A wave of relief washing over him as the sudden surge of power from the engines propelled the aircraft skywards. That said Jimmy, as the Mosquito climbed away into the lightening sky was a close call. Then glancing at his compass, satisfied that the needle was pointing west he called out to Wojciechowski;

'Time to go home.'

'Dom!' Said the Polish navigator. Not so much agreeing with Jimmy, because he hadn't understood a word he was saying. But just telling the crazy English pilot where he would like to go. *Dom!* (Home).

Although a thousand times louder, the screeching of the locomotive's brakes reminded Mayer of a girl in his class at school who used to take great delight in running her nails down the teacher's blackboard. And then there was silence as the great beast came to a halt. Mayer knew they were in a tunnel. Even in the partial darkness, he could make out its arch of smoke-blackened brickwork through the gaping holes in the roof of the wagon. Another miracle. How many more he wondered before the man with the scythe tapped him on the shoulder? Still, he had survived and for now, that was all that mattered. Then the door began sliding open and there grinning from ear to ear like the proverbial Cheshire cat was the man he owed his life to for a second time.

'Thank God for tunnels eh?'

'Definitely! Especially this one,' said Mayer, climbing down from the wagon. 'Given all that bullshit of yours about lightning never striking twice in the same place.'

And with that said, wrapping their arms around each other the two men embraced.

'I didn't think we would make it but we did,' said Otto the grin still fixed to his soot-stained face. And then he noticed the blood on Mayer's hand. 'You are hurt?'

'Ah, it's just a scratch,' said Mayer dismissively. 'I've survived worse.'

Otto frowned but said nothing.

'So Herr *Zugmeister?* (Trainmaster) what do we do now?'

'Well, Tomas and I must wait until our friend our there runs low on fuel or becomes tired of waiting. But better for you if you leave now. It will be light soon and we are not far from the Regensburg junction, four maybe five miles. Not far for a soldier. Certainly not far for somebody who was prepared to walk four hundred miles. Yes?'

Cheeky bugger thought Mayer but he was right, for him five miles was nothing. So with Otto lighting the way with his torch the two men walked along beside the row of wagons towards the front of the train. Reaching the huge locomotive Mayer paused for a moment and glancing upwards he spotted the old fireman looking down at him from the cab. As it was unlikely that Otto hadn't told him of his plan, what must he be thinking Mayer wondered?

Did it have his blessing or was what he was doing seen as an act of cowardice? Quite unexpectedly, the answer came in the form of a gift, as reaching out an arm Tomas dropped the small metal flask he was holding. Watching as it landed safely in the soldier's outstretched hands. Nodded his thanks, pushing the flask into a pocket Mayer continued on to the front of the train. Up ahead, bathed in the beams of light from the locomotives two headlamps was the other end of the tunnel.

'So Franz time for us to say *Auf Wiedersehen*' (Goodbye).

'I like Au Revoir better,' said Mayer holding out his right hand. 'Because I hope one day we will meet again.'

'We will! I am sure of it.' Otto replied, gripping Mayer's hand with his own. 'And next time you will bring your family to see us. Yes?'

'Take care,' said Mayer, squeezing Otto's hand. 'The Russians will be in Berlin soon. Brave as our soldiers are they can never stop them. There are just too many. More than we have bullets to kill them with.' Adding with a cynical smile. 'Only God can stop them and I am not sure he is on our side anymore. So don't try to fight them, Otto. Just survive okay?' Then, after what for Mayer amounted to a small speech, fighting back the overwhelming feeling of sadness which threatened to engulf him Mayer turned and walked away.

Mayer reached the Regensburg junction in less than an hour. Four hours later with the first pale fingers of light permeating the snow-covered branches of the trees lining the track he was standing beside the branch line to Amberg. He had already decided that he would follow the line to Regensburg. For one thing, it was closer to Hohenburg. Secondly, he knew of a place where he could remain hidden until nightfall.

Abandoned over twenty years ago, at first glance the old station building was just as Mayer remembered it. The roof was missing a few tiles and the paintwork around the windows and on the gable end was beginning to peel away. But apart from that, the building had weathered the years of neglect surprisingly well. He recalled hearing his father say that it would make a fine house. With the Proviso that you didn't mind trains thundering past day and night of course. Although never very busy with just four trains a day; one going to Nuremberg the other to Regensburg, both stopping again on their return journeys, it had been a lifeline for the inhabitants of the local villages. But as the route became busier, with more and more train using the line it was decided that the little station was becoming an inconvenience and so the order was given for it to be closed. There were strenuous complaints from the *Burgermeisters* (Mayors) in the surrounding area but in the end, with the efficiency of the line paramount the power of the Reichsbahn prevailed and the little station was condemned to closure.

The door at the rear opened easily enough. A single well-placed kick shattering the lock. Moving from room to room Mayer was saddened by what he saw. Though the ceilings were still sound all were missing their light fittings. Every door had been prized from its hinges and any fixtures removed. All the ground floor windows were missing their panes of glass. In the room fronting the platform the tiled fireplace with its wrought-iron surround which had provided warmth for the waiting passengers had been ripped out, leaving a blackened hole in the wall. The once-proud building reduced to little more than a soulless shell. Finding the staircase was still intact, with one hand gripping the bannister, testing each of the bare wooden treads before giving it his full weight Mayer began climbing up to the first floor. Reaching the landing he made his way towards the back of the building and entered a small room. Kicking aside the stones and pieces of broken glass which littered the floor he lowered himself into a corner. Well, at least its dry thought Mayer surveying the empty room and although the door was missing and the wallpaper peeling away from the walls revealing the mildew blackened plaster underneath, there were worse places to be; Like lying in a shallow hole you had clawed out of the frozen ground, your lice-infested body numbed by the cold. Or huddled together with six other men on top of a Panzer as it rumbled across the vast empty Steppe. Oh yes, there were most definitely worse places to be. Pushing the memories from his mind, dipping a hand into his pocket Mayer removed the brown paper bag which Frau Neusch had pushed into his pocket as they were leaving. Smiling at the sight of the two slices of bread with a generous layer of blackberry jam sandwiched between them. After devouring every crumb and licking the last traces of jam from his fingers, climbing to his feet Mayer removed his greatcoat. Stripping off his jacket and shirt he examined the wound in his upper arm. The splinter had penetrated deeper than he had first thought but at least the bleeding had stopped. Removing the flask Tomas had given him, after taking a generous swig he splashed some of the schnapps onto the exposed flesh, wincing a little as the neat alcohol cauterised the wound. Gritting his teeth, he reminded himself that in all probability the next person to attend to his "scratch" would be his wife, Hannah. She always enjoyed playing the nurse.

Far removed from the theatres of war the village of Hohenburg lay silent, its residents sleeping soundly in their beds. All except for one. Hidden in the shadows, coat collar turned up his back against the wall of a house Mayer looked across at the shop on the other side of the street. Even in the darkness, the painted sign above the plate-glass window was quite visible; *Gemischtwarenladen* (General store). Perfect for somebody who needed some groceries. The light in the upstairs room at the front of the building had been extinguished for what seemed to him like hours. But still, Mayer waited. There was no rush. The important thing was getting in and getting out without disturbing anybody. With the minutes ticking away, fearing that he might fall asleep Mayer made his move. Standing at the corner of the house, satisfied that the coast was clear he quickly crossed the unlit street and ignoring the door at the front he made his way to the rear of the building. Praying that the back door wouldn't be bolted from the inside Mayer forced his bayonet into the space between the lock and the door jamb. Levering it sideways until the gap was wide enough to free the latch and deadbolt from the strike plate. Then with his heart thumping, he placed a hand on the door and pushed. Sighing with relief when it swung open on well-oiled hinges.

With no blinds at the window thankfully for Mayer there was enough light to see by. The shop appeared larger inside than he remembered. Rectangular in shape the area was divided by a central aisle with a long counter running along one wall. Standing on it at one end were a set of scales with a cash register at the other. Behind it, resting on top of a drawer-fronted cabinet was a tall glass display case crammed with an assortment of bottles and jars. At the rear of the shop, cloaked in shadow were a flight of steep wooden stairs leading up to the first floor. But what interested Mayer most was what was on the far wall. Shelves! Each laden with cans of all shapes and sizes. Skirting around the clutter of goods neatly stacked down the centre of the shop; a veritable cornucopia of household merchandise, picking up a hessian sack containing potatoes Mayer began emptying it onto the floor. Cursing under his breath when the contents began pouring out like a mini avalanche, rumbling across the hard wooden floor in all directions. Still as a statue, hardly daring to breathe, Mayer waited. The silence was so absolute that he could hear the ticking of the large circular clock suspended above the counter. Eventually, happy that there was no sound coming from above, sack in hand Mayer approached the wall of shelving.

If Hubert Ploetz had been asleep he probably wouldn't have heard the noise from the shop below. But thanks to his wife's snoring, an affliction which was acquiring an alarming regularity, he was wide awake. Another irritation to be added to the growing list of things about her which he disliked. Like her bad breath and the fact that she was putting on weight at an alarming rate. Something else to make him regret ever marrying the woman in the first place. But of course, he only had himself to blame. At the time her father had owned the house and shop they were now living in and with an eye to the future he had seized the chance to make her his wife. Simply an opportunity to better himself and certainly no love match. A decision he was now beginning to regret. In hindsight, he should have followed his heart and married Mareike Clemens. But foolishly he hadn't and never short of admirer's, she had quickly found herself a spouse. She was a widow now, her husband having died in the first year of the war. Not even killed in battle but crushed by one of their own tanks. She came into the shop quite regularly accompanied by her two adorable children and always gave him a warm smile when he served her. It was then that the dark thoughts would infiltrate his mind. Seeds of evil germinating in his brain. A pillow over her face when she was sleeping? After all, it was common knowledge that his wife had suffered from asthma as a young girl. Or a push when she was standing at the top of the stairs perhaps? Tempting though the thoughts were that's all they remained. Just thoughts. But who knows what might happen if the snoring continued? Well I mean a man can only stand so much. Banishing such ideas from his mind, climbing out of the bed Hubert made his way to the stairs. Probably just that damn cat again hunting for mice but it wouldn't hurt to take a look.

Whatever he expecting to find, nothing could have prepared Hubert Ploetz for what he witnessed. The fact that somebody was robbing his store was quite obvious. What shocked him was that the person in question was a German soldier. Even in the half-light, he could make out the distinctive outline of the man's helmet. And when the thief turned away from him, reaching for something up on a higher shelf, there was no mistaking the Schmeisser slung across his shoulder. Lowering himself onto the top stair the storekeeper sat and watched with amazement as Mayer walked along the row of shelves, removing a tin here, a tin there and depositing them into the sack he was holding. Eventually, satisfied with his "shopping" after stooping to retrieve a couple of errant potatoes, something to eat as he walked the last few miles to his home Mayer opened the back door, and resting the sack on his shoulder, he disappeared outside. Despite hearing all the propaganda and the moral boosting broadcasts by Herr Goebbels Hubert had known that the war was not going well. Deep down everybody knew it really. But if he had needed confirmation that it was truly lost, he had just seen it with his own eyes. It saddened him of course that his country had been defeated. Yet strangely, as he sat there in the half-light the feeling of relief that it was finally over was like the laying on of hands. The cleansing of the soul after confession. Hopefully, it heralded a return to the old days when life was simpler, happier. Climbing to his feet Hubert made his way back to the bedroom and his snoring wife. He would go down early tomorrow morning and re-stock the shelves. Better for all concerned that he should keep what he had witnessed to himself.

Seven

Lauterbruck
Early December 1944

WITH HER BLONDE hair washed and brushed Trudel climbed into bed and pulled the duvet up under her chin. In the bed opposite, after placing the leather bookmark between the pages he had just finished reading Wolfgang pushed the book under his pillow. It was one of his father's old Zane Grey novels. This particular one was entitled *The Trail Driver* and just as his father had been all those years ago, he too was captivated by the story. Hannah knew that there was also a torch hidden under his pillow and the moment she was out of the door, buried under the bedcover he would begin reading it again. Of course, she could have confiscated the torch but she knew he was sensible and that he would only read for a short time so she allowed it. Putting the hairbrush onto the bedside table, seating herself on the end of Trudel's bed Hannah knitted her fingers together and closing her eyes in a soft voice she began leading them in their evening prayer;

'Now I lay me down to sleep, I pray dear Lord my soul to keep. Watch over us from heaven above and keep us in your undying love. Take care of our Papa where ever he may be and bring him home safely to me. Amen'

Planting a kiss on both their foreheads, picking the brass oil lamp off the table Hannah walked towards the door.

'Goodnight *Meine Lieblinge*' (My darlings).

Bathed in lamplight the kitchen still smelled of the days baking. Now all that was left to do was the washing up. Hannah didn't mind, it had been a wonderful afternoon. The three of them working together. Wolfgang had carried up the apples from the cellar; although they only had the two trees this autumn's harvest had been a particularly good one and together they had peeled them. Of course, Trudel had wanted to help but after explaining to her how dangerous knives could be; supplemented by Wolfgang's graphic demonstration of how she might cut off her finger, she contented herself by collecting up the peelings and putting them in a bucket.

As a reward, with the peeled and chopped apples immersed in sugary water, she was allowed to stand on a chair and stir the contents of the large iron pan as it bubbled away on the stove. The most fun was making the puff pastry for the strudel. It was her mother's recipe and her mother's before her so very traditional and one which Hannah hoped Trudel would continue. Hannah's only mistake was in allowed her daughter to become involved in the mixing process. Which resulted in almost as much butter and flour ending up in Trudel's hair as it did in the pastry. Finally, after allowing each of the children to fold the sections of pasty into a plait after brushing on an egg wash it was ready to pop into the oven. An apple strudel both her mother and grandmother would be proud of.

Hannah had just finished drying the last of the bowls when she heard the back door open. Surprised, she quickly turned around, and there framed in the doorway was Franz. At first, she couldn't move. Rooted to the spot she stood staring at him in disbelief. And then he smiled. Overcome with joy life returned to her limbs and rushing across the room Hannah threw herself into his open arms. Whispering his name over and over. He was home. God had answered their prayers and her Franz was home. Freeing herself from his embrace she stared into his face.

'Oh, Franz it's really you? I was so afraid. So afraid... That...'

Placing a finger over her lips Mayer smiled.

'What that I was dead? Do I feel like a ghost?'

Overwhelmed by a sense of relief and unbelievable happiness Hannah began crying. Drawing her closer Franz kissed each tear as it rolled down her cheeks, their salty freshness clinging to his lips. He was home. Somehow, against all the odds he had finally returned to his family.

'I must wake the children. Oh they will be so happy to see there Papa' said Hannah, breaking free from Franz's embrace.

'No!' said Franz, gripping her arm. 'No, let them sleep. You and I must talk first.'

Perplexed, Hannah stared at him. The tightness of his grip and his tone of voice telling her that something was not right.

'What is it, Franz? What is wrong?'

Letting go of Hannah's arm, encircling her waist with his arm Franz guided her across to the kitchen table.

'Come sit down Hannah.' He said, pulling out a chair, 'and I will explain everything.'

Too stunned to speak Hannah lowered herself into the chair, watching as he removed his helmet and weapon. Placing them on the table Franz pulled out a chair and seated himself opposite her, taking hold of her hands he looked into Hannah's face.

'The children must not know I am here. Nobody must

know that I am here.'

Hannah starred back at him nonplussed.

'But why Franz? I don't understand?'

'Nobody must know because I should not be here.' He said, gently squeezing her hands. 'You see I have not come home on leave Hannah, I have deserted.'

Shocked by the revelation Hannah pulled away, desperate to free her hands. But Mayer tightened his grip. Refusing to release them.

'Yes, I am a deserter.' He snapped, angered by the look of revulsion on his wife's face. 'But at least I am alive Hannah. I am alive.'

Stunned at first by the vehemence in his voice, what he had said quickly absolved him of the stigma attached to the word. Yes, he was alive. Her Franz was alive and nothing else mattered. Feeling his grip relaxing, freeing her hands Hannah climbed to her feet and lowering herself into Franz's lap, wrapping her arms around his neck she kissed him hard on the lips.

'Forgive me, Franz, it was just the shock of hearing you say such a thing.'

Franz smiled. That warm loving smile that she had missed so much.

'But what shall we to do when they come here looking for you?' said Hannah, a note of alarm in her voice.

'Nobody will come looking for me *Mein Leibchen* (My darling),' said Franz, encircling her waist with his arm. 'Because nobody knows whether I am dead or alive. I have simply disappeared. Another soldier missing in action. So there is no need for you to worry.'

Somewhat reassured by this revelation, it only took a moment before Hannah's curiosity got the better of her.

'But how is that possible? And how have you managed to get here?'

'To know that,' said Mayer pursing his lips, 'first you must ply me with drink.'

Expressing her annoyance by pouting her lips, getting to her feet Hannah walked across to one of the kitchen cupboards and reaching up she removed a bottle and a glass from the top shelf.

'It's from last Christmas, a gift from Frau Junker. Some of her famous plum liqueur,' said Hannah half filling the glass with the dark amber liquid and handing it to her husband.

Watching as he lifted it to his mouth. Smiling at the look of pleasure on his face as the velvety liquid trickled down his throat.

'Ah, nectar! Pure nectar,' said Mayer holding out the glass for a refill.

'First husband,' said Hannah clutching the bottle to her chest, 'before you get drunk you must answer my questions and tell me what we are to do?'

Putting down the glass Mayer nodded. Hannah was right of course there was a lot to be discussed. There was no point in telling her how thanks to his secondment by the medical officer he had avoided registration. She would just have to take his word that he was not a hunted man. What was important was what they were to do now. During the train ride from Potsdam, he had thought long and hard about this very thing. Finding a hiding place was easy enough. The house had a good cellar. All they needed to ensure was that he wasn't discovered, not even by the children. Feeding him was going to be the biggest problem of all. And it was then that he remembered the sack.

'I have done some shopping,' said Mayer pointing towards the sack he had left beside the back door.

'Show me,' said Hannah, keen to see its contents.

Lifting the heavy sack, Mayer carefully tipped out the contents onto the table.

'Stolen I'm afraid. From the General store in Hohenburg.'

Hannah didn't say anything. Regrettable though the theft was she knew that without the food he had stolen it would be almost impossible to feed another mouth. She had shopped there from time to time and the owner Herr Ploetz had always been very courteous and accommodating. Perhaps they would find some way to repay him in the future thought Hanna but for now, they must only think of themselves. Considering he had "shopped" in virtual darkness, Mayer was quite pleased with the contents of the sack. Mostly tinned meats and fish with a few cans of fruit. And although the two tins of stove blacking were unlikely to find their way onto the menu no doubt Hannah would find a use for them use. With the tins safely stored away at the back of a cupboard, satisfied with their efforts Hannah and Franz returned to the table. Sitting opposite each other, overwhelmed by the day's events, their minds a kaleidoscope of thoughts they lapsed into silence.

It was Hannah who spoke first. Her words accompanied by a warm smile.

'I knew that you would come back to us. The children and I prayed for you every night and now our prayers have been answered.'

Moved by her words Franz reached out and placed his hand on hers, squeezing it gently. It was then that she noticed the dried blood.

'You have been bleeding. Are you wounded, Franz?'

'It's nothing. A splinter of wood took a liking to my arm that's all. Nothing for you to worry yourself about.'

Ignoring his assurance, pulling him up onto his feet. Hannah began unbuttoning his greatcoat.

'Take off your clothes I want to see.'

Knowing that there would be no point in arguing with her Franz removed his jacket and shirt. Sitting her patient back in his chair, holding the oil lamp in one hand Hannah examined the wound. Although Tomas's schnapps had helped it was still enflamed and the area around the torn flesh quite swollen.

'I think there are still some splinters in your arm Franz.'

And with that Hannah walked across to the tall dresser on the other side of the kitchen. Opening one of the drawers she removed a rectangular metal tin. Recognising the family first aid box, Franz decided that purely on medical grounds now might be a good time to sample more of Frau Junker's plum brandy. So while Hannah retrieved the bowl she had used to mix her pastry and began filling it with hot water from the kettle, he topped up his glass.

After glancing down at the three wood splinters and fragments of cloth Hannah had removed from the wound with a pair of tweezers, with his arm neatly bandaged, a yellowing stain showing where the iodine had soaked into the gauze Franz began dressing.

'I should go down to the cellar.'

Putting down the towel she had been drying her hands on Hannah looked across at Franz. Yes, he was right they must see to things before it was time to wake up the children. She could also see that he was suddenly looking very tired. A lack of food together with the three glasses of homemade brandy he had consumed were beginning to have their effect. She had offered to feed him but he had refused. Explaining how delicious and filling the two raw potatoes he had eaten on the way home had been.

'Perhaps before we do I could look in at the children?'

Hannah smiled. How could she deny him?

Yes, but we must be quiet. Wolfgang is quite a light sleeper.'

Leaving his helmet, Schmeisser, and greatcoat in the kitchen Franz followed Hannah out into the small hallway, and together they climbed the flight of stairs to the first-floor landing. Lamp in hand Hannah opened the door to the children's bedroom and peered inside. Thankfully, both children were fast asleep. Stepping aside, taking hold of Franz by the arm she pulled him towards the half-open door. Hardly daring to breathe Franz looked into the room. Trudel was laying on her side, the bedcover pulled over her shoulder her freshly washed blonde hair; which she had insisted on having brushed one hundred times like the princess in the story Hannah had been reading to her, fanned out across her pillow. She still sucked her thumb then thought Mayer seeing the clenched fist with its thumb clamped between her lips. In the bed opposite there wasn't much to be seen of Wolfgang, lying flat on his stomach with the duvet pulled up around his neck. He did seem to take up more of the bed though thought Franz smiling to himself. Another few years and he would be as tall as his father.

The cellar was just as he remembered it. Still filled with all the things they either had no room for or no use for. But that's what a cellar was there for Hannah had always argued whenever he complained as even more clutter was added to the pile already there. Luckily, the old drop-down sofa still occupied the space he had found for it up against the back wall so at least he would have something to sleep on. The workbench with his toolbox pushed underneath was just as he had left it. His wood chisels, mallets, and saws hanging from their respective hooks on the wall behind. With Hannah upstairs finding a pillow and some bedding, after moving things around to make more room, picking up a box of apples he made his way back up to the kitchen. Having agreed that the best excuse for why the cellar was locked was because Hannah had lost the key, by taking out anything she might want it removed the need to get a new lock fitted. "It can wait until your Papa comes home" she would tell the children. So with all evidence of his arrival removed from the kitchen and with Franz safely locked in the cellar, lamp in hand, Hannah climbed the stairs to her bedroom. She wouldn't be able to sleep of course. The excitement at having him home. The relief from the uncertainty of not knowing whether he was dead or alive would see to that. Anxiety would also contribute to her insomnia. For despite Franz's assurance that he would simply be listed as missing in action, presumed dead she still worried. But surmounting all her fears and elation was the pure joy of having him home.

When she reached the bottom of the cellar steps Hannah was greeted by the sight of Franz sitting on the sofa grinning sheepishly and the overpowering smell of human excrement.

'I'm sorry,' said Franz weakly. 'But I didn't know where else to do it.'

'Franz it's disgusting!'

'I know. I think perhaps raw potatoes and plum brandy are not something which should be enjoyed together.'

'I don't wish to know that,' said Hannah staring at the

The Letter

bucket in the corner, 'I just need you to dispose of it. Now!'

'But what about the children?'

'Wolfgang is at school and Trudel has gone to the market with Frau Junker. She likes helping her carry her shopping home.

'Perhaps I could eat first?' said Franz, eying the contents of the tray Hannah was holding.

'Now Franz or I will give your meal to the chickens'

She would too he thought. So swallowing his protest Franz picked up the offending bucket and made his way up the cellar steps. Smiling inwardly, putting down the tray Hannah crossed to the back wall, and reaching up she pushed open the small window.

With the air, a little fresher, seated side by side on the sofa Hannah and Franz began eating the meal she had prepared for them. The remains of yesterday's rabbit stew supplemented with a few dumplings made from the leftover pastry mixed with the grated potato.

'Was it one that Wolfgang caught?' asked Franz.

'Yes. Did you enjoy it?'

'Yes, nothing better than rabbit stew,' said Franz smiling.

'Oh,' said Hanna, frowning 'and since when did you become so fond of rabbit stew?'

'It's a long story. I will tell you one day I promise.'

With that, the pair lapsed into silence. Sitting like a couple of teenagers who have been left alone in the parlour for the first time, each waiting for the other to say something.

'We have chickens now,' said Hannah. Not at all sure why she was even telling him.

'Yes, so I noticed. I spotted the hen house when I looked out of the window this morning.'

'Our son built it,' she said proudly. 'With some help from Herr Rueckerl. He said we would need a safe place to keep them because of the foxes.'

Although he tried to stop himself, Franz suddenly began laughing.

'And what is it you find so funny? Said Hannah crossly.

'I'm sorry *Liebchen* (darling) but chickens! You don't even like chickens. You are frightened of the damned things.'

'The children wanted them,' said Hannah, staring back at him. 'And with food becoming scarce I thought it would be a good idea.

Franz nodded. She was right it was a very good idea.

'Besides which, 'said Hannah, keen to wipe the stupid grin off his face 'I don't have to go near them. Wolfgang feeds them and cleans out the hen house and Trudel collects their eggs.' Adding for good measure. 'Perhaps now you don't think it is so funny?'

'No! No! I think it is an excellent idea,' Franz replied, inching himself along the sofa towards her. 'Free eggs. What could be better and when they stop laying a nice roast chicken for dinner. Perfect!'

'We can't kill them,' said Hannah, pulling away from him.

With a loud groan, Franz dropped his head into his hands.

'No don't tell me,' said Franz. 'Trudel has given each of them a name. Yes?'

The guilty expression on his wife's face telling him instantly that he was right.

'Well, you know how she is with animals. She likes to give

them names,' said Hannah, reminding him of the two snails Wolfgang had put in a jar for her. Even they had been given names.'

'Yes,' said Franz smiling, 'even though nobody could tell which was which not even Trudel. Ah well, let's hope these chickens of yours go on laying for a long time.'

Resting her head on his shoulder Hannah took hold of his hand.

'I knew you would understand. I know you would never do anything to upset your darling daughter.'

'Of course,' said Mayer, stroking his chin thoughtfully, 'we could always tell her that the fox had got them.' It was then that he thought she was going to hit him. But instead of which she kissed him.

Hannah knew it wouldn't be too long before Wolfgang noticed that the cellar door was locked. She would find him down there sometimes rummaging through Franz's toolbox. It wasn't that he needed any of the tools. It was just his way of coping with his absence. A way of feeling closer to his father. Puzzled as to why his mother had locked the cellar in the first place, Wolfgang's first thought was to borrow some tools from Herr Rueckerl and fit a new lock. "It's quite easy for me to do mother," he told her. But she had said no. There was nothing in there that they wanted she told him. Besides which the door was old and needed replacing anyway. A job for your Papa when he returned home. And with that, the matter was closed.

It was on the morning of the third day when they first made love. A purely spontaneous act. Not something brought on by passion or a sudden lusting for each other's bodies. Quite a playful thing, to begin with. Wolfgang had gone off to school and after much pleading, Hannah had allowed Trudel to go and visit with her adopted *Grobmutter*

(Grandmother), Frau Junker. Allowing her and Franz to enjoy breakfast together in the kitchen. A moment of normality.

'I think you should take a bath, Franz,' said Hannah, placing her knife and fork side by side on the plate.

'Why?' Said Mayer, grinning. 'Do I smell?'

'No, but you should get out of that uniform and put on some other clothes. Besides which it might become difficult later and then you will begin to smell.'

Franz smiled. After going for months without a bath now he was having two in the space of a few days. Fifteen minutes later with his clothes piled up on a chair, Franz found himself luxuriating in a bath of hot water. The aroma of sandalwood as he rubbed the bar of soap into his hair reminding him of bath-time with the children.

'I've boiled some water,' said Hannah pushing the bathroom door shut with her foot before emptying the contents of the large copper kettle into the bath.

'Hey!' Shouted Franz, drawing up his knees to avoid the jet of boiling water. 'Just be careful where you are aiming that thing. And look away woman, can't a man have some privacy.' Quickly covering his genitals with his hands in a show of modesty.

'Oh! Said Hannah, putting down the empty kettle. More than a little piqued by his rebuke. 'And since when did you become so shy? Still why should I care, from what I remember there's not much to look at anyway,' and scooping up a handful of soapy water she flung it into his face. Immediately, two things happened in quick succession; Franz hauling himself out of the bath and Hannah dashing for the door.

Racing across the narrow landing, flinging open their

bedroom door Hannah rushed inside, slamming it shut behind her. Standing with both her hands pushing against it she watched in horror as the handle began turning. With the catch released and Franz pushing against the other side slowly but surely, she was forced back. Abandoning all hope of keeping him out Hannah quickly ran around to the far side of the double bed, watching in horror as the naked figure of her husband entered the bedroom.

'Now Franz just you keep away. The children will be home soon.'

Wiping the last of the soap suds from his face Franz looked at her and smiling at her lie he moved towards her. Knowing that unless she jumped out of the window there was no escape for her now Hannah leapt onto the bed. But before she could scramble across it to safety Franz reached out and grabbing her by the ankle he pulled her towards him, her skirt riding up and revealing the pale flesh of her thighs. Rolling onto her back, her chest heaving Hannah watched as Franz climbed onto the bed. Straddling her like a horse with droplets of water dripping onto her face Franz hovered over her. Suddenly, overwhelmed by a surge of passion, reaching up Hannah wrapped both of her hands around his neck and pulled him towards her. Her lips seeking his. Her tongue exploring his mouth. Slowly, one by one Franz unbuttoned her blouse. Waiting patiently while she pulled her arms out of the sleeves before reaching around behind her and unhooking her brassiere. Cupping his hands he began caressing each of her rounded breasts. Her moans of pleasure when he squeezed her nipples between his thumb and forefinger inflaming his senses. Reaching down Franz pushed his hand under skirt, sliding it slowly up between her thighs. Running her thumb across her moistened lips Hannah arched her back. Trembling as his fingers found her, Groaning with pleasure as they explored the velvety softness of her hidden place. Opening her legs she pulled him towards her, desperately wanting him inside her. Gasping as he pulled down her underwear. A feeling of ecstasy coursing through her veins as he entered her. The rhythmic undulations of their bodies like the incoming tide on some far-away shore.

For what seemed like the hundredth time Mayer stripped, cleaned, and reassembled the Schmeisser. The gun had become like an old friend. A constant companion. Besides which if the Russians reached Hohenburg before the Americans, he might have to use it. But oh how he longed to escape the confines of the cellar. To walk out in the garden, to say hello to his neighbours and of course play with his children. By answering his countries call to arms he had missed so much of their childhood. Times that could never be reclaimed. Occasionally he would catch sight of Trudel walking back from the hen house carrying a bowl of eggs. The urge to call out to her. To see her running towards him. The feeling of her arms around his neck was almost overwhelming. But he knew he must be patient and to just give thanks that he was able to see her at all. So far the food was lasting well, supplemented by the rabbits Wolfgang had managed to catch in his snares. The chickens were also playing their part. Franz joked that it was because they had overheard their conversation about what would happen to them should they fail to keep the family supplied with eggs.

But life also had its compensations. Every night when the children were fast asleep Franz would sneak into their bedroom and the couple would spend the night together. Lying in each other's arms like a pair of young lovers until the early hours. That was until the night Mother Nature intervened. As storms go it wasn't particularly violent but the rumble of thunder and flashes of lightning that accompanied it were still enough to terrify one young girl. Suddenly, without warning the bedroom door opened, and clutching her teddy bear in her arms Trudel raced across to her parent's bed. Flinging back the cover, arms outstretched Hannah wrapped her distraught daughter in her arms. Oblivious to what was happening, the first thing Franz knew was feeling Hannah's foot in his back and the next minute he was lying in a heap on the floor. After that, they knew things had to change. So now it was Hannah, wearing nothing but her dressing gown who visited him. Not every night though. For her moments of passion were all very well in a warm comfortable bed. Not so enjoyable in a cold, damp cellar. Franz grumbled of course but Hannah was adamant, reminding him that she was getting too old for lumpy sofas and knee-tremblers up against the cellar wall and that was that.

Occasionally, when circumstances allowed they would sit together on the sofa in the front room holding hands their fingers entwined. Each finding contentment in the silence and solitude. At other times they would talk. Usually, it would be about the future and what it might hold for them as a family. Having been a carpenter before joining the Wehrmacht, with a country needing rebuilding Franz knew he would have no trouble in finding employment. Even though she never questioned him, sometimes he would talk about the war. He never mentioned the bad times, of course, those he kept hidden away. Just snippets from those moments which had brought a little light into the darkness. Like the old Gefreiter with the beautiful baritone voice and the officer's Doberman which he and Neubauer had eaten. And of course Giebeler's famous condom calamari. But mostly he talked about the Neusch's. How much he owed them that could never be repaid. Their heartbreak over losing their son. The table with its secret hiding place, filled with his radios. Frau Neusch's delicious blackberry jam and

Otto's trick with the Schnapps bottle. As she listened Hannah knew she also owed them a great debt, the life of her husband, and one day God willing she hoped to thank them in person. And so the hours became days and the days became weeks. Everything settling into what almost seemed like a normal routine. But then one morning everything changed.

It began with the unexpected arrival of Herr Rueckerl at the back door clutching a rusty biscuit tin in his gnarled hands.

'Keys,' he said to Hannah when she opened the door, 'Young Wolfgang tells me that you've lost the one to your cellar?' The old man said, rattling the tin. 'Bound to be one it here that will fit. Been collecting them since I was a boy.'

Horrified Hannah just stared at him. Then quickly recovering her composure;

'That's very good of you Herr Ruecherl but there really is no need. I know when Franz comes home he will want to change the door anyway.'

'Nonsense, it will only take me a minute. Besides I think you're boy put my bag of nails in his toolbox and I might need them.' And with that, before Hannah had a chance to do or say anything the old man stepped into the kitchen.

'No need to show me I know where it is,' he said walking across the kitchen and out into the hallway.

The first Franz knew of Herr Ruecherl's arrival outside the cellar door was when the old man inserted a key into the lock. Watching in horror as he attempted to turn it. Sighing with relief when it was withdrawn.

'Ah I thought that one would do it,' said Herr Ruecherl a little disappointedly, tossing the key back into his tin. 'Never mind we'll soon find one that does the trick you mark my words.'

Frantically, Hannah tried to think of some way of stopping him. But apart from physically restraining him, there was nothing she could do. He was determined to open the damn door.

Finding another suitable candidate, before the old man could insert it into the lock both he and Hannah were distracted by the sound of vehicles driving past the front of the house. Certainly not cars judging by the noise of their engines. And then a loudspeaker crackled into life.

Even though the window in the cellar was wide open Franz couldn't hear the noise of the engines. If he had he would have recognized the sound immediately; an Opel 3.6 the type fitted to the Wehrmacht's workhorse the good old Opel Blitz truck. But he could hear the loudspeaker though, although not clear enough to make out the words the man was bellowing into it. Still, whoever they were thankfully they had stopped Herr Ruecherl from rummaging around in his tin box for another key.

The next thing Franz heard was the back door being slammed shut. After waiting for a few minutes, with no sound coming from the rooms above putting on his uniform jacket Franz picked up his Schmeisser, and making his way up the stairs he unlocked the cellar door. From the living room window, he could see the street quite clearly. Hidden behind the full-length curtain he watched as family groups, parents and children filed past. All walking towards the centre of the village. Common sense told him he should return to the cellar. But curiosity won in the end and although he knew it was foolhardy, dangerous even he found himself walking towards the kitchen. Leaving by the back door after checking that there was nobody around, he ran to the end of the garden. Climbing over the low fence, hidden from view by a row of conifers he made his way behind the row of detached houses.

There were three trucks, all parked in line alongside a grassy area the size of a football pitch. Two of them had canvas covers the third had just the bare metal frame. Standing beside them, each armed with a rifle were six German soldiers. Having paid a visit to Hohenburg less than an hour ago the reason the small convoy had stopped on its way through Lauterbruck was simply that the NCO in charge, *Feldwebel* (Sergeant) Gaschler had seen an opportunity to acquire more "volunteers".

'Good people of Lauterbruck,' he called out in a loud voice, slowly strutting up and down before the assembled villagers his overly long greatcoat brushing the ground. 'Your Fuhrer has need of you. At this moment of danger, our beloved Fatherland needs you.' Pausing for a moment to allow his words to germinate. 'The enemies of the Reich are at our gates and in this grave hour every man is called upon to do his duty.'

Stunned the villagers listened in silence. Many of them gazing across towards the two canvas topped trucks and seeing the faces of men and young boys staring out at them from behind the tailgate. Having issued his proclamation Gaschler now shouted out his orders.

'Men under the age of seventy and boys over the age of twelve, step forward.'

Nobody moved.

It was always the same thought Gaschler. A little prodding was usually required. A little gentle persuading. And with that he gestured to the squad of armed soldiers, watching as they pushed their way into the crowd. They would soon weed out the less fortunate ones. It was all so incredibly easy thought Gaschler, allowing himself a self-satisfied smile as he watched the soldier's herding the collection of men and boys onto the grassy area and forming them into a single line. Yes, there had been some mutterings and a bit of pushing and shoving but no real resistance. Of course, there wasn't any need to parade them like this. It served no real purpose. He could simply have loaded into the truck and driven away. But actually, he quite enjoyed this part. The subterfuge. Convincing them that they were not being press-ganged but simply being given the opportunity to demonstrate their love for their country. A lie of course because scrapping the barrel was precisely what they were doing.

It was then, just as Gaschler was beginning his so-called inspection that Wolfgang made his move. Pushing past Herr Ruecherl, breaking free from the crowd he raced across to the line of men and boys. Elbowing a space for himself between two youths. Hannah's first instinct was to scream. Her second was to go running after him. But in the end, she did neither. It was as if her whole body had been turned into stone. All except for her knees which had suddenly grown very weak. Thankfully, before she collapsed onto the ground, reaching out a hand Herr Rueckerl grabbed her by the elbow. What was the boy thinking of? He was only ten years old.

Although he had never actually witnessed the Fuhrer doing this in person he had seen it on the newsreels being shown at the local cinema. Film clips of Herr Hitler walking along a line of ordinary men and youths. Bestowing a smile here and there. Exchanging a handshake with a lucky few. Patting a young boy on the shoulder. He had even grown a "Fuhrer" moustache but then shaved it off because he thought it made him look more like Charlie Chaplin.

'So who have we here then?' Said Gaschler, stopping in front of Wolfgang.

'Wolfgang Mayer sir,' Wolfgang replied, pulling himself as

upright as possible without actually standing on tiptoe.

'So Wolfgang Mayer you want to be a soldier do you?'

'Yes!' Said Wolfgang, proudly sticking out his skinny chest. 'My Papa is a soldier. He is a Sergeant like you.'

'Is he now?' Said Gaschler, admiring the boy's pluck.

'He is fighting the Bolsheviks.'

It was at that moment that Gaschler experienced an unexpected pang of guilt. Seeing this young boy standing before him, filled with an eagerness to fight for his country had suddenly removed the scales from his eyes as it were and for the first time he saw what he was doing for what it was. But the feeling wasn't allowed to survive for long.

'How old are you?' The smile had gone now along with the guilt. Sentiments are all very well but duty must always come first.

'I will be twelve soon.' Wolfgang lied.

It might have helped Wolfgang's cause if he had chosen to stand somewhere else in the line. With height potentially being a deciding factor, positioning himself between Deiter Schmitt and Peter Alsdorf, two of the tallest boys in the village only served to make him appear shorter.

Distracted by a sudden movement in the crowd, looking over Wolfgang's head Gaschler watched as a woman pushed her way to the front of the onlookers. The boy's mother no doubt judging by the look of anxiety on her face he thought to himself. A pretty looking thing, not like the one he had waiting for him at home.

'So almost twelve eh?' Said Gaschler, bending forward so that his face was directly opposite Wolfgang's. 'Did you hear me asking for boys who were almost twelve?' A hard edge to his voice. 'No! I asked for boys over twelve.'

The Letter

Emphasizing the word "over".

Wolfgang dropped his head. It was not going as well as he had hoped.

'Go home boy!' Shouted Gaschler, his patience finally exhausted. I'm not here to steal children. Now bugger off before I give you the back of my hand.'

With his hopes crushed, Wolfgang walked dejectedly back towards the sea of watching faces his face flushed with embarrassment.

Overwhelmed by a feeling of relief as he watched a crestfallen Wolfgang making his way back towards the crowd of onlookers, his mother Franz slumped back against the wall of the building he was hiding behind and lowered his Schmeisser. Much as he would have wanted to, he knew he couldn't have used it. Not even to save his son. For Hubert Ploetz, watching proceedings from the back of the lorry, there was only a feeling of indifference to what was taking place. He was so pre-occupied with how he came to be here in the first place that even if an elephant had been performing handstands in front of him he wouldn't have noticed. He had protested of course, quite vehemently. He was needed to see to the running of the shop he argued. But the sergeant hadn't listened, simply telling him that his wife looked capable enough to cope on her own. In hindsight calling the NCO a fat oaf probably hadn't been a wise thing to do of course. But he hadn't been able to stop himself. What was strange though was that although he was being taken off to fight in a war, uppermost in his mind was the thought of how much he was looking forward to getting a good night's sleep.

Exhausted by the day's events, for once Hannah was pleased to be spending the night alone in her bed. She had made her peace with Wolfgang. Telling him she wasn't angry with him but also explaining that as the "man of the house" how much she and his sister needed him. She also told him how proud his father would have been in showing such bravery. As for her husband risking everything by leaving the house. Now that was a different matter. But luckily for him, with the children within earshot, she had resisted the temptation to take down the large iron frying pan hanging on a hook beside the oven and hit him over the head with it. He had protested of course; how was he to know who they were? They could have been the Russians of the Americans. She hadn't listened of course. But in the end, they were both relieved that it had ended well.

For two days the thought persisted. Burrowing into his brain like an insidious worm. And that night Franz reached a decision. Unlocking the cellar door, with the small oil lamp in his hand he climbed the steps and made his way to the front room. Navigating his way around the furniture he seated himself at the desk which had once belonged to his father. Made from ash and inlaid with strips of mahogany it looked almost as new as when his father had bought it over forty years ago. The six drawers all had their original brass handle and escutcheon. Two even had a key. Placing his hands palms down Franz ran his fingers over the polished inlay, the feel of the leather evoking memories of his childhood. Pushing his thoughts aside he opened the top left-hand drawer and reaching in he removed a writing pad and two envelopes. Taking Kohlar's pay-book and tag from his jacket pocket, turning to the appropriate page with a pencil he had found in his toolbox he began filling in the missing details.

Fallen on; 20/10/1944 – Buried at; Rozan Poland.

The date was not specific but he knew it had been towards the end of the month. As for the place, well a forest was a forest but at least Rozan was a place on a map Slipping both

into an envelope, after sealing it he wrote on it in capital letters;
PLEASE TAKE THIS ENVELOPE TO THE TOWN HALL IN HOHENBURG.

The next item to be removed from his jacket pocket was the envelope on which Otto had drawn his map. Turning it over, Mayer copied the Bodelschwingh Weg address onto a clean envelope. Satisfied that he had it down correctly he pulled the writing pad towards him. Was he tempting fate he wondered? Or was he doing the right thing? Then the little voice in his head had its say and wetting the pencil lead with his tongue he began writing; *My Dear Friends, if you are reading this letter then it is because I am dead.*

Although there were no images just the sound of children's laughter Hannah's first thought was that she must be dreaming. But when she opened her eyes the sound was still there and it was coming from Wolfgang and Trudel's bedroom. A happy noise and yet it turned her heart to ice. Climbing out of bed she slipped on her dressing gown and torn between hope and fear she made her way to the children's bedroom. Tiptoeing across the landing she peered in through the half-open door. The fearing part of her wasn't surprised to see Franz sitting on the end of Trudel's bed. Hope hadn't survived very long. Just the time it had taken for her to cross the landing. The fact that he was wearing his uniform confirming her fears. He was leaving. Her Franz was going back to the war.

Then Wolfgang noticed her first standing in the doorway.

'Look *Mutti* (mother), Papa has given me his penknife.' Holding up the double-bladed knife for her to see.

Hannah smiled. But it was the smile of a clown. A badge of defiance worn by countless wives and mothers whenever the spectre of war darkened their door. Carrying off their husbands and sons on its chariot of delusion.

'Yes but you must be careful, knowing your Papa it will be very sharp.'

It was then that Franz turned towards her. His eyes, his whole being begging her to forgive him. To understand.

'Look Mama,' cried Trudel, her voice filled with excitement. 'Papa had some made some dolls for me. See!' Holding up the four peg-dolls Franz had carved for her from scraps of wood he had found in the cellar.

'And have you given them names yet?' asked Hannah smiling.

'No, not yet. Will you help me chose Mama?'

'Yes, when you come home from Frau Junkers I will help you chose. I promise. But now I must prepare breakfast or Wolfgang will be late for school. Perhaps your Papa would like some of our eggs?'

'Yes!' Squealed Trudel. 'He must, I know he will like them.'

Their goodbye was brief. They had learned from past experience that it was better that way.

He had tried to make Hannah understand the reason for what he was doing. Tried to explain the feelings of guilt and shame which were threatening to engulf him. But he knew it was hard for her. He was home. He had survived the war. He was safe. And to her, that was all that mattered. Was he being selfish perhaps? Maybe he was. But hiding in a cellar, like a coward while old men and young boys were being sent off to fight was something his conscience wouldn't allow. They had argued briefly, something they rarely did; the last time had been over what colour to paint the new shutters he had made for the windows. On that occasion, she had got her way. But not this time. Franz wouldn't be

The Letter

swayed. Yes, she was right, he had done his bit. Those who had fought alongside him would say he had done more. But in the end, it wasn't about doing your share, it was about doing the right thing. That was what truly mattered and for him, this was the right thing to do. Hannah had almost broken down when he told her about the letter he had written to the Neusch's but somehow she had managed to hold her emotions in check. It was just a letter he told her. And besides, she wouldn't have to post it because he would be coming back to her. Then a final hug and he was gone.

Alone in the empty house, with no more tears left to shed, Hannah sat gazing out through the window. She had tried so hard to understand why he was doing it. A part of her even understood the reason for it but it was only a small part. The rest of her raged against him. He had been safe. The family had been united. Even in a war-ravaged country, they had a future.

Now the waiting must begin again. The awful day-to-day anxiety. The unseen burden every soldier's wife and mother carries with her. Then Hannah spotted Frau Junker and the two children walking along the road towards the house. Was it that the time already? Pausing in front of her dressing table mirror she hastily applied a few dabs of powder to her face to hide the redness around her eyes. Then closing the door behind her she hurried downstairs into the kitchen. Hopefully, Frau Junkers would leave the children at the door as she usually did. It was going to be difficult enough explaining to the children why their father had left so quickly without having to include Frau Junkers in the conversation.

Although farther away than Ansbach he had chosen Regensburg for two reasons. Firstly, with seven platforms its station was much busier. Secondly, it was also on the mainline which meant more trains. And more trains meant more passengers coming and going. More opportunities for him to go un-noticed amid all the hustle and bustle. He didn't have a plan. At times like this, all you could do was trust to luck. His had been pretty good up to now so hopefully, it would last. He waited until well into the afternoon before venturing onto the station itself. Moving along the crowded platforms, trying his best to appear as inconspicuous as possible. Greeting the occasional inquisitive look which came his way with either a smile or a scowl. A few soldiers were standing about, mainly in small groups smoking and chatting together. None of them he noticed were armed. Which made his old friend the Schmeisser something of a liability. Moving to the back of the platform, Mayer watched as yet another train pulled up alongside the wide platform. He noticed this one was filled with young children. Each one wrapped in a warm coat and clutching a cardboard box or small case. All of them were wearing a name-tag attached to a piece of string looped around their neck or threaded through a buttonhole. Refugee children from one of the big cities thought Mayer, possibly Berlin. Sent away by anxious parents to escape the bombing.

It was while he was watching the children being led away by their adoptive parents that a vague sort of plan began forming in Mayer's mind. Somehow he had to make carrying a weapon a positive thing rather than a negative one. And to do that he needed to find himself some travelling companions.

He had seen them arriving earlier. Watching as they jumped down from the back of the trucks like trainee paratroopers and running into the station to get out of the rain. They all looked very young but they were well armed and wore regulation uniforms. A few, probably those with a larger head were even wearing helmets. Mayer also noticed that

The Letter

two of the stronger-looking youths were each carrying a machine-gun. Once inside the station's concourse, forming the hundred or so soldiers into a ragged formation the Gefreiter in charge, probably no more than eighteen himself marched them to the end of the platform. This thought Mayer could be just the opportunity he had been waiting for.

Crossing over to the platform Mayer made his way along to where the group of young soldiers had congregated. The majority of them, having decided that they could be in for a long wait had already squatted down on the platform. Sitting back to back or if there was space, sprawled out full length on the ground. Strangely there was no sign of an officer which was good news as far as Mayer was concerned. With nobody to outrank him, it certainly made his plan a lot more likely to succeed. "His troop train had left without him and he needed a lift." As simple as that! Nothing elaborate or complicated. What he would do when they got to wherever it was that they were going was something he would deal with when it happened. The important thing was getting onto the train with his new band of brothers. Oh, and staying alive of course. It was all very well having a conscience and doing the right thing just as long as you didn't end up getting killed.

Then he spotted the two *Bahnhofswache Officers* (Railway station police) making their way along the platform towards him. Their distinctive white armbands stitched onto their coat sleeves, a holstered pistol attached to their belts. Stopping every now and then to scrutinise an individual's papers. They liked hunted in pairs. It made them more intimidating.

Bugger! Thought Mayer, this was the last thing he needed.

'Not a particularly pleasant occupation but sadly a necessary one wouldn't you agree Sergeant?'

Mayer hadn't noticed the officer. He had been too busy watching those bloody policemen. He was almost as tall as Mayer, smartly dressed in a full-length greatcoat and peaked cap. The shoulder epaulettes denoting his rank as that of an Oberst. Judging by the tracery of lines etched into his face he must be well into his seventies thought Mayer coming to attention. Maybe even older.

'Yes, Herr Oberst, most necessary.' Mayer replied. Stiffening slightly when the officer glanced at the machine-pistol slung across his shoulder. Perhaps he should have left it at home after all.

'You are returning to your unit perhaps?' Said the officer, his words laced with ambiguity.

'Yes, Herr Oberst but unfortunately I have missed my transport,' said Mayer, trying to make the lie sound as convincing as possible.

Just for an instance, a flicker of amusement manifested itself in the officer's eyes. Clearly, he hadn't believed a word Mayer had said. Then it was gone. Replaced by a look so piercing that Mayer felt like a butterfly about to be impaled by a lepidopterist and added to his collection.

'It is of no interest to me why you are here Sergeant,' said the elderly officer, staring into Mayer's face. 'I will be frank with you. As you can see the soldiers under my command are very young. Raw recruits in fact with no experience of war.

Instinctively, Mayer glanced across at the group of young soldiers.

'And so,' the officer continued, 'the services of a seasoned NCO like yourself would be a great benefit to me.'

Mayer remained silent. He had a fair idea of what the officer had in mind but he didn't want to go jumping the gun.

'So a simple choice for you Sergeant. You can place yourself under my command.' Pausing he turned his gaze to where the two Bahnhofswache officers were berating a soldier over an irregularity in his travel papers. 'Or you can take your chance with our two friends over there. Which is to be?'

It was what the English would have called "Hobson's choice". You either accepted the horse Mr. Hobson offered you or you ended up walking. Only in Mayer's case, it was a little more serious than that. If he didn't accept what was being offered there was the distinct possibility he would be shot. So in the end it was a relatively easy choice to make.

'Sergeant Mayer reporting for duty sir,' said Mayer, pulling back his shoulders.

'Excellent!' Said the officer, a smile adding a few extra lines to his face. 'As I said I am not interested in what you have done Sergeant or why you are here? All I demand is your loyalty to me and the men under my command. Is that understood?'

'Yes, Herr Oberst.'

Good! Then we understand each other.' Adding by way of a promise rather than a threat. 'Don't let me down Sergeant or I will shoot you, make no mistake.'

With formalities concluded, he reached out a hand. 'I am Oberst Kellermann and I am in command of this company if you can call it that. It seems much has changed since I last had the honour of serving my country. Back then a company was at least two hundred and fifty men strong. It seems now everything is getting smaller.

'And also younger Herr Oberst,' said Mayer, shaking the officer's hand while at the same time nodding towards his new charges. Children dressed as soldiers waiting to go off to war.

Kellermann smiled. 'Yes, so it would seem.'

'Can I ask where we are going Herr Oberst?'

'To the Western front Sergeant. To the Seigfried Line.'

Well thought Mayer, the west was a decidedly better direction to be going in. After fighting the Ivan's for over three years, taking on the Americans should be an easier proposition. Sadly he was soon to find that war was never that predictable.

With clouds of steam belching from its boiler the soot-blackened locomotive chugged into the station, slowly coming to a halt alongside the platform. Fixed to a wooden pole and secured by a length of wire to its front buffer was a white flag.

'Ah! Transportation,' said Kellermann, aware of the flag's significance.

Filled with an overwhelming sense of relief Mayer began striding towards the group of soldiers. Shouting out in a loud voice.

'Right on your feet. *Schnell!* (Quickly!) *Schnell!*' (Quickly!)

Pleased to see the majority of the conscripts hastily scrambling to their feet. Mayer instilled a sense of urgency into those who were a little slow in obeying the command with the toe of his boot. The sooner they learned he could be a bit of a mean bastard the better for all concerned.

Eight

Abandoned Farmhouse – Muehlhausen
Late January 1945

AFTER CHANGING TRAINS twice Kellermann and his company finally arrived at Rottenburg station. An hour later, with a welcome meal under their belts, they were loaded onto trucks and transported to a section of the Seigfried Line's west wall. While not the most salubrious of places to be spending Christmas at least the bunker they had been assigned to was warm and dry so there were few complaints. A hot meal was provided every evening, usually, a stew of some sort supplemented with loaves of fresh bread. Mayer had also managed to acquire some *Ersatz coffee* (acorn coffee) and a half dozen tins of jam from a fellow Panzergrenadier assigned to quartermaster duties in the field kitchen. So by saving a little of the bread from their evening meal, most mornings the company was able to enjoy a meagre but nourishing breakfast. With little to do except patrol a section of the "dragon's teeth," a name given to the huge cone-shaped concrete tank traps which ran for miles in each direction it seemed boredom would be their main enemy.

Thankfully it never arrived. Mayer made sure of that. He had learned from long experience that soldiers and idle hands were never a good combination, especially when the soldiers in question were mostly teenagers. They moaned of course. Was it really necessary to dismantle, clean and re-assemble their weapon twice a day? Well, Mayer thought so. He insisted on it. He also insisted on inspecting their kit too. Assigning a loader to each of the two soldiers entrusted with an MG-42, just as he had done with young Kohlar Mayer showed them how to join the short belts of ammunition into one continuous strip. With no ammo to spare, training the two young soldiers to work together as a team was restricted to the changing of the gun barrel and loading and unloading the belts of ammunition. It wasn't ideal but Mayer knew that to get the best from a weapon like the MG-42 working well together as a team was essential. He also knew that while this constant repetition might seem boring and unnecessary to them that it would pay dividends when they had to use the gun in action. Mayer also ensured that they all wrote home to their families. He had written to Hannah. Just the one letter. Letting her know that he was safe. Asking her to forgive him and telling her again how much he loved her. That same night as he stood outside looking up at the stars he found himself thinking about the poem he had written to her shortly after they had declared their love for each other. Reciting the words in his head.

> *When you sleep I will be your dream*
> *When you smile I will be content*
> *When you cry it will be from happiness*
> *When you are sick I will care for you*
> *When you are afraid I will protect you*
> *When you are uncertain I will reassure you*
> *When you are in pain I will comfort you*
> *When you are sad I will be your clown*
> *When I am gone I will be your memories*

He had written her other poems over the years but this was

the only one he could remember word for word.

After almost a month of enforced inactivity, their new orders finally arrived. Together with a battalion of lightly armed Volksgrenadiers and a mortar company they were to advance across the Rhine and take up a defensive position near the small town of Muehlhausen. It didn't come as a surprise, certainly not to Kellermann. Word had reached him a few days earlier that the Colmar region had been lost and that the remnants of the Nineteenth Army had retreated across the Rhine to regroup. With the whole of the Alsace region now in French and Allied hands, the danger was that the US seventh Army advancing from the south would try to cross the Rhine at Chalampe.

'If they do,' said Kellermann ruefully, it seems we are to be the "*Warnung Klingel.*" (Warning Bell)

While not perfect, as a defensive position the abandoned farmhouse with its cluster of outbuildings had much to commend it. Located on rising ground with broad fields intersected by hedgerows and small clumps of stunted trees stretching out in front, it was certainly not an ideal terrain if you happen to be an attacking infantryman. Bordering it on one side was a long serpentine lake. On the other was an apple orchard, its trees running in rows along the side of a low hill. Kellermann had suggested to the Hauptmann in charge of the Volksgrenadiers that taking up a position beside the orchard would strengthen both their positions and stop the enemy from outflanking them. But he had refused. Deciding instead to move closer to the outskirts of Muehlhausen. Even Mayer could see the stupidity of it. In an exposed position like that and with most of the Volksgrenadiers armed with only a *Panzerfaust* (anti-tank launcher) or a machine-gun they were asking for trouble. Thankfully, the NCO in charge of the mortar company was more cooperative and soon had his men digging in where

Kellermann had suggested.

The first contact with the enemy came two days after their arrival. A quiet affair. Young Feldbauer had spotted one of their patrols and much to Mayer's annoyance he had opened fire on them with his MG-42. Ah well, at least they know where we are thought Mayer before giving the young soldier a bollocking.

'Idiot! You fire on my orders. Not until then. Understood?'

'Yes Sergeant,' said the terrified youngster, before adding 'I think I hit one of them.'

'Did you now?' said Mayer, 'Proper Dead Eyed Dick eh? Well, I suppose we had better go and take a look.' Calling out for one of the other soldiers to follow him, un-slinging his faithful Schmeisser Mayer climbed over the low wall and hugging the hedgerow he walked out into the field.

They found the body of the American soldier lying in the bottom of a shallow ditch. And it was then that Hirzel, the young soldier who had accompanied Mayer began throwing up. Well, even Mayer had to admit it wasn't a pretty sight. Half the man's head and face had been shot away, his helmet containing what remained of his brains. Like most soldiers regardless of nationality, the soldier's pay book was where Mayer expected to find it. Tucked into a top pocket, it revealed that the soldier was a private and that his surname was Buchner. Such irony thought Mayer, an American with a German name being killed by a German. More importantly, it showed that he belonged to the 103rd Infantry Division of the American 7th Army.

The TORN Fu d2 radio which they had been issued with had never functioned properly. Even communications between themselves and the Volksgrenadier battalion who had a similar set had been sporadic. The young signalman had tried his best, Kellermann had accepted that. He had even clambered up onto the farmhouse roof and rigged up an aerial to try and achieve a better line of sight. But it had made no difference. So after writing the information onto a sheet of paper, as a reward for having accompanied Sergeant Mayer young Hirzel was given the task of personally carrying it back across the Rhine. "Swim across if you have to," the officer had told him. "But it is imperative that the information you are carrying is received by the Army command in Mullheim."

Two days later, just as dawn was breaking the Americans attacked. The previous day Kellermann and Mayer had held a council of war. Having fought in the First War the officer knew just how valuable Mayer's experience of fighting in this one would be. Confirmation of this coming as they watched the enemy's mortar shells raining down on the farmhouse and outbuildings from the safety of the line of trenches Mayer had made them dig some fifty yards to the rear. A lesson learned from the Ivan's in Stalingrad. Sadly for the Volksgrenadier battalion, their Hauptmann's inexperience was to prove fatal. Exposed to the deluge of missiles their only option was to retreat into the town itself. While in the short term this ensured their safety, when the barrage ceased and the American infantry advanced, trapped in the narrow streets and at the mercy of the Americans heavy machine guns it soon became a death trap.

With the bombardment over, leaving the safety of their trenches Kellermann's company took up their previous positions. The two gun-pits for the MG-42's were untouched but the farmhouse itself had suffered. Windows had been blown in, their glass and frames shattered. One of the end walls was demolished, the section of the roof it had once supported threatening to collapse at any moment. A fire had also broken out in one of the barns, clouds of thick black smoke drifting up into the sky. Could have been much worse though Mayer. But best of all, they hadn't sustained any casualties. Kneeling next to him behind the low wall Kellermann surveyed the fields in front through his binoculars.

'Let's see how bold they are eh Sergeant?'

He didn't have to wait long to find out.

Initially, the two companies of American infantry advanced cautiously. Hugging the lines of hedges which pointed like arrows toward the cluster of buildings. A thousand yards from their objective and the order was given to attack. Breaking cover they fanned out across the open ground and began running towards the farm. After backing away from the wall Mayer began moving from position to position. He had spoken to them all collectively the previous evening. Explaining the strategy for the battle to come. Ensuring each one of them fully understood their role and the importance of fighting as a unit. But now that the moment was upon them with their nerves jangling from fear and excitement it didn't hurt to remind them.

'No firing now. You wait for my command. Understood?' Adding with a grin. 'First, we will see how they like our mortars.'

Without the benefit of radio communication with the mortar company, to make the most of their collective firepower Kellermann and the NCO in charge, an Obergefreiter by the name of Woelke had devised a simple semaphore system. The waving of a red flag would be the order for the mortars to commence firing. A black flag to cease.

The moment he saw the red flag Woelke gave the order and instantly the crews of the four GrW 34 mortars leaped into action. Well trained, loading and firing with efficient precision the three soldiers in each team were soon sending round after round hurtling into the sky. Moments later, yelling at the top of his voice Mayer shouted out the same command, and nine hundred yards from their objective the American infantry suddenly found themselves advancing into a wall of death.

In minutes, with mortar shells raining down together with the merciless firepower of the two MG-42's the area in front of them quickly became a killing field. Although it was something those in command liked to keep to themselves, every allied infantryman had heard stories about this awesome weapon. They had even been given a nickname; "Meat grinders." So-called because with their rate of fire there was no way through the hail of bullets. No lulls between bursts so you could find cover. If they found you they simply chewed you up.

'Cease fire!' Yelled Mayer. 'Cease fire!'

The American's were retreating. They had had enough so time to conserve ammunition for the next time. And there would be a next time he had no illusions about that. There was silence at first, then one of the young soldiers began shouting out, punching the air with his fist. Soon another followed, then another and soon the whole company was shouting and cheering as if they were at a football match and their team had just scored the winning goal. Mayer smiled, letting them enjoy the moment. They had done well but he wasn't going to tell them that, well not yet anyway. Let the excitement calm down a little first.

The following day was uneventful. The American's would have plenty to be thinking about before they launched another attack thought Mayer. Kellermann had hoped they would have received fresh supplies of food and more importantly, ammunition by now but none had arrived. Woelke had also expressed his concerns, informing Kellermann that his supply of mortar shells was worryingly low. For both men, the lack of radio contact was as frustrating as it was worrying.

'So Sergeant what do you suppose they are up to?'

'I think they would like to out-flank us Herr Oberst but they know that means crossing open ground and they have already seen what our mortars can do. If they have armoured units close by then they will wait. If not and we lose this cloud cover,' said Mayer looking skywards, 'then they will ask for air support.'

'So all we can do is wait. Wait and pray.'

'Or we could withdraw Herr Oberst. Without reinforcements, we cannot hope to stop them. Not a whole Infantry division.'

Kellermann thought about what Mayer had said for a moment. The Sergeant was right of course, alone they had no hope of holding them at bay. And to make matters worse, without radio contact there was no way of knowing if they would be reinforced.

'We still have a good supply of ammunition. Yes?'

'Perhaps enough for two days if we are careful. But that will depend on how often they attack Oberst,' said Mayer. What about our friend Obergefreiter Woelke? Without his mortars, we could find ourselves in serious trouble.'

'The same I think,' said Kellermann, a worried frown appearing on his face.

Early the next morning the American's launched another mortar attack, the majority of the shells falling onto and around the orchard. Mayer knew this was not simply bad aiming on their part. They were hoping to get lucky and put their own mortars out of action. Eventually, the shelling stopped and the rest of the day passed uneventfully. On

The Letter

two occasions they heard the roar of aircraft engines overhead but mercifully the cloud cover was still holding. The only other moment of excitement was the arrival of "reinforcements" in the form of young Hirzel.

'What's this then,' said Mayer smiling as he caught sight of the young soldier walking into the yard. 'Too fond of us to stay away eh?'

Catching his breath Hirzel grinned. He had just walked the last five miles in a little over two and a half hours. Quite an achievement for a fifteen-year-old boy burdened down with two boxes of MG-42 ammunition.

'And I see you've even brought us some presents too.'

Surrounded by a sea of smiling faces, dropping the ammo boxes onto the ground Hirzel finally found his voice.

'I could have carried more Sergeant but it was all they would let me have.'

I'll bet the little bugger would have done too thought Mayer, nodding his head.

'You delivered my report?' Said Kellermann striding across from the farmhouse. A hint of anxiety in his voice.

'Yes Herr Oberst,' Hirzel replied standing to attention. 'Your report was delivered as you instructed.'

'Good! You have done well, extremely well and your return is most welcome. 'Three cheers for Hirzel.'

'Hurrah! Hurrah! Hurrah!'

'Feeling hungry?' asked Mayer when the cheers subsided.

'Yes Sergeant,' said Hirzel, subconsciously licking his lips.

'Feldbauer!' Shouted Mayer. 'Seeing as one of Hirzel's presents is for you, go and warm up some soup for our young hero and see that he gets his two days bread ration.

The rest of you back to your positions. Quickly now!'

The next day the weather gods were less generous and with a gap appearing in the cloud bank, swooping down like birds of prey the two P-51 Mustangs began strafing the farmhouse. The 12.7 mm rounds from their twin Browning machine-guns tearing furrows in the earth before impacting the walls and roof of the buildings. Banking sharply, they circled away, gaining altitude before diving down for a second low-level run. The deafening roar of their Rolls Royce Merlin engines and the chatter-chatter-chatter of their machine guns striking fear into the young German soldiers.

'Short bursts Feldbauer. Don't waste ammunition.' Mayer called out in a loud but calm voice as he raced across the farmyard towards the front wall. Dropping to his knees, he peered out across the patchwork of fields. Watching the ranks of American infantry, encouraged by the air-strikes, advancing towards them. Having learned from their previous ill-fated assault, although in greater numbers they were strung out this time with two-man teams armed with a Browning light machine-gun laying down covering fire. Mercifully, before the two planes could carry out a third attack the cloud cover returned. Cheated of their prey, with a defiant roar from their engines the two Mustangs climbed away into the sky. No sooner had the noise of their engines faded away when the American's mortars opened up, this time targeting the farmhouse and outbuildings.

Through the sounds of the explosions, Mayer heard the screams of the wounded. Young voices filled with terror and pain. But this time there was no pulling back. With the enemy advancing towards them this time they must stand and fight. Thankfully, Woelke's mortars were still in action their shells exploding among the ranks of advancing infantry with devastating results. Then quite suddenly, like a storm which had blown itself out the firing subsided and a lull settled over the field of battle. Seizing the opportunity, doubled over Mayer moved from position to position. Ordering the dead and the wounded to be taken to the farmhouse. Praising the young soldiers for their bravery. His voice and words imbued with confidence.

'We're almost out of ammo Sergeant,' said Raupp, a tall strapping teenager who was manning the other MG-42.

'Don't worry we'll be supplied soon,' said Mayer reassuringly. 'In the meantime do as I showed you. Just a gentle squeeze on the trigger. You use fewer bullets that way. Okay?' Ashen faced, Raupp, nodded.

Moving away, Mayer crossed to where a group of young soldiers was dug in beside an old stone barn.

'Chin up lad's division will send us reinforcements soon.'

'Pfalzgraf said he heard tanks Sergeant.' One of them replied anxiously.

'No,' said Mayer grinning. 'If the Ammies had any tanks we would have seen them by now. Just keep your heads down and don't waste ammunition.'

As he spoke the American infantry opened fire again. No mortars this time thank God thought Mayer as he dashed across to the farmhouse door.

Given the number of times that the old stone building had received a direct hit from a mortar shell it was a miracle that it was still standing. But standing it was, a testament to the workmanship of those who had built it. The chimney stack had been demolished together with a large section of the roof. Its terra-cotta tiles littering the ground like a discarded pack of cards. The framework of timbers exposed to the elements for the first time in a hundred years. Forcing open the door Mayer stepped inside, his eyes immediately drawn towards the row of corpses stretched out along the far wall. Each of the eleven bodies covered in a layer of plaster-dust like a dusting of icing sugar on a cake. The rest of the room was filled with the wounded. The more seriously injured laid out side by side on the tiled floor. With the ones that could still walk, sitting propped up against the walls. Some had their wounds bandaged, others simply covered the torn flesh with their hands. The cloying odour of blood and iodine permeating the dust-laden air. Now and then the silence was broken by the sound of a young boys voice pleading in vain for his mother.

As afforded by the privilege of rank Kellermann occupied the room's only piece of furniture. A three-seater sofa, its rich velvet upholstery faded and worn. Standing beside him was the young Gefreiter.

'I have done all I can Sergeant,' said the young NCO. 'But in the *Deutsches Jungvolk* (German Young People) they only taught us first aid I'm afraid.'

Smiling, Mayer placed a hand on the young Gefreiter's shoulder.

'See what you can do for the young ones.'

As the NCO moved away Mayer stared down at the elderly officer. Kellermann's uniform jacket and shirt had been unbuttoned and pulled back. His exposed hairless chest was swathed in a blood-soaked bandage. The young Gefreiter had done his best but the wound inflicted by the piece of shrapnel was too deep. The jagged edge of the metal protruding from the lacerated flesh pushing against the layer of gauze each time Kellermann dragged air into his lungs. It was obvious that the man was dying. Drowning in his own blood. He might last an hour. Probably less. Certainly no longer.

Having accepted the baton of command, Mayer focused

his thoughts on the three options open to him. Retreat. Fight on. Or surrender? Although the more preferably of the three he knew that attempting to retreat without the cover of darkness would be suicidal. The Americans would be on them like a pack of hounds. They could always fight on of course until they ran out of ammunition. But then what purpose would that serve other than the loss of even more young lives. No, though it pained him to admit it his only choice was to surrender.

Although left with no alternative, it was still not an easy decision for Mayer to make. When you had fought and struggled for as many years as he had the act of surrendering felt like a betrayal. A slap in the face for all the brave soldiers who had laid down their lives for their country. But in his heart, Mayer knew that now was the time. To sacrifice the lives of these young boys for a cause which he knew was already lost would be immoral. Better a POW camp than a hole in the ground. "Germany will need men like you" Otto had told him when they said their farewells. Perhaps he was right. It will certainly need young boys like these. They truly were Germany's future. What it was Eismann used to say when the odds against you were too great, "Live to fight another day". Well, not this time Herr Oberst. This time it is just to live. The time for fighting is over.

Pulling a grubby white handkerchief from his pocket, Mayer knotted an end of it around the muzzle of his Schmeisser and walked towards the door. Reaching for the door-handle he suddenly spotted Hirzel sitting on the floor with his back against the wall. The young soldier's pallid face was freckled with dried blood. A swathe of bandage concealing the deep gash in his forehead. A blood-soaked field dressing covering what little remained of his left ear. Squatting down beside him, Mayer removed a packet of cigarettes and a box of matches from his pocket. Lighting one of the cigarettes, after dragging on it to ensure that it was alight he stuck it between the young boy's thin lips. Gazing up at him Hirzel managed a half-smile and for Mayer that was thanks enough. Returning the crumpled packet to his pocket, after casting a last look around the room Mayer made his way to the door.

Once outside, yelling 'Cease fire! Ceasefire!' Mayer began running across the farmyard towards the low wall. Almost immediately after a few sporadic shots, the firing stopped. Dropping onto his knees Mayer raised the machine-pistol above the wall and began moving it slowly backward and forwards. Initially, nothing happened but then above the rattle of gunfire Mayer heard a voice calling out in a distinctive American accent. "Hold your fire! Hold your fire!" Twice more the voice called out before the guns finally fell silent. It was then that Mayer climbed onto the wall and raised his Schmeisser with its token of surrender in the air.

When the mortar shell landed, the soldier alongside Private Lipski simply disappeared. His body reduced to a jigsaw of flesh and bones. Unaware that his fellow soldier had unwittingly saved his life, blown sideways by the blast Lipski found himself lying face down in a shallow ditch. Unaware of the blood trickling out of his left ear all he knew was that apart from a loud buzzing in his head all sound had ceased to exist. Satisfied that he was bodily intact and that his arms and legs responded to his instructions Lipski began crawling forward. Reaching the end of the ditch he dragged himself up onto his knees and peered out. It was then that he saw the German soldier standing on a wall waving his gun. Instinctively, Lipski tucked the butt of his carbine into his right shoulder, and taking aim he pulled the trigger.

The Letter

Contrary to what old soldiers would have you believe, Mayer heard the crack of the carbine. But by then he was already falling backwards off the wall, the bullet it had just fired buried deep in his chest. Lying spread-eagled on the ground Mayer was aware of the blood soaking into the fabric of his jacket. Strangely there was no pain, just an overwhelming feeling of weariness. An irresistible urge to close his eyes. But the desire to see their faces one last time was stronger. With his faithful Schmeisser slipping from his grasp Mayer reached across and unbuttoned the top-flap of his uniform jacket. Dipping his blood-soaked fingers into the pocket taking hold of the leather wallet he slowly removed it. After flipping it open, feeling with his fingertips until he found the serrated edge of the photograph he gripped it between thumb and forefinger and pulled it free. With the last of his strength ebbing away, unable to raise his arms Mayer tried desperately to lift his head. But the earth had already laid claim to it. All he craved was one last glimpse of their faces. Sadly for Mayer, the Angel of Death was in one of his less charitable moods.

Looking down at the body of the dead German soldier Lieutenant Southworth couldn't help feeling a sense of sadness over what had happened. All the guy had wanted was to surrender. He had bawled Lipski out of course. Hell, he had even threatened to have him court-martialled for disobeying orders. But given the fact that he was as deaf as a post after the explosion, it was all just hot air. For the German, it was a case of being in the wrong place at the wrong time. Or maybe just plain bad luck. Call it what you like these things happened in a war. The real irony was that normally Lipski couldn't even hit a barn door. Pushing the thoughts from his mind he turned and walked away. The important thing was that they had taken the German position. It had come at a high price and there were a lot of GI's who wouldn't be going back home. For those who had survived what shocked them, was finding that they had been fighting against a bunch of kids for Christ's sake. A misconception quickly dispelled by their hard-nosed Company Sergeant. His laconic explanation putting the whole thing into context.

'It don't matter much who's pulling the trigger, it's the gun what does the killing.'

Nine

Lauterbruck
Late June 1945

IT HAD TAKEN them a little over an hour to find the small village. Now all they needed to do was find the right house. Fortunately, a chance encounter with Herr Ruecherl, who had decided to take a walk after an over-indulgent lunch of sausage and homemade saurkraut provided them with the necessary directions. Although neither, Lieutenant Southworth or Private Lipski spoke any German the mention of the name "Mayer" had proved sufficient. And after a series of gestures and arm waving followed by a show of fingers indicating the number of the house, with a shake of the head Herr Ruecherl watched them drive away.

The house was modest in size. Detached with a ground and first floor. Set into the gable end of the pitched tiled roof was a small square window allowing daylight into the loft space. Decorative lace curtains covered the downstairs windows, their pale blue shutters adding a much-needed touch of colour to the drab timber walls. Leading up to the solid wooden door were a set of wide steps. A small front garden separated it from the road enclosed by a low picket fence and gate. Attached to the gate post was the number eight.

'This is it I guess,' said Lieutenant Southworth, applying the jeep's handbrake. 'The old guy said number eight.'

Private Lipski didn't say anything, he just sat staring across at the house.

'You figure we're doing the right thing Lieutenant?' He said nervously.

'This was your idea remember?' Said the Lieutenant, not unkindly.

Unable to deny the fact, with a brown manila envelope clutched in his hand Lipski climbed out of the jeep, and opening the gate he walked up the steps to the front door. Knocking twice before stepping back and waiting for a response.

A few moments later when the door was finally opened it was difficult to tell who was the more surprised, Lipski or Hannah. Lipski because the woman standing in front of him was obviously very pregnant. Hannah because the last person she expected to find standing outside her front door was an American soldier. After staring at each other for what seemed longer than it was, it was Lipski who broke the silence.

'Frau Mayer?' He had rehearsed the two words over and over in his head for so long it came as a relief to say them out loud.

Hannah simply nodded. Her mind struggling to comprehend what this man was doing here?

'Howdy Mam,' said Lipski, thankful that they had at least found the person they were looking for. 'My name is Lipski. Leroy Lipski and I...' But that was all that he could get out. The speech he had prepared about how sorry he was. How the whole thing had been an accident on account of his busted ear-drum. Not another word passed his lips. Which was just as well really because she probably wouldn't have understood a word he said anyway. Instead, he simply thrust out the hand holding the manila envelope, silently praying that she would take it just so he could get the hell out of here. Thankfully, Hannah did just that. It was an automatic reflex. Like taking a letter the postman was delivering. Relieved, throwing up his hand in a salute Lipski turned away and descending the steps two at a time he hurried along the path towards the gate.

With Private Lipski seated beside him, yanking on the gear stick Lieutenant Southworth pushed his foot down on the accelerator and the jeep pulled away.

'That was a fine thing to do Lipski. It truly was. Not many guys would have done what you just did and that's a fact.'

Lipski remained silent. Simply staring ahead through the windshield as the jeep made its way along the narrow tree-lined road. For the first time in his life "The Lip" as his buddies called him, was lost for words. He had known all along that coming face to face with a woman he had made into a widow was never going to be pleasant. He was prepared for that. He just hadn't expected her to be pregnant that was all.

For what seemed like a long time Hannah stared after the jeep. Watching until it had disappeared from view before turning away. Her fingers had already given her a clue as to what the envelope contained. Subconsciously tracing the outline of the wallet as she watched the two American soldiers driving away. Re-entering the house Hannah made her way to the small front room. Closing the door behind her she walked across to the desk. The flap hadn't been stuck down so the contents of the envelope slid out easily onto the polished leather surface. Although the war had been over for weeks and many soldiers had already returned to their homes Hannah had never given up hope that one day her Franz would walk in through the door just as he had done many times before. Seeing the proof that this would never happen laid before her on the desk-top was like having a knife pushed into her heart. Lipski had done his best to clean off the blood and when she eventually came to look inside Franz's pay-book she would see that he had also recorded where he had died and the date.

It was a fine wallet. Frau Junker's late husband had made it for her. It had been a hobby of his making things from scraps of leather. He told Hannah that he did it to make some beer money but she knew the real reason was that he simply enjoyed creating things. The satisfaction of craftsmanship. It had been her present to Franz on their first wedding anniversary and now it had come back to her. She also remembered him taking the snapshot of her and the children. And how annoyed she had been that he hadn't let her brush her hair before taking it. Hannah also knew that the dark stain on the back had been made by his blood. Lifting it to her mouth she pressed it against her lips. It was all she had of him, a dark shadow on the back of a photograph.

It had been three days since the visit by the American soldier. But with uncertainty replaced by reality, hope replaced by despair it was the nights Hannah feared most. Alone in the darkness with just her thoughts and fears for company. Although she was puzzled by what he had done, she was also grateful to him. Such kindness from an enemy was not something she had expected. He had been so young too. Why he had returned Franz's wallet she would never know. She wished now that she had asked him. There were other questions too; was he there when he was killed? How had he died? But then she reminded herself that neither of them would have understood what the other was saying anyway. No better to just be thankful for what he had done. At least she had something which had been dear to him. A tangible link to his existence. A wealth of memories crafted in leather.

The following morning with the letter addressed to the Neusch's clutched in her hand, accompanied by her two children Hannah made her way to the centre of the village. It was at this time that the postman from Hohenburg delivered and collected the mail. He only visited one day a week so she didn't want to miss him. Halfway along the road, they encountered a small group of women enjoying the sunshine while passing the time of day. Normally Hannah would have stopped for a gossip, but having seen her approaching the women had already turned their backs on her. She understood why of course. With little hope of disguising the pregnancy word of her condition had quickly spread. And knowing that her husband was away fighting in the war the name-calling had begun. Adulteress. Harlot. Quickly followed by the finger-pointing. Old men, they may be but it seemed that one of them still had some lead in his pencil. Hannah had confided the truth to Frau Junker. Telling her everything that had happened. She had understood of course. Even why Franz had done what he did. Telling Hannah that any decent man would have done the same. As for the womenfolk, well their bitchiness was only to be expected. Adding 'But at the moment what concerns them most is knowing which of their husbands couldn't keep his sausage in his trousers?'

Hannah saw his van first, parked alongside the village square. Then she saw the postman walking towards it. Fearing that he would drive off before they reached him, she handed the letter and a handful of coins to Wolfgang. Watching as he raced away down the road. She needn't have worried. Spotting the young boy running towards him all arms and legs, the postman released his grip on the door-handle. There was always a latecomer. Sliding to a halt in front of the postman, gulping down a mouthful of air

Wolfgang handed him the letter. Watching as the elderly man scrutinised the address. Satisfied that it was in order, pushing the envelope into his leather satchel the postman reached out a hand.

'Eighty Reichspfennigs.'

Picking through the coins his mother had given him, Wolfgang selected the required amount and placed it into the man's outstretched palm. Watching as he counted them with his eye.

Satisfied that he had been given the correct amount, depositing the coins in his coat pocket with a curt nod of the head the postman climbed into the van.

Standing together Hannah and the children watched as the post van drove away. Staring after it until it disappeared around a bend in the road. Then turning away, hand in hand the little family began walking back along the road. She had done what Franz had asked of her and although it was a simple thing, doing it had filled her with a sense of contentment. Tomorrow she would tell the children what had happened to their father and show them the photograph he had carried in his wallet. Today they would just enjoy walking home in the sunshine and leave the tears for another day.

About the Author

Barry Cole was born in Yorkshire and after leaving the army he began contributing stories and articles to the monthly magazines of two Native American charities. With a love of film, he then studied for two years at the London Screenwriters Workshop.

Barry's first book, *The Time Bandit* was published in 2016, followed by a historical novel *Shingas* a few months later. His third book *The Conquistadors Horse* was published in 2018 and has been optioned as a short film by Looking Window Pictures.

His latest book *The Letter*, inspired by the Battle of Stalingrad has recently been published by Michael Terence Publishing.

After living on a narrowboat for several years Barry has now returned to his roots in North Yorkshire.

Other Books by Barry Cole

For Children:
The Time Bandit
The Conquistador's Horse

Historical Novel:
Shingas

Available worldwide from Amazon

www.mtp.agency

www.facebook.com/mtp.agency

@mtp_agency

www.ingramcontent.com/pod-product-compliance
Lightning Source LLC
Chambersburg PA
CBHW020903080526
44589CB00011B/421